The Culture of Digital Fighting Games

This book examines the complex network of influences that collide in the culture of digital fighting games. Players from all over the world engage in competitive combat with one another, forming communities in both real and virtual spaces, attending tournaments and battling online via Internet-connected home game consoles. But what is the logic behind their shared playstyle and culture? What are the threads that tie them together, and how does this inform our understanding of competitive gaming, community, and identity?

Informed by observations made at one of the biggest fighting game events in the world—the Evolution Series tournament, or "EVO"—and interviews with fighting game players themselves, this book covers everything from the influence of arcade spaces, to the place of gender and ethnicity in the community, to the clash of philosophies over how these games should be played in the first place. In the process, it establishes the role of technology, gameplay, and community in how these players define both themselves and the games that they play.

Todd Harper is a Postdoctoral Researcher at the Massachusetts Institute of Technology's MIT Game Lab.

Routledge Studies in New Media and Cyberculture

The Culture of Digital Fighting Games
Performance and Practice

Todd Harper

Routledge
Taylor & Francis Group

LONDON AND NEW YORK

First published 2014 by Routledge

2 Park Square, Milton Park, Abingdon, Oxon OX14 4RN

711 Third Avenue, New York, NY 10017, USA

*Routledge is an imprint of the Taylor & Francis Group,
an informa business*

First issued in paperback 2017

Library of Congress Cataloging-in-Publication Data
Harper, Todd, 1978–
    The culture of digital fighting games : performance and practice /
Todd Harper.
        pages cm. — (Routledge studies in new media and cyberculture)
    Includes bibliographical references and index.
    1. Violence in video games.   2. Combat.   I. Title.
    GV1469.34.V56H37   2013
    794.8—dc23
    2013028533

ISBN: 978-0-415-82130-8 (hbk)
ISBN: 978-1-138-71011-5 (pbk)

Typeset in Sabon LT
by Apex CoVantage, LLC

To my mother, who encouraged me to think this was possible.
To Mia, who believed in me even when I didn't.
And to everyone who helped me to prove them both right.

Contents

Figures

Acknowledgments

It would be impossible to acknowledge the huge list of people who helped to make this book a reality, but I will attempt to enjoin that challenge nonetheless. First and foremost my thanks to Mia Consalvo, who has been mentor, guide, and sounding board for the past seven years. Without her help and advice (and more than occasional prodding) the research that this book is built on would never have been finished, never mind the actual book itself. Secondly, my thanks to my coworkers at both the GAMBIT Game Lab and now the MIT Game Lab—Philip, Rik, Mike, Clara, Matt, Owen, both Jasons, Drew, Sara, Marleigh, Gene, Patrick, Konstantin, and Abe—who supported this endeavor both professionally as my colleagues and personally as my friends. Special thanks to Abe Stein, who not only encouraged me but also went above and beyond, providing incredibly helpful 11th-hour reading and support for the manuscript itself.

Thank you to T. L. Taylor, who suffered like a champ through months of me losing my mind over Twitter and email, for her patient reminders that it wasn't quite as bad as all that. As long as we're at it, thank you to the many scholarly friends I've made at conferences like AoIR and DiGRA over the years: Kelly Bergstrom, Nick Taylor, Adrienne Shaw, Mark Chen, Shira Chess, Alison Harvey, and many, many more. When my anxiety started to dip into the ridiculous, one of you was always there to snap me back to reality (probably more times than I deserved). Please know that a desire to keep up with the great work you are all doing motivates me.

As this book owes much to my doctoral dissertation, thank you to my doctoral committee: Jenny Nelson, Christine Mattley, and Bernhard Debatin. As well, thank you to Nathan Dutton and Cynara Medina, my compatriots, for being part of our mutual doctoral survival pact. Finally, thank you to the Ohio University School of Media Arts and Studies for taking a chance on me in the first place.

Thank you to Felisa Salvago-Keyes and Andrew Weckenmann at Routledge/Taylor and Francis, both of whom showed extraordinary patience in dealing with a new author who had a tendency to rapid fire stupid questions via email. You are both saints.

A particular thank you needs to go to Christopher A. Paul, whose contributions to the existence of this book are many and too varied to list here. Suffice it to say, the ability to get hyped up about basically anything—even your neurotic friend's impending book preparation-related meltdown—and use that enthusiasm to solve problems is a rare gift. Cherish it.

Finally, thanks to all my friends and family who ever believed that I could do something like this. Guess what? You were right!

1 Introduction

Like a lot of research, this book has its roots in my own personal experience with fighting games. The story begins in Waterbury, Connecticut in the summer of 1991, just outside the mall-side entrance of a drug store in the city's largest shopping mall. Sitting there was an arcade machine of *Street Fighter 2*, one of the oldest digital fighting games in the history of the genre, and certainly one of the most iconic. A gamer even at a young age, I found something fascinating about that *SF2* machine. Dubbed *The World Warrior*, the characters of *SF2* were colorful, brassy, and unique. Massive, muscled Zangief the Russian pro-wrestler would face off against an emaciated Indian yogi named Dhalsim inside a digital recreation of a Cold War-era Russian steel mill. Dhalsim's digitized (and not at all Indian) voice rang out "Yoga fire!" as he inhaled and then spit fire across the field, the fireball connecting with Zangief and briefly causing his entire body to black out, engulfed in a sprite art rendition of flickering scarlet flame. My favorite World Warrior at that early age was the only female fighter in the group, a Chinese martial artist named Chun-li, who had a nimble, acrobatic, and showy style.

At the time I lived in Plymouth, a small town outside of Bristol and a good 20 miles from Waterbury. Whenever we arrived at the Waterbury mall, I hoarded my quarters and begged my parents for leave to run off to the drugstore to play *Street Fighter*. One of my most salient memories of those times was when another player—an Asian teenage boy who was much older than me—stepped up to the machine and put in a quarter. Suddenly, he was challenging me, and we were duking it out—digitally—for the right to keep playing. If I lost, then my game was over and my quarter was through. This game was entirely different than the other arcade games I had come to love: shooters, like *Centipede* or *Gauntlet,* or side-scrollers, like *Super Mario,* which I could play until the game itself did me in. With *Street Fighter*, if I wasn't skilled enough to beat my opponent, then my quarter was gone for good.

I'm not quite sure how, but I managed to beat him, and believe me when I tell you, it had to have been a fluke. I remember watching him turn to me with a frustrated expression, saying in an exasperated tone, "Oh, usin' cheesy throws!" I also recall not understanding what he was talking about;

my young ears heard "chinsey" rather than "cheesy," and I assumed he was telling me the name of the secret technique I was using to defeat him. I can only imagine his exasperation when I turned to him and said, bright with pride at my perception of his approval, "Yeah! Chinsey throw, for sure!"

Flash forward to 2004 and a long history with fighting games to that point. It's an endless series of playing not in the arcades, for the most part, but buying home console ports and playing against the computer, enjoying the style of the game but not having another person to play against. In those instances where I could play with friends, I was always hopelessly outmatched and a terrible loser. *Street Fighter 2* gave way to other games: *Mortal Kombat, Soul Edge*, a number of *Street Fighter* spinoffs, including the *Street Fighter Alpha* prequel series, Nintendo's *Smash Bros.* series, and even a truly awful American-produced game by California developer Interplay called *Clayfighter*. Something about the aesthetic and the play of fighting games—even the really bad ones—drew me in and did so with a vengeance. I played any that I could get my hands on, but always alone, and almost never in the arcades, which were few and far between in the various places I have lived since that fateful discovery of *SF2* back in Waterbury two decades ago.

However, in the age of the Internet and YouTube, I became aware that there was a side to fighting game play I'd never seen or experienced. Friends who enjoyed fighting games referred me to sites and videos. I learned of events such as the Evolution Championship Series (or EVO) Tournament, where serious, dedicated fighting gamers met to battle against each other in a competition that had a lot in common with competitive sports. One landmark wake-up call to the alternate possibilities of fighting game play came when a friend linked me to a YouTube video of professional Japanese player Daigo Umehara, facing off against American pro-player Justin Wong, in the finals at EVO 2004. They were playing *Street Fighter 3: Third Strike*, one in a long series of *SF2* successors that had been released.

The video[1] is maybe hard to understand if you don't know the intricacies of the system, but the crowd reaction that accompanies it gives even a lay viewer a taste of just how incredible that moment was for the people who experienced it. Daigo—playing Ken, the male character in white— performed a counter play of masterful skill at almost literally the last possible second, counterattacking to take the win and the tournament. In sports terms, it was the play of the century. To me, it was an example of a world of fighting game play that was beyond the scope of what I knew. Who were these professional players? What was this event that attracted such a massive crowd? Perhaps most importantly, how did they acquire their incredible skills and what seemed like, to me, superhuman reflexes? In essence: Who *were* these people? At the time I was completing my master's degree at Syracuse University, however, and had little time to explore the issue, either as a player or a scholar.

ENCOUNTERING HARDCORE PLAY: DRIVING ME UP THE BRAWL

Skip ahead four years to March 2008. Now a student at Ohio University, I eagerly wait in a midnight line at the local Wal-Mart to acquire a copy of the latest installment of the *Super Smash Bros.* franchise: *Super Smash Bros. Brawl* for the Nintendo Wii. I've been a series fan since it debuted on the Nintendo 64 with the original *Super Smash Bros.* Since then I'd purchased the GameCube version, *Super Smash Bros. Melee*, and was now quite pleased to get my hands on the newest installment. Particularly interesting to me was the fact that with the Wii's online capabilities, you could play *Brawl* with random strangers around the world from the comfort of your own home. Finally, I would get a chance to play against other people instead of only by myself against CPU opponents.

It's important to understand that *Brawl* has seemingly little in common with *Street Fighter 2*. In *Brawl*, there are up to four players instead of only two, and controls are highly simplified compared to the more complex motions required in *SF2*. Also, the *Smash* games include a number of random elements, such as items that drop from the sky to be used against your opponents (everything from bombs and laser guns to paper fans and hamburgers) and stage elements that can be just as much a hazard as other players. Some stages are relatively tame: flat, featureless planes. The majority, however, are rather more extreme: a boiling underground cavern where lava flows appear out of nowhere; a slippery iceberg floating in an Arctic sea; and even a Pokémon-themed stage where giant destructive laser beams and occasional reversals of gravity are a taste of the random possibilities.

What I experienced online, however, told a different story about the game than the description I just gave you. Rather than the vast range of stages and selectable characters available, my online play with anonymous opponents worldwide had a very homogenous tone. Match after match, I played against a very narrow range of characters on a limited selection of stages, time and again. The most common stage was "Final Destination," a holdover from *Brawl*'s predecessor *Melee* that is a single, featureless platform. Rather than seeing the wide range of Nintendo characters that the designers added to *Brawl*, I often would fight matches where I was the only person *not* playing a given character. After a certain period of playing an unending tide of matches against three Solid Snakes, Ikes, or Kirbies on Final Destination again and again, I gave up on online *Brawl*. My frustration with the process had reached new heights. Why were these people playing this way? Wasn't the random nature of the game—all the potential wackiness and unexpected twists—the fun of the experience?

Like the YouTube video mentioned above, this experience caused me to question just what was going on here. In considering the *Brawl* situation, my mind returned to an Internet meme that had surrounded the previous game, *Smash Bros. Melee*. The joke ran that serious *Smash* players would adhere to a "Fox only, Final Destination, no items" rule of play. That is to say, they would turn off items entirely, only choose the Final Destination stage, and all players would choose the character Fox, who (in *Melee*) was considered one of the strongest characters. As the meme went, anyone who embraced this sort of play was taking *Smash* a little bit too seriously.

Naturally, as a meme, this was an exaggeration; even a cursory glance at online communities provides a page or two that identify the meme as a parody of tournament-legal play, which typically bans items and stages in order to keep the match fair ("No items. Fox only. FD", 2008; "Tournament legal (SSBM)", 2010). Of course, the idea of the meme is to criticize or tease these serious players, heavily implying that their playstyle effectively strips all of the actual fun out of the experience; consider the related TVTropes. com page "Stop Having Fun Guys," which once referenced *Smash* players directly with language that has since been removed[2]: "while most Stop Having Fun Guys are Tournament Players, **not** *all* the **Tournament Players are Stop Having Fun Guys** [emphasis original]."

CONCEPTUALIZING PLAYSTYLES: CASUAL, HARDCORE, AND PERFORMANCE

My awe at the skills of hardcore *Street Fighter* players and my combination of curiosity and, in the spirit of full disclosure, annoyance at online *Brawl* players provided the seed of this study. As many scholars have suggested (see van Manen, 1990), our lived experience can provide the entry point for a better understanding of what's going on with a given phenomenon, though we have to be careful not to let our own experiences unduly bias our analysis. These two narratives of fighting games suggested that there were other ways to think about and play these games that I hadn't even thought or conceived of yet. More to the point, it would be worth finding out just what those perspectives were.

In interpreting cultural texts (like video games), one always has to consider the context in which they're consumed (McKee, 2007). I began to wonder: What *is* the context of these hardcore players? What would lead players to experience the game in the ways that they do? More to the point, the culture of competitive play wasn't just about how you play, but about being a competitive player in the first place. How could a playstyle turn into a way of understanding the self? Where did competitive players' orientation toward the play of these games become part of their self-concept and social interactions? And finally, what might we learn about games *and* their players by examining that context?

Though it may seem odd to some readers, the more I thought about the situation, the more I came back to the work of feminist scholar Judith

Butler (*Gender Trouble*, 1990; *Bodies that Matter*, 1993). I have an interest in feminist and queer theory, so I had some exposure to a notion that Butler dealt with heavily: gender performativity. Butler wanted to situate the idea of gender in the realm of discourse and social interaction. By separating gender from the physical body, she hoped to argue for ways in which gender could be problematized—hence the title of her first book, *Gender Trouble*—and resisted.

Butler's argument is that gender isn't something we just have naturally that we can't do anything about. Instead, she explains that gender is about performance. We constantly do and say things—and people do and say things *to* and *around* us—that construct us as gendered individuals, over and over again. Society is constantly asking us to respond to it in gendered terms, so we have to engage in this performance all the time. Sometimes we can consciously change the performance if we want to resist, but that's not always possible; sometimes we have to conform to survive. While this is a simplification of a very complex idea, the basic notion is that our identity—or part of it, gender in this case—is related to the things we do, every day, just as part of living with other people in the world.

The research that went into this book sought to explore the possible link between this performativity idea, of identity concepts created and recreated over time through social interaction, and the play of digital games, particularly in social contexts. Some have argued that the primary way in which digital game texts convey ideological information is through "procedure" (Bogost, 2007): the actual *process* of gameplay—interacting with the rules, fiction, goals, and other aspects of experiential play—models systems, and thus conveys rhetorical information about how those systems work. That said, a growing number of scholars (see Sicart, 2011) have emphasized that we can't forget the player in all of this, and that only thinking about the procedural parts of gameplay, the mechanics and rules, is missing a critical part of the equation.

The primary question here is: If gameplay interactions are discursive, then can gameplay itself be a type of identity performativity? Certainly, we know that gameplay—particularly public gameplay, in spaces like arcades—can and does represent a discursive relationship, both in the immediate literal sense of onlookers (Lin & Sun, 2011) or in the broader context of gaming culture (Crawford & Rutter, 2007). What the literature on gender performativity suggests is that social performances are one part of a broad, discursive web through which fighting game players understand themselves as individuals—as members of the fighting game culture—and their relationships to others through that lens. As an example, consider this question: Do casual or hardcore gamers, in adopting their preferred playstyles and interacting with other players socially in the context of those playstyles, help create the identity concept of being "casual" or "hardcore" in the first place? What relationship does the practice of actual gameplay have to the performance of identity?

In early 2008, *New York Times* reporter Seth Schiesel wrote on how the sales figures for video games in the previous year suggested a fundamental shift in the demographics of gaming. The article claims that the decline of sports games and single-player action games—long considered the bastions of the stereotypical hardcore gamer—and the rise of more socially-oriented and less "hardcore" systems and games, such as Blizzard's popular *World of Warcraft* and the family-friendly Nintendo Wii, are evidence that what society conceives of as a "gamer" is shifting. As the title of his recent book, *A Casual Revolution* (2010), suggests, Jesper Juul examines of the rise of casual games and the people who play them. The idea of the hardcore player—the diehard gamer, with all of his/her attendant stereotypes of behavior and demographics—appears to be on the way out.

Yet the vibrant communities of self-described hardcore fighting game players that congregate online suggest the hardcore identity and mindset are not going away, though they may be changing. Events such as the EVO tournament still draw massive numbers of players who adopt a more hardcore style of play. What's left is a question of what being a gamer even means, and perhaps most importantly, what do *gamers* think being a gamer means? How is that hardcore identity constructed and expressed, both to other gamers and to the world, and how reliant is it on styles of play for maintaining itself?

SITUATING GAMEPLAY

The questions I just described are broad in scope, drawing on both game studies literature as well as research on gender and performance. The next step is determining which parts of gameplay it makes sense to look at. The actual act of playing a game is a dense experience, packed with numerous simultaneous influences, some even competing with one another. Picking out which ones are the most important to examine in answering these questions is difficult. However, guided by the literature I've mentioned, I identified three aspects of gameplay that were the most critical:

Play practice is about how games are actually played. Play practice refers to the ways in which players interact with the rules of the game, how they control the game through technology and interfaces, and the decisions about interfacing with the game text that players make.

Normative play is, on the other hand, about how players feel games *should* be played. Rather than play practice, which is the act of literally interacting with the text, normative play refers to social contexts, mores, norms, and other cultural, contextual factors that guide thinking about how the ideal experience ought to be. Statements like "It's not a real fighting game unless it has [x]" or "Real players don't do [y]" are in some way about normative play.

And finally, *social play* is about how players play together. Issues of social play focus on the ways that interacting with other players becomes part of the gameplay experience, and incorporates aspects of both play practice and normative play. Social play encompasses not only how players *literally* play together—in other words, interact with a text together—but also how they engage in the culture of gameplay together. Online forums and communities, tournament events, and fan work are all aspects of social play.

Gameplay is not static, but rather something experiential and fluid. This book works under the assumption—grounded in theory—that gameplay is not limited to the act of engagement with a particular game; rather, players also engage games through social contact inside gaming culture and through the consumption of related texts. This is what Mia Consalvo (2007), building on the work of Genette (1987), refers to as the "paratext" of gaming. Also, my own previous work on gameplay (Harper, 2006) has suggested that even the act of *observing* a game and socially engaging the player can present, in its own way, a type of play.

THE RESEARCH

This book is based on a year-long study of the fighting game community that involved observing players and talking with them about their experiences. The goal of that research was to identify and explore the ways that these three aspects of play mentioned above are performed. How did "serious" fighting game players choose to play? For that matter, how did they come together to talk about play, or to play together? Seeing and hearing for myself the various aspects of how serious fighting game fans went about engaging with their passion was the critical thing.

To that end, in July of 2009 I took a trip to the Evolution Championship Series tournament, one of the biggest fighting game tournaments in the world, and certainly the largest in the United States. That year was slated to be particularly exciting, as it was the release year for *Street Fighter 4*, the first "new" release in the *Street Fighter* series in over a decade at that point. For three days I attended the tournament, watching people play against each other and interact in a place dedicated to fighting games, culminating in the high-energy finals on the third day. Between the various things I observed and the conversations I had with players on the tourney floor, I was able to get a broad picture of many different pieces of fighting game culture.

From there, I recruited and interviewed members of the fighting game community, fans not just of *Street Fighter*, but a variety of games, including the *Soul Calibur* series by Namco-Bandai Games and players of the aforementioned *Smash Bros.* titles by Nintendo. Recruiting participants was difficult, for reasons that are discussed in more detail later in the book, but in total I spoke to 10 players: Ibrahim, Evan, Isaac, Jordan, Aaron, Jeff,

Matthew, Nicholas, Garrett, and Gene[3]. Drawing on what I had seen at the EVO tournament for inspiration, I asked these players about their history with fighting games, how they played, and how they interacted with other fighting game fans. What unfolded were stories about crowding around *Street Fighter* cabinets in mall arcades, forum battles over the banning or use of characters in *Smash*, and the history of a player's beloved arcade stick, the weapon of choice for the serious fighting game fan. The many topics and stories I heard from the players who approach these games with such passion went a long way to answering my many questions, and taught me that more than a few preconceptions I had of just how competitive fighting gameplay works were in serious error.

DEFINING FIGHTING GAMES

Of course, if one wants to study the fighting game culture, it's important to know what even constitutes a "fighting game" in the first place. After all, combat and fighting are not uncommon in video games of all types; at the broadest level, the range of "fighting games" is potentially endless. Does *any* game that involves fighting—everything from first-person shooters to *World of Warcraft* to even some hockey games—in some way become a "fighting game"? Common sense tells us it's rarely that easy, and as we'll find later in this book, even players who've been dedicated to these games their entire lives have competing definitions of just what are the precise elements that constitute a fighting game. The companies that make and distribute games, the stores that market them, and the gamers who play them all have specific, and sometimes conflicting, ideas of how to define games.

Before moving into specifics, here I offer some information and context that will create a working definition of "fighting game" that is used throughout the book. The explanation focuses on three areas: the idea of genre (how texts are grouped together), the developmental history of fighting games, and finally some in-depth description of iconic games relevant to this research—particularly the games that were played at the EVO tournament in 2009. The intent here isn't to define once and for all what a fighting game is; rather, this chapter will provide a sense of how the term is used and what sort of games are being played in the culture.

FIGHTING GAMES AS A GENRE

At the most basic level, the idea of genre is about "taxonomy" (Feuer, 1992, p. 138): taking a group of texts (like games) and classifying them according to observed qualities. For example, a TV show that is 25–30 minutes long, filmed with a three-camera setup in a studio and dealing with the comedic ways that characters interact, is probably a "sitcom." For games it's much the same; games like *Madden* that simulate real-life sports are usually called "sports games," while those that use statistic mechanics and fantasy settings like *Final Fantasy* fall into the "role-playing game/RPG" genre. The idea of genre is something that consumers of media are used to engaging every day for a variety of reasons.

That being said, many people who've studied genre (Altman, 1984; Neale, 1990; Mittell, 2001; see also Feuer as previously noted) have argued that it's usually not quite that simple, and that genre is as much about the cultural context in which people consume media. It's easy, they argue, for us to believe that genre is something that just "happens," occurring naturally, when the truth is that each new entry into a genre helps to change and shift its boundaries. Role-playing games are a good example; in the 1990s, during the era of the Nintendo Entertainment System, Western-created games like the *Ultima* series and Japanese titles like *Dragon Quest* and *Final Fantasy* were all simply called "RPGs." Twenty years later, western games such as Bethesda's *Elder Scrolls V: Skyrim* retain the label of "RPG," while games with a more Japanese aesthetic and style (like the aforementioned *Dragon Quest* and *Final Fantasy*) have developed an entirely new sub-genre: "Japanese RPG/JRPG." What used to be any game involving blowing things up ("shooters") now may be classified as "rail shooters," "first-person shooters," and many more variations. It's made obvious just by looking at games historically that genres shift over time.

To add another level of complication, identifying just how genre should be classified in video games is tricky work, with roots going all the way back to early arguments about whether games are primarily stories/narratives or if they are instead systems or simulations first. In *The Medium of the Video Game*, Mark Wolf (2001) comes down on the ludic side, arguing that what gets done in a game—what players do—is the most critical way to group game texts, supported by scholars like Apperley (2006). On the flipside, people like Ewan Kirkland (2005) take the opposite view, arguing that for the most part it's the thematic elements of a game—his example is the use of suspense movie tropes in the horror game series *Silent Hill*—that drive a game's genre. My own work on the subject[4] suggests that genre is somewhere in between these two poles, depending on how they combine gameplay and fiction to make certain ideological arguments. For our purposes, this book considers both gameplay elements and thematic elements when considering a game's genre.

Coming back to Wolf, his description of the "fighting" genre from *Medium of the Video Game* at least provides a useful starting point for determining which games fall into this category:

Games involving characters who fight usually hand-to-hand, in one-to-one combat situations without the use of firearms or projectiles. In most of these games, the fighters are represented as humans or anthropomorphic characters. This term should not be used for games which involve shooting or vehicles (see Combat and Shoot 'Em Up), or for games which include fighting like *Ice Hockey*, but which have other objectives (see Sports). Note: Many fighting games can also be cross-listed with Sports. For related games, see also Combat.

Examples: *Avengers*; *Body Slam*; *Boxing* (with Sports); games in the *Mortal Kombat* series; *Soul Edge*; games in the *Tekken* series; *Wrestle War*. [emphasis all in original] (pp. 124–125)

Certainly, this definition helps narrow down the range of potential games by setting aside the notion that any game with fighting in it is necessarily a fighting game. Looking at our previous list, for example, we can take off hockey games: they may include fighting but are primarily about representing a real-world sport.

Another useful point of entry to the potential ambiguity in these definitions comes from the market. After all, game retailers and distributors need to package their product so that potential consumers can recognize it, grasp the essential characteristics of the game, and (ideally) take an interest and buy it. They want to attract buyers, and more specifically, the right demographic of buyers. Of course, this means that what ends up being the "marketing" genre of a game—the genre that it's being "sold as"—can sometimes be at odds with other genre classifications.

Take, for example, Microsoft's online marketplace for the Xbox 360, with everything ranging from full games designed specifically for the 360, to add-on content, to downloadable arcade games and ports of games from other consoles and platforms. Their "fighting" genre includes games that, as I'll mention later, are staples of the fighting game community: various *Street Fighter* and *King of Fighters* incarnations, *Soul Calibur*, and *Marvel vs. Capcom* games. However, it also includes games that more rightly belong in Wolf's "Combat" genre of side-scrolling beat-'em-ups, like *Final Fight Double Impact* and *El Shaddai*. It also includes a variety of "ultimate fighting" and pro-wrestling games that straddle the line between fighting and sports, perhaps. It even includes *Left 4 Dead 2*, which is a first-person shooter and not in any way like iconic fighting games such as *Street Fighter*.

Take a look at the "Fighting" genre pages for various consoles on the website for the game retailer Gamestop, or on Amazon.com (which lists the driving combat game *Twisted Metal* as a "fighting" game) and the story is much the same. It's clear that in this case marketers have an investment in grouping games together in a way that drives sales, rather than in a way that's focused solely on their qualities; if anything, marketers take the most top level elements of these games and then string them together on that alone.

Finally, there's the issue of players themselves in general, and fighting-game players, specifically. As Chapter 3 will discuss in more detail, players can have some very particular ideas about what exactly constitutes a fighting game in the first place. Even a game series that meets many players' understanding of what a fighting game is—the *Super Smash Bros.* games, for example—can become contested territory, depending on who you talk to. As mentioned previously, when it comes to genre, context is very important. The diehard *Smash Bros.* tournament fighter, the casual *Marvel* fan, and the *Street Fighter* arcade veteran are all coming from different places when it comes to imagining what fighting games are. Yet each of these players wants to engage a game with the fighting game "feel."

FIGHTING IN TWO OR THREE DIMENSIONS

According to Brian Ashcraft (2008), the earliest fighting games found in the Japanese arcade scene were Sega's 1976 *Heavyweight Champ*, a boxing game, and a smattering of karate or kung fu-related games, such as *Karate Champ* (1985) and *Yie Ar Kung Fu* (1986), which tried to simulate more realistic, competitive martial arts. He explains that these games didn't reach high popularity because shooting games had major dominance in Japanese arcades at that time. That said, these games have little in common with how fighting games are understood today.

The title that changed it all was Capcom's *Street Fighter 2* in 1991. A sequel to a little-known game[5], *SF2* featured highly stylized (and somewhat stereotypically ethnic) characters, each with a repertoire of special techniques that had very little indeed to do with realistic martial arts in any way: an Indian yogi breathed fire, a Chinese acrobat/martial artist delivered kicks so fast that the eye couldn't track them, and a green-skinned Brazilian beast crackled with self-generated electricity. The goal of the game was simple: reduce your opponent's health to zero within 90 seconds by using kicks, punches, grapples, and the aforementioned special attacks, while protecting your own health by dodging or blocking your opponent's attacks. Whoever won two rounds first was declared the winner.

It's no wild leap to call *SF2* the progenitor of the modern fighting game. Ashcraft goes on to describe how other companies, such as Neo Geo developer SNK, would create their own spins on the *Street Fighter* mystique, using the same general elements and reconfiguring them in different ways. One such game—Data East's *Fighter's History*—was reportedly so close in execution and tone that Capcom sued them in the United States for copyright infringement (Dannenberg, 2005), though they lost the suit. However, for many years the *Street Fighter* series was the grand dame of the fighting game world. The original *SF2* would go through five separate incarnations between 1991 and 1994, with each new edition adding new characters and moves, and otherwise refining the game engine (Horwitz, n.d.). It also sparked a number of spinoff series (including the three *Street Fighter Alpha* games, among others) and two direct sequels: *Street Fighter 3* (1997) and *Street Fighter 4* (2009). Both *SF3* and *SF4* have followed the series tradition of multiple versions as well.

However, the *SF* series—and the many games it's inspired over the years—are specifically what the community calls "2D fighters." In a 2D fighting game, there's no third dimension for on-screen action; characters can move left or right, jump or crouch, but they can't move into or out of the foreground/background[6]. Even *Street Fighter 4*, which made the series switch from sprite-based to 3D model-based graphics, follows this structure. To compete, in 1993 Sega created their *Virtua Fighter* series of games. Although a lot of what was in *SF2* went into *VF*—life gauges, special attacks, stylized characters, and a focus on one-on-one competition—the designers at Sega used 3D models that could move around a 3D battlefield. Now, instead of just left and right, players could move in circles around the opponent. Also, it was now possible to win the match by hurling the opponent off the side of the arena, a type of win that would come to be called a "ring out," and that would go on to become a staple of 3D fighters.

Just like *SF2*, 3D games like *Virtua Fighter* also sparked the development of followers and innovators. Among the best-known of the 3D fighter series to emerge are the *Tekken* and *Soul* series of games by Namco (now Namco-Bandai). While the *Tekken* games, currently on their sixth incarnation, focus on hand-to-hand martial arts combat, the *Soul* series—starting with *Soul Blade* and then the *Soul Calibur* games up to the recently-released fifth game under that name—introduced weapon combat to the mix. However, both games are touchstones for the basics of 3D fighting games: the ability to move around your opponent in any direction, and the ring out victory by knocking the opponent off the arena floor.

That said, this 2D/3D dichotomy isn't the only mode that exists for fighting games. Nintendo subsidiary HAL Laboratories created *Super Smash Bros.* for the Nintendo 64 in 1999, launching a franchise that would appear twice more on Nintendo home consoles: *Super Smash Bros. Melee* on the GameCube and *Super Smash Bros. Brawl* most recently on the Wii. The *Smash* series takes popular characters from various Nintendo properties and pits them against each other in combats of up to four players. The controls are somewhat simpler than the complex motions of *SF* games, usually requiring only a directional input and a single button to pull off, but for the most part the basic building blocks of 2D fighters are here: characters move on a 2D plane, using attacks to weaken their opponent.

However, unlike the featureless backdrops of *Street Fighter*-style games, *Smash* stages have more in common with 3D fighters: the stages are large, irregular, and freely navigable, sometimes even featuring damaging hazards and other gimmicks. On top of that, usable items—everything from paper fans to laser guns—appear at random and are usable by players as well. The goal in a *Smash* game isn't to deplete the opponent's vitality, but rather to knock an opponent clear off the stage. Rather than counting down health to zero, as a *Smash* character takes damage, his/her damage "percentage" goes up; the higher that number, the easier it is to send that character flying with a powerful attack. Interestingly, a 3D-based game series in a very similar vein—the *Power Stone* games—were created by Capcom for the Sega Dreamcast as well, with a later compendium re-released on the Sony PlayStation Portable. However, the *Power Stone* games were less popular and well-known compared to *Smash*, likely because the latter had the force of many popular and beloved Nintendo properties behind it.

A WORKING DEFINITION

So, taking all of this into account, we circle back to the question we had at the start: just what *is* a fighting game? For this book's purposes, we can take a few of the common and important aspects from the discussion above and create the central points of a working definition.

First, **these are games of close-quarters combat.** For the most part, fighting games involve physical combat between the on-screen characters. Sometimes elements of that combat might involve projectiles; as an example, Ryu of *Street Fighter*'s iconic attack is the "Hadouken," a ball of energy he throws from his hands. That said, the focus of a match is rarely to out-shoot the opponent, *Halo*-style, using these moves. Their role is to give some fighters variety and extra capability to control space on the field, or as fighting game fans call it, to "zone." So for our purposes, fighting games are close-quarters combat games about martial arts action. The combat may be silly or wacky in appearance, but it retains the flavor of physical, melee combat with or without weapons.

Second, **characters in these games have standard and special attacks, or "moves."** The mode is that each selectable character has a range of standard (sometimes called "normal") moves that are available with the press of a single button, such as *SF*'s Roundhouse Kick or the *Soul* series' Horizontal Slash. While each character executes these differently in terms of animation and frame rates, etc., the execution is the same. On the flip side, characters typically have "special" moves (or even highly complex and limited-use moves, called "supers" or "ultras") that require more complex controls, but offer specialized and powerful capabilities compared to the more vanilla and utilitarian "normals." Ryu's Hadouken mentioned above, for example, is executed by hitting down, down-toward, and toward the opponent, along with using a punch button. The payoff for the more complex input is that he has an attack that he can use at range. While this is a simplistic description—in execution, there's a massive variety of techniques available to an advanced player—it gives a sense of the basics expected from a fighting game.

Third, **match parameters are quantified on-screen in some way.** Put more simply, things like life bars, the time remaining in the match, and other aspects of the fight are not left ambiguous; they're quantified and shown on-screen during the fight and are visible to all. Some games have secondary gauges that are also there for the player. Many games with "super" moves have an entire "super gauge" dedicated to showing that resource. The Arc System Works fighter *BlazBlue* often has a specialized gauge specific to each character, thanks to their designs; Rachel Alucard controls the wind and thus has a meter for how many times she can use that power, while Bang Shishigami uses nail-based projectiles and so has a nail counter for how many more he can throw.

Fourth, **fighting games are competitive.** The goal of a fighting game match is to determine a winner, be it in a game against the computer or against another person. Some home console versions have extra modes that don't meet this feature—such as *Marvel vs. Capcom 3*'s "mission mode," intended to teach players attacks and combinations of moves—but these modes are almost always couched in terms of bonus/extra content, a service to the fans. In general, in a fighting game, the goal of a match is for one player to reduce the others' health (or similar resource) to zero.

Finally, and most importantly to fighting game fans, **these games allow for multiplayer competition.** This is really the distinguishing feature of fighting games, especially as compared to what Wolf called "beat 'em ups[7]." Think about it: conceptually, playing *Street Fighter* against the computer and playing a game of *Final Fight* don't have much difference. They even feel the same in execution: The characters in *FF* have basic attacks and more complex special moves, a quantified health gauge . . . everything listed above. What really sets *Street Fighter* apart is that two human players can go up against each other competitively. As we'll see later in the book, it's this competitive drive that draws in fans and has contributed so much to the culture of fighting games as a whole.

While this definition is a little broad, it covers a wide range of games—just like the fighting game community, which has its core popular games and its more esoteric outliers as well. However, these qualities are the basics that the games they enjoy have in common, and they're useful for understanding not just the variety of fighting games people play, but also the more intricate and complex things about the way their fans play them.

CHAPTER DEVELOPMENT

The chapters of this book cover what I learned from engaging with serious fighting game players about their play and their communities. Through recounting their stories and analyzing their practices, I argue that both these players and the games they play are at the center of a nexus of different defining factors. The way that serious fighting game fans approach the act of playing involves literal gameplay, true, but it also involves a complex network of social expectations, historical contexts, technological constraints, and attitudes toward play. What comes out of that are two things: a set of activities—a performance—that defines the player as a "fighting game fan," but which also defines what "fighting games" are in the first place. As the players continue to play and engage, they are continually defining themselves as players and the games they play in a cycle.

Arcades—public commercial spaces for playing digital games—may be dying out in the United States, but to the fighting game community they are an important historical context. Chapter 2 discusses just how important they are by examining the different aspects of the arcade experience that are still influencing fighting game fans today, especially in an era where online play through home gaming consoles and computers is the norm. Echoes of the arcade are present in the fighting game community in many forms: the technology of arcade sticks, the etiquette of multiplayer play, even the expectations of competitive play. Many fighting game fans were introduced to the hobby via the arcade despite its massive decline, as well.

However, this story is as much about where fighting games are as it is about where they came from. Chapter 3 looks at the practice of play: the rules—social or otherwise—that govern play in these communities. What are the preferred ways to play for these fans? Perhaps more interestingly, what happens when group A thinks the game should be played one way, and group B thinks it should be played another? This chapter follows two critical paths: that fighting games are competitions that deserve a level playing field, and defining the qualities of an "ideal" match, which exhibits all the different qualities that the fighting game culture holds dear.

Chapter 4 brings the focus away from playstyle and toward the social aspect of fighting game culture. The central idea in this chapter is that for fighting game fans, there is a core conceit that's impossible to get away from: these games are meant for competing with people, not playing against a computer. In this chapter I'll discuss the ways in which fighting gamers come together socially, both online and off: the affordances and limitations unique to online play, as well as the ways in which social events like tournaments serve simultaneously as competitions and social gatherings.

Chapter 5 is less about where and how fighting gamers play together, and more about their various online communities. Online forum spaces provide places not only for fighting game fans to gather, but perhaps most critically, places for them to meet up, arrange play events, and to distribute and debate—officially or otherwise—information about the way games "should" be played. As the forums tied to the EVO tournament, Shoryuken. com or "SRK" is a locus of this activity, but no matter the game and the players, there's a web community doing this sort of work. In this chapter we'll look at how these communities bring players together and, in the case of debates over playstyle and player culture, can also split them apart.

A person's identity is a complex thing; in Chapter 6, " 'Asian Hands' and Women's Invitationals," I look at how being a fighting game fan can and does intersect with other ways of defining oneself, with particular regard to ethnicity and gender. As the source of many of the games that fighting game fans love to play, Japanese culture (and southeast Asian cultures in general) has a complicated relationship with fighting game culture in the

United States, especially since some of the world's top-ranked players come from Asian countries. On top of that, despite the rapidly growing number of women who play games or identify as gamers, the fighting game community remains a very male-dominated space that is in many ways hostile to women players. This chapter will discuss some of the discourses around race and gender that haunt the community, and how they shape what it means to identify as a serious fighting game fan.

In the last chapter, I reflect on the stories and experiences that make up the snapshot of the fighting game culture that this book represents, and discuss in detail the major conclusion: being a fighting game fan means performing that identity on multiple levels, from adhering to a certain playstyle to embodying certain discourses about where and when these games should be played in the first place. In the end, what a fighting game even is sits at the center of all these various influences, and to those players who don't perform play in the same way, it can often feel as if they're not even playing the same game anymore. This final chapter will bring the discussion back to the theories I mentioned earlier about performance, and suggest some ways in which this understanding of one diverse and fascinating community can inform how we understand other digital game player cultures.

NOTES

1. The video, dubbed "EVO 2004 Moment #37," can be viewed online at http:// www.youtube.com/watch?v=jtuA5we0RZU. For reasons that will become apparent later in the book, the commentator interestingly refers to this as a rare instance of Umehara being "actually angry."
2. The text at TVTropes.com for this trope—http://tvtropes.org/pmwiki/pmwiki. php/Main/StopHavingFunGuys—used to be much more explicit in referencing *Smash*. The trope's picture was even a screenshot of the stage select screen for *Smash Bros. Melee*.
3. These are pseudonyms used for research reporting purposes.
4. See Harper, 2010. Though that analysis of *Persona 3* focuses on procedural rhetoric, I argue that the procedural and the fictional are working together to create large-scale rhetorical frames.
5. Its predecessor was the original *Street Fighter*. The first *SF* had very simplistic controls compared to *SF2* and only had one selectable character, series icon Ryu. However, the seeds of what would eventually become the core concept of the *Street Fighter* series were still there.
6. An exception here is SNK's *Fatal Fury* games, which had two to three "lanes" in a stage that one could move between. However, as SNK's fighting games developed into the future, this stage setup turned out to be an infrequently-used gimmick rather than a serious interface change.
7. Compare video of a *Street Fighter 4* match—http://youtu.be/hp Com3opMdc#t=03m10s—with play of recently re-released, *Dungeons and Dragons*-themed beat 'em up *Shadows over Mystara*: http://youtu.be/ 3I2poY6lBMU. In both scenarios, the players are using specific controller combinations to perform combat maneuvers, but there is a clear difference between the one-on-one competition of *SF* and the cooperative combat of *Shadows over Mystara*.

2   The Arcade Ideal

What sort of image does the phrase "game arcade" conjure up? For some it might evoke a fun fair at a theme park or playground: an open-air gathering of various skill games like skee-ball and the like. For others—such as myself—it conjures up memories of dimly lit, cramped spaces inside other commercial venues, like shopping malls and movie theatres. Row after row of games inside their brightly-colored cabinets, each showing equally vibrant images to draw you in and pull your quarters into their hungry coin slots. Not to mention the cacophony of mixed sounds; the chiming tones of a crane game versus the staccato of gunfire from a shooting game multiplied by the cheers, groans, and conversations of the human element.

And of course, you can't forget the people in this image, either: players moving from machine to machine trying to find a game they like, or huge crowds of players—usually young men—clustered around one game that allowed head-to-head competition, an appreciative crowd watching a very public performance of play. This second image is very much intertwined with fighting games and fighting game culture, as this chapter will discuss. The arcade represents a point of entry for considering the environment and circumstances of fighting game play, one of the most basic but also most critical aspects of play within the community. Looking at the environment of play provides insights not only into how fighting games *are* played, but also how the people who play them feel these games *should* be played. Understanding their preferred environment—and the influences that helped create it—is a window to the community's normative constructs, especially when it's spread across geographical and temporal space.

Fighting games, particularly the *Street Fighter* series, became highly popular in the 1990s, despite a decline in arcade play (Horwitz, n.d.). Comparatively, in Japan, arcades and gaming centers are still quite popular, and fighting games in particular have a thriving arcade culture there (Ashcraft, 2008). Yet for fans of fighting games, this arcade experience—standing at an arcade machine, surrounded by other players cheering and yelling, fighting an opponent one-on-one in public—remains very salient, even for those players who did not have the chance to experience it firsthand. Echoes of the arcade experience press into the future in the form of the way fighting games are played now, and many of the ways in which current fighting gamers play are designed to evoke the feel of this experience.

Thus this chapter focuses on the arcade as a critical influence on fighting game culture, which manifests in a few different ways: the arcade as a social space (both physical and imagined), the arcade as technology and apparatus, and finally the arcade as a focus for acculturation. Examining these influences we find that the arcade is a place both real and imagined, where technology and playstyle come together to both bring people into the fighting game community fold and to teach them the basics of what that means.

THE ARCADE IN CONTEXT

The earliest days of video games were characterized by arcade machines or cabinets: tall, person-height enclosures featuring a control setup—typically a joystick and a series of buttons, though variations existed—and a monitor and speakers which displayed the game's audio/visual elements. The public's image of the arcade includes all sorts of elements, but one of the most durable and widespread is the aforementioned crowd of rowdy, enthusiastic players surrounding a single cabinet. Academic research on arcades is somewhat difficult to find, but a few sources tell the story of the arcade as a space that triumphed in the early days of gaming popularity and then began to wane over time, for a number of reasons. Dmitri Williams (2004) discusses a cultural shift away from public spaces and into the home as technology improved. According to him, play moved "away from social, communal, and relatively anarchic early arcade spaces, and into the controlled environments of the sanitized mall arcade (or 'family fun center') or into the home" (p. 40).

Both Williams and Kline, Dyer-Witheford, and De Peuter (2003) also describe a situation where the development of home consoles that let consumers play video games in the home rather than in separate public spaces was a major factor in the decline of the arcade. More to the point, at first consoles like the Atari 2600 and the Nintendo Entertainment System—the dominant forces in the 70s and 80s—didn't necessarily produce "arcade-authentic" reproductions of games. However, as time wore on and the home console (and PC) became increasingly powerful and available, the "home version" of games became more faithful. *Pac-Man* on the Atari 2600 was a blocky, highly incomplete version of the arcade cabinet (that nevertheless sold plenty of consoles for Atari) but by the time the PlayStation emerged in 1994, home versions of arcade games were functionally identical to their source material. As we'll discuss in more detail in Chapter 3, this faithfulness is a critically important factor in the relationship between fighting game competitors and home console versions of fighting games.

One respondent in this study, Evan, had some experience working in arcades, and shared with me a few anecdotes that speak to the economics of arcades versus home consoles. When I asked what games he plays in the arcades versus at home, he mentioned *BlazBlue* and *Tekken 6* as games he plays at home, primarily for economic reasons:

> *BlazBlue*, I had to give that a try on console 'cause it was just too much stuff going for me to be popping quarters in there to learn a completely new system. . . . I got *Tekken 6*, I tried getting into that, but that's mostly on console, which is . . . the whole *Tekken 6* was basically just the current economy of arcades thing, where the *Tekken 6* cabinet costs, like, a billion dollars and there's not enough *Tekken* players to get a machine that costs a billion dollars, so we opted out of that one, yeah.

The idea here is that Evan would prefer to play everything in the arcade, but when that model is pay per play[1] it's not economically feasible to learn a new game and its systems in the arcade. The expectation, of course, is also that in a public space you'll be fighting against other people, and so in a low-skill scenario you may have to spend considerable money just to be beaten down by those more experienced.

Evan also notes that most fighting game arcade cabinets are modular—"we just need a board, and they can fix the sticks or hook that up however they want to"—but that the *Tekken* series cabinets are "dedicated," meaning they have to be purchased wholesale and have many side expenses that up the cost even further. Thus those games tend to be more expensive, but "if you jack the price up to sort of help recoup things, people will complain a lot, so." In short, this economic imperative is both powerful and cyclical. Home console ports are cheaper than the arcade, and as time goes on have greater fidelity to the original, which drives arcade business down, and so arcade owners either have to charge more per game to recoup, or rely on more "gimmick"-like sources of income, which makes arcades less attractive to audiences like hardcore fighting game fans.

In his examination of public opinions of and academic research on gameplay, Williams identifies a moral panic-like stance about gaming in the early 1980s that reflected shifts in and concerns about "family values" in the United States: "[w]hat was once considered a harmless fad could now be seen as fostering a range of ills including drug use, gambling, and prostitution" (p. 63). However, he also describes a time when arcades were praised as places where people could be social and play together, breaking boundaries of class, ethnicity, and age (though, sadly, not so much gender; digital games remained a male-coded activity).

Williams would go on to write more on this notion of games—and particularly arcades—as social spaces, and of the power and appeal of social play. In particular, he discusses the notion that at the arcade, what really mattered more than anything was skill at playing games: "[t]here was no gender or status bias in arcade competition, and the machine didn't care if the player was popular, rich, or an outcast" (p. 8). What was critically important was that the arcade presented a space to engage an activity with other people. As we'll discuss in this chapter, this element of arcade play is incredibly important to the fighting game community, who have not only adapted their play to allow it, but have in fact centered their organizational play behaviors around it.

Considering that many of the most famous fighting game titles—in fact, nearly all of them—come from Japanese companies such as Capcom and Namco-Bandai, a brief look at the arcade scene as it exists in Japan is helpful if only to highlight its relationship to U.S. fighting game culture. As one of my interviewees, Jordan, put it, "I mean, Japan . . . the arcades, and the density of the area that you can get all the best people, like, intermingled and playing together all the time." Comparatively, he mentioned how in the United States, competitive players are spread over a much wider area, particularly since the east and west coasts have some of the largest concentrations of those players.

Brian Ashcraft, a writer on Japanese gaming culture for the gaming news site *Kotaku*, wrote a book on Japanese arcades—*Arcade Mania: The Turbo-Charged World of Japan's Game Centers* (2008)—which describes a much more vibrant, varied, and widespread culture of arcades than is found in the United States. Interestingly, many of the attractions found in Japanese game centers are "fun fair"-style games, such as pachinko or crane games, that are more resonant with the "family fun center" conception of the arcade space. Yet the fighting game culture consistently paints the Japanese arcade scene as a flourishing Nirvana of strong competitors that gives those players an edge over Americans and their comparative lack of physical meet-up spaces. In Chapter 6, I return to this difference between the US and Japanese arcade scenes and how it affects the community's ideas about race and ethnicity in the fighting game culture, specifically an assumed relationship between Asian players and naturally high skill levels.

EVO itself—the pre-eminent fighting game tournament in the United States of which much of the information in this book is an analysis—has roots in the culture of the arcade, if not so much the literal space of one. Seth Killian, one of EVO's initial organizers, related this part of EVO's history both to me personally at the 2009 event and to *Kotaku* a year earlier in an interview (Crecente, 2008). At first nothing more than a competition between highly skilled fighting game fans arranged over usenets, the EVO tournament was hosted at various arcades across the country before settling down in Las Vegas and—thanks to an explosion of interest that would "require more cabinets than exist on the whole continent"—switching from arcade machine play to using home console versions, a decision Killian describes as "extremely hard."

Killian expresses sentiments about the arcade that I came to find are echoed quite powerfully by the community of which he is an icon. His interview with *Kotaku* describes arcade play as a "crucible" in which a number of factors[2] come together in gestalt to create a powerful feeling of affect, in particular a social one. His description—and as you'll see below, the descriptions provided by other players as well—speaks to the competition, the closeness with other people, and the sense of both rivalry and camaraderie that a social, physically-oriented head-to-head activity can provide as what he (and presumably others) love about it. Noting that he doubts fighting games would have become so popular had they never come out in the arcade, he finishes by saying "EVO isn't about bringing back arcades, but preserving this fire, this passion, this connection."

THE ARCADE AS SPACE

So, we know that the arcade was in many ways a place for social play, and that legacy has in some way moved forward to inspire, if not the fighting game community itself, then the institutions that support it, like the EVO tournament. We also know that various forces aligned that have caused the literal arcade space—the physical manifestations of it described above, like the fun fair or the mall arcade—to, if not die out, then dwindle substantially. The question that remains is, how do echoes of the arcade still exist? What was playing games—particularly fighting games—in the arcade like, and how do various spaces for fighting game play *now* echo, recreate, and reconfigure that experience?

A recent and very telling real world example that highlights both the changes US arcades are going through, as well as their importance as a space to fighting game players, is the story of a famous New York City arcade: Chinatown Fair (see Figure 2.1). In many ways, the "old" Chinatown Fair was the perfect example of the type of arcade where fighting game culture had its infancy and development: it was a "dim, dank and narrow battlefield of wall-to-wall Japanese street-fighter games" (Gregory, 2012), a place that even a longtime fan described as "a sort of dank, musty hole in the middle of Chinatown . . . [i]t wasn't a large place, nor a particularly well-kept place by any means, but it was a sincerely cool little spot, especially if you dug competitive fighting games" (Navarro, 2012). Certainly, these mental images evoke more of that "anarchic early arcade space" Williams discusses; my own memories of arcades in the mid- to late 1980s–90s echo very similar spaces, dimly lit and tucked away from everything else.

Problematically, though, the "old" Chinatown Fair wasn't financially tenable in the eyes of its manager, Lonnie Sobel, who told the *New York Times* "No, [the arcade]'s not exactly the same as it was before. If it was, it wouldn't be in business now." And in the eyes of everyone who witnessed

Figure 2.1   Street Fighter cabinets at the "old" Chinatown Fair, February 2011. Photo by Dan Dickinson, used with permission under Creative Commons License 2.0.

Chinatown Fair's 2012 reopening after a protracted time being out of business, the space was definitely not the same. Consider this description from the same article:

> The old arcade has been washed in bright candy colors, flashing lights and carnival-style music, the background of an animated movie. A pink Baby Air hockey table sits by the door, near [tic-tac-toe-playing chicken] Lillie's former performance space. The Wizard of Oz coin pusher game draws the biggest crowd.

Indeed, the photos that accompany this and other stories about the changes to Chinatown Fair show a brightly-colored space full of flashy carnival games like skee-ball, rather than a dark corridor lined with *Street Fighter* machines. The end result is more of Williams' "family fun center" than the arcade that fighting gamers came to the genre through.

That much becomes obvious simply by reading the reactions of longtime fans to the change. Joshua Kopstein (2012), writing for online tech and media outlet *The Verge*, provides a very telling anecdote along those lines:

> Before we could even get inside, various cries of anguish coalesced into an informal sidewalk assembly that seemed to vaguely resemble

a funeral. "It's a trap!" yelled one distressed fan as he emerged from the arcade's legendary threshold on the south end of Mott Street. Chinatown Fair . . . had undergone some drastic changes, and some of the regulars were none too happy about it. "They should have let it stay dead," another arcade veteran loudly proclaimed in a harsh tone.

For an arcade that was once synonymous with fighting games in the area (Fishbein, 2012), this sudden transformation to an entirely different space—one notably devoid of the fighting games it used to host—was striking and disappointing for many fighting game fans. Alex Navarro lamented the transformation to a family-friendly space, wondering what would come of spaces that were, perhaps, specifically *not* family-friendly, a thing he associates with the "old" Chinatown Fair and arcades like it. Bound up in these rejections of the change are some very deep and telling statements about the relationship between fighting game fans and that prototypical arcade that the pre-change Chinatown Fair represented. A space that's not "for kids" and which might be a little dirty, a little messy, maybe even "anarchic" as Williams put it, but was ultimately theirs.

This desire and nostalgia for the arcade space is, as previously discussed, a motivator behind the EVO tournament having strong roots in the arcade tradition. In its earliest days, EVO was primarily an arcade tournament that took place in arcades across the country before expansion moved it outwards to increasingly larger venues[3], and advancing console technology made it possible to play arcade-perfect versions of those arcade games on home consoles, such as PlayStation or Xbox. Seth Killian stated outright that the EVO tournament itself attempts to capture the feel of the arcade, even now that it's moved to console-based play.

The setting itself had strong echoes of the arcade space, with a monitor as a focal point and a cluster of people around it spreading outward from the two (or more) players at the epicenter. Particularly on days one and two, when the elimination pools were still filled with competitors playing through their matches, the relatively intimate setting of the pool booths—a table no more than a person height across with a TV and enough room for two side-by-side chairs—gave rise to batches of small groups together in this mold. Similarly, the bring-your-own-console spaces and even the booths for both Capcom and Namco-Bandai to feature their upcoming and current games were roughly the same: a TV and enough space for a few people to stand close together around it, connected in sequence. These close gathering points, with a small cloud of onlookers centered around the two people playing the game, had considerable resonance with the crowds one might find at a game arcade. In the BYOC and test booth areas, even the "I've got next" practice, where the next player in line indicates that they will play the winner of the current match, was common[4].

Yet among all of the players I interviewed, there are aspects of the arcade experience—playing alongside another person in a physical space being watched by a crowd, for example—that are resonant among all of the respondents regardless of their history. Those respondents who had attended tournaments or events like EVO in the past—particularly those who have attended an actual EVO tournament—spoke to their great affection for such situations, where players are gathered together in a physical space to play matches against one another while other enthusiasts are there to watch and take part. Interestingly enough, in describing the Japanese arcade experience, Ashcraft (2008) notes that in Japanese arcades, standing next to the other player side-by-side was a detriment to machine use/coin drop in fighting game cabinets. As he tells it, once arcade managers in Japan developed two linked cabinets that were back to back, so challengers *couldn't* look at each other while playing, business took off. Such cabinets, sometimes called "candy cabinets," are the norm in Japan compared to the US.

One might wonder why this mode of play, with its emphasis on cohabiting space and playing in person, would be so dominant, particularly in a world where online-capable consoles with arcade-perfect home versions ("ports") of most fighting games are commonplace. Wouldn't online play offer a better opportunity to fight against many different types of opponents, without the cost and effort involved in finding a physical space to do it in? The answer, almost universally, was that it does not. Although some of the reasons why are related to the technology of online play, many of the reasons that the respondents I spoke to avoid online play—either altogether, or only using it in highly specific circumstances—dealt with its impersonal nature, and the behaviors enabled by anonymity. The arcade ideal of two people face to face in the proverbial ring stands as a contrast to online play; in a world where fighting games can and often are played online, the players I spoke to not only rejected that mode of play, but have embraced a different one with a far greater resource cost by comparison.

This isn't to say that all the players interviewed eschew online play. Ibrahim noted he still plays online in games that he does not take "seriously," which can easily be read as another way of saying "competitively," yet Nicholas got his start playing online. Garret actually finds that online matches can be rewarding "if you find good players," but that in the end, "I'd say that playing online is good for learning but not competing. It's much better to be face to face." The general thrust of these statements seems to be that the limitations of online play hold it back, but it's better than nothing. Later we'll discuss what it is about the online play experience that contributes to this scenario, but for now it suffices to know that while online play is a possibility, playing in an offline space is the preferred mode.

THE ARCADE AS TECHNOLOGY

More than just being a physical space, the arcade presented a very specific kind of interface with games as well. The arcade cabinet is such a widespread image that practically anyone can envision what one looked like: somewhere between 5' and 6' tall, with a recessed area about head height for the screen and a flat shelf at just above waist height with between two and four joysticks with accompanying buttons. Of course, this was provided that the game was controllable with joysticks; cabinets for racing games often featured a single wheel as interface instead[5]. Standing in front of one of these is a much different experience than sitting at home on the couch, facing the TV with a console controller in your hand.

For games played in that context, there are a wide variety of possibilities for controlling the on-screen character. While the single joystick and button setup of the Atari 2600 echoed the arcade, over time the control pads for consoles like the NES and PlayStation would come to only vaguely resemble their arcade forebears. The typical method of control for most console games is an input device that for our purposes will be called a "pad:" these are often rectangular or wing-shaped devices that are included with the console at point of sale, including a series of individual face buttons, typically a "cross pad"—a +-shaped directional controller—and one or two analog "thumb sticks." This distinction between how arcade games and console games are controlled, however, leads to an important example of how arcade technology moved out of that space and into the fighting game culture broadly.

A phenomenon I noticed while observing play at EVO was the ubiquity of something called the arcade stick (see Figure 2.2). Those devices, by contrast, are a different animal; the ones I observed at EVO were typically

Figure 2.2 An EVO 2009 competitor's arcade stick in between match downtime. Photo by author.

in a relatively large wood housing, roughly the size of a large city phone book, with two rows of face buttons and a single tall joystick. The term "arcade stick" comes from the fact that these sticks are built to resemble the joysticks and buttons that are used to control arcade game cabinets, particularly fighting game cabinets. The double rows of three buttons echo the control scheme for the original *Street Fighter 2*, which offered three types of punch and three types of kick. In fact, this faithful resemblance to the arcade layout is quite important; consider that most modern game console controllers also involve joysticks (in the form of analog sticks) but their layout is not intended to evoke a specific arcade aesthetic in most cases.

Of course, beyond controlling the game, arcade sticks are also a form of personal expression. The ones that I observed at EVO also served to identify a certain gamer chic; these controllers are often housed in quite large wooden "boxes," and while some players left their stick boxes unadorned (see Figure 2.3), others decorated them.

It's not entirely clear why some players leave their arcade sticks unadorned, while others choose to decorate them in various ways. Certainly, one possible reason for decorating a stick is to show fandom for a particular game, and in fact some sticks had art on them from media that have nothing to do with fighting games. In chapter 4, I discuss in greater detail the relationship

Figure 2.3   An example of a totally unadorned arcade stick at EVO 2009. Photo by author.

between the iconography found on decorated arcade sticks and what it says about fighting gamers and their relationship to broader fan cultures. Suffice it to say, however, that whether they were plain wood frames or layered with pieces of anime-style character art, the arcade stick was everywhere at the EVO tournament.

Also, the creation and modification of arcade sticks is a pursuit all its own, separate from their use as controls for playing the game. One of my interviewees for this research, months after the study had ended, emailed me to share a link to a video[6] demonstrating an arcade stick that was made with advanced, responsive LED lights on the buttons. The video, which is four minutes long, shows a number of fascinating but totally unnecessary effects: a "Simon"-style memory game that the user can play with the buttons, as well as flashing patterns that can be programmed with the stick itself. Doing a little research on the Internet on unusual arcade sticks, as inspired by the video I was sent, even produced a picture of a completely functioning PlayStation2 compatible stick that was built in a Rubbermaid plastic storage container[7].

In talking about case mods—alterations to a computer case that are decorative, functional, or sometimes both—for PC gaming, Bart Simon (2007) observes that they're a way to perform a number of different ideal identities for the modder; as he puts it, "[w]hat started as a practical solution for cooling overclocked systems has become, among gamer-modders, a means of self-expression and, importantly, a means of demonstrating machine knowledge and skill" (p. 187). The mods can show off an artistic skill through aesthetic beauty, but it can also show off expertise and knowledge through a beneficial effect on computer *or* by the fact that specialized knowledge and skill is required to create one in the first place.

Simon is quick to point out, however, that a case mod cannot *only* be artistic: "a crucial component of a quality case mod is not only that it works but that it works well in terms of computer performance" (p. 190). It's quite likely that this is what's going on with arcade sticks like the ones I just described; it's critical that they're functional, but showing technical expertise in adding superfluous but interesting aesthetic modifications is its own way of both participating in and paying homage to the culture of fighting games. It's worth noting, for example, that the flashing LEDs are a callback to the noise and flashing lights that were the occasional hallmark of the physical arcade experience.

Certainly, reflecting on the previously discussed importance of the arcade experience, the prevalence of arcade sticks made a certain amount of sense. If replicating the feel of the arcade is important, then using a controller that duplicates that experience is a logical extension of that. However, it seems unlikely that a group of respondents that puts such an emphasis on the context of play and the proper play environment would embrace widespread use of a particular peripheral *only* for that reason.

A secondary concern here is cost. A look at the official stores for two arcade stick manufacturers mentioned by respondents—Hori and MadCatz—shows sticks costing, at the time of this writing, well over US$100 ("Real Arcade Pro. EXSE", 2009; "Xbox 360 Real Arcade Pro. VX SA", 2013; "GameShark Store—Arcade Sticks", n.d.): a non-trivial amount of money, to be sure. What advantages does the arcade stick offer over the alternatives that justifies the cost and accounts for such widespread use? The answer involves a number of factors, but it contributes to the idea of a "comfortable environment."

Almost every interview respondent reported owning and using an arcade stick; even players on the more casual end of the spectrum such as Isaac and Jordan. In general, their logic was quite specific: arcade sticks offer a level of control that a pad does not. The reasons for this are numerous, involving everything from the speed of button presses to the ways in which moving an object with one's thumb is different than doing so with the palm of the hand, the wrist, or even the entire arm. Ibrahim gave a quite detailed explanation of how this works:

Todd: I'm guessing that people who learned how to play in arcades tend to favor arcade sticks and people who learned on home systems tend to favor pads? Is that a . . .

Ibrahim: Yeah. Although a lot of people who came to the scene much later and played on home systems have seen the advantage that people with sticks have, and just forced themselves to learn how to play it. A good example of that is, if you've ever seen that video on YouTube of the master Tetris player? The speed that he can move a stick—because he's moving it with each of his fingers individually and his palm—he could not possibly do on a pad with just a thumb, because he's inputting five inputs in the amount of time it would take you to move your thumb once.

Todd: I hadn't even thought of that. I just thought I sucked. [laughs]

Ibrahim: [laughs]

Todd: Granted, I don't think I would do any better with an arcade stick. But . . . you know, I'm actually sitting here holding my hand like an idiot, trying to think "Okay, if I was holding the stick, how would it move?" But that's a good point.

Ibrahim: Well with a stick, each of your five fingers can move the stick, plus your palm. With a pad you only really have your thumb, so while one finger is reflexing [sic] from having to press the stick, the next finger is ready to fire.

Jeff also spoke to the relative difference of performing inputs on an arcade stick, physically. He described the difference between holding a pad and attempting to reach every face button with one's thumb, and hovering a hand over an arcade stick where each fingertip is poised to strike a button; a player can make more precise button strikes, and a greater number of them, with the fingertips than with only the thumb. Thus on a simple level of human anatomy, an arcade stick presents a better, more facile control setup than a pad.

Beyond the physical ability to input buttons, however, there is also the actual construction of the stick itself, compared not only to pads, but even between different types of arcade stick. Notable here is the distinction between quality parts and the styles of both American and Japanese-style arcade stick parts. Jordan, Jeff, and Ibrahim in particular had much to say on this subject, referencing Japanese manufacturers Sanwa Denshi and Seimitsu. The situation they describe is one where sticks with Japanese parts—particularly parts from those manufacturers—are superior to those made in the United States by manufacturers such as Suzo-Happ. Jordan put it thusly:

So part of the advantage of the custom build things, and part of the reason they're so expensive, is that they'll usually come with authentic parts, so they'll either be Sanwa parts or Seimitsu parts, and as I understand it, it's mostly a matter of preference, but they're more durable, they're more accurate, the buttons are a lot more sensitive . . . like Sanwa buttons, you can . . . you think you're resting your hand on them and you're engaging them. They're super sensitive . . . and in most of the kind of things where, like, if you haven't experienced it and you look at what people are paying and you look at how obsessed people are you think it's like technology fetishism, right? Like, "oh, this is authentic and that means I'm great because I have authentic," well, no, actually it's a hell of a lot more playable on good parts.

Jeff made a similar mention to the high sensitivity of Sanwa buttons: "You can literally, um, hold a piece of paper—like notebook paper?—and just push it against the buttons, like, holding the other end of the stick, and it'll count the button being hit, just a feather's touch will make these buttons go off . . ." Descriptions of non-Japanese sticks focused on the stickiness of the buttons, and the unresponsive nature of the control stick. Their observations closely mirror a thread on SRK that discusses the various technical advantages and disadvantages of Sanwa and Seimitsu parts compared to those from other manufacturers ("The Sanwa and Seimitsu FAQ", 2006).

These factors encourage the idea that if you aren't using an arcade stick with the proper parts, you're already at a disadvantage against serious fighting gamers who are. Most respondents echoed that, although Ibrahim did note that for 3D fighting games—such as his chosen *Soul Calibur 4*—the difference isn't as critical as it is for 2D games, which require more precise inputs. As for Ibrahim himself: "I prefer to use stick because I grew up on the arcade system, and it feels most natural to me." Isaac describes it as a generational thing, suggesting that players who didn't grow up playing on arcade cabinets (as he did: "I have to make my joystick resemble the American arcade experience that I . . . was inculcated with, you know?") don't have the right context to prefer sticks over pads.

However, learning to use an arcade stick is an important part of the process for people without arcade experience; it isn't as if the stick itself presents an immediately-accessible comfortable playing environment. Quite the contrary; some of the respondents I spoke to who had not always used a stick were emphatic that learning to use one properly—particularly if one is used to a pad—takes practice and acclimation time. My own inability to use an arcade stick provided a useful entry point to discussion on this topic. Both Jordan and Jeff responded by mentioning that it was primarily a matter of time and exposure, though they differed on what the length of that time period might be *like*; Jeff suggested a relatively short 24 hours, while Jordan indicated it could be a much more conservative six–eight weeks. Recall too that Ibrahim speaks of players unfamiliar with arcade sticks who "force themselves" to learn to use them as part of the entry cost to the culture of serious fighting game play.

Interestingly, Evan told a slightly different story. Having played primarily on arcade machines his whole life, playing *without* an arcade stick presents a challenge of its own. On the subject of the adjustment period mentioned previously, he had this to say:

> [Adjusting] isn't a problem with me since I've been playing at home and in the arcade for as long as I remember, so I, um . . . actually the reason I got an arcade stick is actually going the other way, and being frustrated that stuff that I was doing all the time was harder to get in the . . . when I played at home, so it was just like, using the arcade sticks at home, since I was switching back and forth and doing worse on the controller, probably, but it was things that I knew that I could do that I couldn't get out because of the way the buttons were laid out, so.

In either case, learning on a pad or an arcade stick initially seems to have a great influence on preference. Because playing on them has such a wide range of differences, switching from one to the other isn't easy.

Jordan's feeling is that despite their learning curve, the technical advantage of sticks contributes to a comfortable and level playing environment because it is a way the technology can contribute to—rather than detract from—the experience. It's worth noting that my discussion of arcade sticks with Jordan followed from speaking on another similar topic: the ideal TV or monitor to use while playing. At EVO during the *Street Fighter 4* finals, the players once requested that a different TV be swapped in for the one that had been used up to that point. I was unclear on the reason why, and he explained that depending on the TV/monitor, there could be perceptible lag time between inputs on the controller and their appearance on screen, which then led to a discussion of the influence of technology on play:

Todd: So, but it does . . . it kind of seems like about minimizing the interference of technology on . . .

Jordan: Yeah, certainly.

Todd: . . . what's going on in the match.

Jordan: Well, I mean . . . that's kind of a broad way of putting it.

Todd: Narrow it down for me?

Jordan: My only quibble with that is, if you think about arcade sticks, right? I mean, people clearly have preferences—arcade stick over controller—but then what's your button layout, are you using . . . what kind of parts are you using? It's like the . . . the technology needs to facilitate the match, not . . .

Todd: Interfere with it.

Jordan: Yeah.

The link between the lag on a monitor (and finding a monitor with the least amount of perceptible lag) and an arcade stick, in this situation, is that in both cases the technology should be something that makes play easier, not more difficult.

One striking example of controller use that I observed personally was during the *Soul Calibur 4* finals at EVO. At one point, a competitor who had been using an arcade stick up to then suddenly switched to a console control pad after losing a match. Since arcade sticks had been the norm at the event, this struck me as odd. That impression was confirmed by the sudden explosive and, to me, inexplicable booing that occurred when the crowd noticed it. Confused, I turned to nearby attendees who were also watching the finals, and asked why the crowd had suddenly turned against this player. One of them informed me that the character he went on to pick for the match that followed—Hilde—had a particularly powerful combination of moves that is easier to perform on a pad than on an arcade stick, and thus his switch in controllers was proof to the audience that he was about to pick the character in question.

It's also worth noting that just because arcade sticks are the norm, that doesn't necessarily mean they're always the rule. At the EVO tournament in 2010, there was a rather infamous match between veteran fighting game champion Justin Wong and Vance "Vangief" Wu, a player known for using a default control pad instead of an arcade stick. They met in the *Super Street Fighter IV* finals and while the match was close, in the end Vangief was able to hold his own and win against an extremely skilled opponent who was using an arcade stick. Watching video of the match[8] is actually quite instructive on the impact of this decision; the seasoned veterans giving play-by-play commentary mention the pad use multiple times with undisguised incredulity/surprise in their voices. Interestingly, his victory over Wong gave Wu a sort of folk-hero status, including a number of Shoryuken.com threads discussing his pad-use style and, perhaps more tellingly, a Facebook fan page titled only, "The robot, Vangief!"

While there's a bigger context regarding Hilde and her unpopular combination attack that I'll return to later, both that example and the community-shocking victory of what was dubbed "Padgief" speak to situations when certain technology choices are part of creating the "best environment" for intended play. Since the moves that the Hilde player wanted to perform were easiest to do with a pad, he used one. While I wasn't on hand to question the crowd about Vance Wu, one assumes that he chose to use a pad because it presented the best choice for his particular playstyle. The "norm"—in this case, arcade-stick use—is pervasive, but only to the extent that it facilitates play in the right manner. If arcade sticks were not widely seen as an effective tool for optimum play, their use may not be nearly as widespread.

There is also a resonance here with the narrative that David Sudnow (1995) presents in his book *Ways of the Hand*. Sudnow tells his story of learning to play improvisational jazz piano. For him, part of the journey was one of coming to grips with an interface: specifically, his hands and a piano keyboard. When he began, there was a period of looking at the keys to make sure his finger positions were correct, but the more he played— and practiced, and internalized—the more automatic and non-conscious his actual hand movements became. In the process, he was able to devote more of his attention to the higher-level issues of playing jazz improv piano. Narratives about using an arcade stick seem to follow the same trajectory. Although the stick presents a point of interface—it literally controls the game—practice with it is intended to make it become so natural, so effortless, that the possible noise (Consalvo, 2009b) created by using the interface is minimized, or even obliterated. In short, using the right technology and adapting to it helps to bridge the gap between the more high-level issues of skill and strategy in the mental realm of play, and the execution of those strategies on-screen.

THE ARCADE AS ACCULTURATION

Another interesting question is: How did the arcade influence players in terms of their entry into fighting game culture in the first place? Looking back on the anecdote that opens this book, I was clearly too young and too inexperienced to understand all of what was going on when I stepped up to a *Street Fighter 2* machine and was challenged by an anonymous stranger. Still, there was something that drew me back to the activity over and over again as I continued to develop an interest in fighting games. A noticeable trend among the players I spoke to during this research was that arcade play served as a gateway to a broader interest in fighting games. Even for players whose interests diverged away later in life, that early arcade fighting experience presents something that drew them in.

Many of the players I interviewed were in their early to mid-20s at the time; only a few were about to enter (or had already entered) adolescence when *Street Fighter 2: The World Warrior* (*SF2*), the game's first iteration, hit arcades in 1991. Yet many of them describe playing *SF2* in the arcade as one of their earliest experiences—if not *the* earliest experience—they had with fighting games in general. Even players such as Ibrahim, who would later in life shift his focus to 3D fighting games such as the *Soul Calibur* series rather than 2D games like *Street Fighter*, started with arcade play of *SF2*:

Todd: Interesting. Back in the *Street Fighter 2* days did you mostly play in arcades, or did you play at home, or a combination of both . . .?

Ibrahim: Well yeah. At first, for a long time, arcade was the only option, so it wasn't until it came out on SNES that people were able to play it at home, so for the first three, four years it was exclusively in the arcades.

Todd: So you said you played exclusively 2D games for a while, so you started with *Street Fighter 2* and the 18 versions of that, I'm guessing.

Ibrahim: Yeah, yeah.

Gene had a similar experience; he played the *Mortal Kombat* games in the arcade, only playing *SF2* once it came to a home console, but those early arcade experiences with *Mortal Kombat* helped to spark an interest in fighting games that would eventually lead to his current engagement with the community, even as he left *Mortal Kombat* behind.

Isaac, the oldest respondent at 36, had a strong friendship in his youth with another player, and one of the foundations of their friendship was that they would play *SF2* against each other in the arcades while he was in college. Though they have since fallen out of contact, Isaac expressed a desire to get in touch with him again, because of his fond memories of those early days. Evan, too, had a fighting friend and rival in his earliest years playing *SF2*, which he describes in relative detail:

Started, waited forever to get on and then started playing and then I . . . probably played there for about . . . I dunno. A couple years? Through all the different versions, there's upgrades, Championship Edition and on through, like, Hyper Fighting stuff, and one of my best friends . . . I really remember meeting him playing *Street Fighter* there, so we would go there and play and we got pretty good for local players.

In both of these cases, it is the combination of the arcade and a close personal relationship that is the salient memory; the two are strongly linked together. In fact, for Evan, the arcade experience was so formative that he would go on to eventually work in the arcade he played in as a teenager, running fighting game tournaments and encouraging the owner to support fighting games in purchasing decisions. Gene describes going to the arcade after school every day, and even mentions "defending" its honor against players from another arcade who came to challenge players there.

The decline of the arcade means that not all respondents—particularly the younger ones—had access to arcades; Nicholas, for example, was too young to have played heavily in the arcades in the early days of fighting games, being only seven when his game of choice, *Super Street Fighter 2 Turbo*, was released. Yet even without the actual arcade setting, arcade cabinet play was still a very common "first experience" with fighting games. Jordan notes that his first experiences with fighting games were playing both *Street Fighter 2* and *Mortal Kombat* at a local bowling alley. That being said, Jordan's first identified *meaningful* investment in play came on a home console; specifically, the release of *Street Fighter Zero 3* (*Alpha 3* in the United States) in the late 1990s. Then there are players like Garret and Aaron who, while having a small amount of scattered arcade experience, have for the most part been home console players of their chosen games.

However, even those players who didn't have regular access to arcades still describe situations where social game play pulled them into the community of play. In the process, they became acculturated to some of the hallmarks of arcade-style play—playing in-person, going to local meetups, tournament play—that the community values. There's a very common thread where players I interviewed would either engage with a home console port, or play a new arcade game, and in the process end up having a match with other players already in the community. Online forums such as SRK and 8 Way Run also become prominent figures in these narratives at this point, a topic I discuss in greater depth in Chapter 5. Ibrahim, Jeff, Garret, and Aaron all tell stories where an initial foray into play led them back to forums, which then led them to other avenues of play that were different than their previous modes. Ibrahim and Garret, players of *Soul Calibur 4*, were introduced to 8 Way Run[9], and from there made connections with other local players. Those connections then branched out into regular, in-person play in their area, which led to tournament participation, and in general served as their gateway into serious fighting gaming.

Evan's experience as an arcade player in Philadelphia is much the same. His local arcade—at which he frequently helped arrange tournaments—hosted an *MvC2* tournament in October of the game's release year. A number of players from nearby New York City who were regulars at Shoryuken. com were in attendance: "It was the first time I got to see people from other places, and they played different characters . . . they had a different style of play and stuff, so. They told us about SRK while they were there, so I think I just went home that night and signed up and got an account, but uh . . . that was sort of the introduction to tournaments." He was surprised at first that players from as far away as another state might show up to participate, but their distinct style of play and encouragement brought him to SRK, where he then branched out to contribute to the fighting game culture and develop his own skills, including arranging more tournaments at his local arcade.

What is notable about these instances is that they inevitably lead the respondent to revise their patterns and styles of play. Forum participation leads to regular social play, or at the very least a period of regular social play that may be interrupted by more practical concerns (e.g. a few respondents, such as Jeff, who stopped playing briefly due to financial factors, or Jordan, whose play is limited by his graduate work taking up the majority of his free time). As is explored further in the following chapter on social play, the "right" way to play is against other people, not against the computer, which these experiences support.

Some respondents had different stories about their entry into the serious fighting gamer way of play that have some relation to the arcade ideal. Isaac's is perhaps the most striking, tied as it is with his personal history as described above, but also to his desire to attend EVO in 2009. Diagnosed with stage-four lung cancer and told by doctors he didn't have much time to live, he made it a life priority to attend EVO that year. Rather than being drawn in by experiencing an instance of serious fighting gamer-style play and moving to a forum, he was driven by his memories of arcade play in his youth. The memories he describes include very vivid, visceral language, and it is clearly his emotional and even physical resonance with the arcade experience that drove him to participate in an event like EVO: "One, because I should have been there to begin with because I love that environment and just never could break away from work but this is . . . my circumstances and all the extra time I had made it impossible not to go. Unforgivable if I were to skip that opportunity to do what I love, and I'm so glad I went."

He goes on to describe an instance of play where he went to a retro arcade bar in his hometown, and played the original *Street Fighter 2* arcade cabinet against a stranger:

> It's that . . . I didn't know who I was dealing with, and one of the dude's friends was talking shit and I was kicking his ass but I was sweating really bad . . . technically there's another aspect of someone playing right next to you, you can really hear him touching the keys and if you're really careful, people will look at your fingers and see what you're charging for, what you're about to do. That's something you don't get. You hear the environment and you feel the recoil of somebody else slamming buttons on the same machine. You're rubbing shoulders. There's . . . right there, there's already some primal thing about two dudes ponying up to save their quarter, you know? The practice of losing and reaching to your pocket to see if you have a quarter and bending down and sticking . . . there's like, a submission there, which you try to minimize subtly but you can't help it as a man, you know? So there is that aspect of rivalry at the arcade that you can't repeat online.

He then notes that his experiences with EVO, while not in the same literal frame—EVO matches were played at small tables, on televisions, with home console ports—gave him much the same feeling out of playing at the tournament that he did playing in arcades. The vividness of his description stands out—it's highly likely that Isaac's context makes him more reflective in this situation than the other respondents might be—but other players interviewed described enjoying the affective dimensions of play in person.

Aaron, for example, was not able to attend EVO 2009, but looked forward to attending the event in 2010. He spoke about the differences between an in-person competitive fighting game and other competitive online games, such as Blizzard's real-time strategy title *Starcraft*; for Aaron, the difference between the team play of an RTS and a fighting game is that a fighting game is as much about connecting with your opponent as it is about actual competition. Much like Isaac, he believes that playing a fighting game in person gives a player a chance to "connect with the person next to you" that online play, for example, does not. Similarly, part of his desire to attend EVO in 2010 was to compete in a scenario where the opponent isn't just the person next to you, but "your own nervousness;" the in-person setting adds an entirely different dimension to the experience resonant with Isaac's description as well.

These various responses point to an ideal scenario of which serious fighting gamers should aspire to be a part. Arcade cabinets and settings themselves feature prominently in the history of almost all of my interviewees, and even those without arcade access frequently were drawn into the hobby by isolated play on arcade machines. While online play is a possibility in the current technological landscape, it's seen as a lesser alternative to play in person. It can provide many of the benefits that respondents were looking for in play—access to a variety of opponents, convenience—but usually at a great cost in both technical difficulty and dealing with players who have differing ideals about play, or who are simply antagonistic or sore losers spurred on by the relative anonymity of online play.

Play in person, by contrast, provides a number of benefits, primarily social and affective ones. Respondents spoke to the positive feel of the crowd, particularly at events like EVO, and the affective dimension of having your opponent in close physical proximity. Entry into the culture, often via forums such as SRK, would then lead inevitably to a greater amount of social play on a regular basis, and the experience of playing in person is often transformative for respondents, encouraging their further participation. Finally, the experience can even deepen the challenge for some, adding a dimension to the fight beyond just controlling characters and predicting an opponent's moves. As Taylor and Witkowski (2010) observed with *World of Warcraft* players at the DreamHack LAN gaming event in Sweden, play in public adds a new social dimension to the activity, with players on display.

Interestingly, this also has some resonance with Jansz and Martens' (2005) findings that players at LAN events were more motivated to attend by the desire to socialize in and around the gameplay space than for the competition itself.

ARCADE NORMS AS COMFORTABLE PLAY ENVIRONMENT

What the above examples suggest is that the material and social conditions of the arcade—everything from the ways in which games are literally controlled to the geography of social interaction around a machine—constitute a set of norms for both the players at EVO and those I spoke with during interviews. This is not necessarily to say that these players adopt the norms of the arcade solely on that merit alone. There are a number of contextual factors that make the arcade experience salient. However, the sort of situations in which many of these players find themselves most "comfortable" at play have a resonance with the arcade setting, even among those players who never had the chance to experience arcades firsthand.

The end goal is to create a play environment that is both comfortable and enjoyable. In most cases, the arcade ideal provides that. Arcade sticks are precise, easy-to-use controls (once the player acclimates); offline play on a lag-free LCD monitor minimizes the negative impact of technology on the match itself. As many players mention—Evan refers to it as "the greatest thing ever"—the feeling of a crowd surrounding you while you face off against a skilled opponent who's right next to you in physical space lends a unique and important quality to fighting-game play. Thus, situations like the EVO tournament arise. They're not simply a way for players of like mind to meet, but a physical space where the comfortable, enjoyable pursuit of fighting-game play is maximized.

However, there are also clear situations where the arcade ideal cannot provide what players want. As the arcade institution dies out in the United States, home consoles more and more provide the most accessible, and sometimes only, outlet for play. Despite lag and "haters" who are poor sports thanks to the relative anonymity of Internet socialization, online play presents an opportunity for engaging in the activity that, in the days before online console play, would have been denied to those players entirely. Some, like Ibrahim, engage in online play only in a "casual" sense, never playing a game they are serious about for fear of hurting their offline game. Others, like Nicholas, embrace the rare opportunity to engage players from all over the world in their chosen game. Interestingly, EVO provides a little of both in this scenario: although it is a once-a-year event, it gives players the opportunity to meet and engage with players they might otherwise never encounter.

It should be noted that the ramifications of this ideal play environment both extend outward into other areas, and also are fed into by those other areas. The arcade ideal influences social play, for example—the focus of the next chapter—but the way in which fighting game culture is created and maintained reinforces the arcade ideal as well, creating a cycle. Arising from these material conditions of play are social play and play practices, which have their own strong influences on the fighting game phenomenon.

NOTES

1. It's worth noting that we tend to think of the quarter as the default pay unit for arcade games, but in fact many games nowadays require $0.50 minimum, or more. Also some arcades, particularly those associated with a corporation or franchise, don't take actual money. Instead players buy tokens, and games function on an [x] tokens per play basis.
2. Factors that, in the article, Killian suggests he doesn't entirely understand and isn't 100% able to identify.
3. And necessitated its settling down to one city, specifically Las Vegas, though the tournament is held at a different hosting hotel each year.
4. This is one of those moments where the one quarter = one play idea comes back into play as an issue of practice: it's common, in arcade settings, to set your quarter on the physical machine in order to tacitly say, "I've got next game" while others are playing.
5. Or a literal reconstruction of a motorcycle, for Sega's *Hang On series*, or one big flashing button for *Dragon's Lair*; while obviously not all arcade games involved a joystick and buttons, these other examples are exemptions that prove the rule, by and large.
6. At time of this writing, this video is still viewable on YouTube: http://youtu.be/G-ADymPCP0I.
7. Viewable at http://tinycartridge.com/post/89530544/ps2-arcade-stick-built-inside-a-rubbermaid. What's interesting about this design is that it gives an idea of how comparatively little electronics are going inside these sticks; it's likely that the large size of common arcade sticks has more to do with arcade aesthetics than strict functionality.
8. Available online at http://youtu.be/JgAi-nIQibU.
9. And its spiritual predecessor, Caliburforums.com; according to both Ibrahim and Garret, a schism in the community and internal shuffling at Namco-Bandai led to the creation of 8 Way Run.com.

3 Play Practice

So far we've considered a material, historical, and cultural influence on fighting game culture in the form of the arcade. The questions to which we now turn are: What are some of the norms of play practice in that community? When these players decide to engage with the game, which aspects of gameplay do they find desirable, and which do they find less desirable (or even worth prohibiting)? To answer these questions, this chapter focuses on two major and related areas: the qualities of an "ideal" match, and the critical importance the fighting game community puts on the "level playing field," or the game-as-skill test. By looking at actual examples of gameplay practice, cultural mores, and values attached to certain gameplay practices—practices that the community values or doesn't value, approves of or disapproves of—we can get a clearer picture of how the community defines both itself and the games with which it engages.

In attending multiple large fighting game events, I was able to see what specific types of play—strategies, choices, and norms—found the audience's approval, and those of which they were not so fond. Sometimes, this intersected with the notion of fairness and broken-ness; the multiple discussions of *Soul Calibur 4* character Hilde in this chapter highlight one such congruent point, and the clash between "casual" and "hardcore" players is another. What players approved or disapproved of, though, was not always based on the ideal of maintaining a level playing field. Sometimes it was about what sort of match is enjoyable to play in, interesting to spectate, or is perceived to have a positive impact on the fighting game community.

On the issue of the level playing field, this chapter primarily looks at the issue of game balance: which elements of a game contribute to or detract from the perception that a given game's ruleset and characters are "fair." Part and parcel of that is an analysis of moments when a game is considered "broken," a common term in gaming culture for games or game elements that are unfair or unbalanced. The word "broken" conveys considerable meaning on its own, implying a game that features one of these unfair mechanics is not fulfilling its primary function, or has a serious and fatal flaw (hence, broken). Since the individual character—i.e. Ryu from *Street Fighter*, or Voldo from *Soul Calibur*—is one of the most important ways in which a fighting game player engages the mechanical ruleset, a look at which characters are perceived as broken points to prevailing ideas about fairness and its place in the fighting game culture.

DRAMA, SKILL, AND EXECUTION: QUALITIES OF THE IDEAL MATCH

What is it that makes an ideal competitive fighting game match in the first place? Which styles of play do players desire and respond to? Both the matches observed at the EVO tournament and the experiences of the players interviewed paint a particular picture of which styles of play are rewarded or rejected, and which elements of the match contribute to the idea of a satisfying gameplay experience.

The final day of the EVO tournament—the day when the final tournaments for each game were held—had a distinct character compared to the previous two. The bustling, busy, visually stimulating aura of the first two days seemed to put the emphasis on gameplay: the participants were obviously there to play in matches, to play fighting games with others, and to generally take part in the event. The third day was entirely different. Changes in lighting and physical space helped to convey a complete change in mood: now the participants were there to watch. The lights were dimmed, the exhibits and freeplay stations were cleared away, and the seating was increased to focus on the main stage. This isn't to say that watching matches wasn't part of the experience on days one and two; quite the contrary, some pool matches involving famous players drew such large crowds that the organizers had to force people to move simply so the competitors could play the game at all. However, on the first two days the "watching" part of the experience seemed to run concurrent to the "playing" part. On day three, "watching" was foregrounded to the exclusion of all else.

That being said, "watching" should not be construed as "not participating." In fact, some of the more intense examples of how the participants valorized or rejected certain types of play come from crowd responses to public matches. As mentioned before, this brings us back to the idea of the gaming paratext (Consalvo, 2007): the act of playing the game is not limited just to the literal act of holding a controller and engaging the game itself, but in consuming and taking part in peripheral activities related to the games. In fact, it was the crowd's participation as observers that helped to best identify how different styles and forms of play were held up as good or desirable, compared to which ones were instead considered negative in some way. Watching for which events received a positive response and which received a negative response from the crowd—indicated by cheering, booing, and other crowd activity—helped create a sense of how tournament participants performed being good (skilled) players.

In terms of crowd response pointing to particular types of play, there are both general themes that hold across certain scenarios, and specific examples from certain games that are endemic to that game alone. One of the prevailing general themes was technical excellence. Consistently, across both official matches, I observed on the main-stage pools and casual matches in the BYOC zone that a player who was able to perform special techniques, moves, attacks, or defenses that were difficult, flashy, or both, received accolades and cheering from the crowd. I make the distinction between "difficult" and "flashy" based on the way in which fighting games are played. Controlling one's character involves multiple aspects of control and timing; most attacks and defenses require varying amounts of actual physical interaction with the controller, ranging from pressing a single button to throw a punch to performing a series of directional inputs on the joystick followed by multiple button presses to perform a highly complex attack or pattern of attacks. On top of that aspect, however, there's also the issue of timing: Your attack must fall into a time when the opponent is defenseless, otherwise your opportunity will be missed and the opponent may counterattack. So, technical skill may refer to performing a particularly difficult or hard-to-use attack all on its own, performing a relatively simple input under difficult circumstances, or both.

One common example of this is what are called "supers": techniques that require some degree of resource build-up or expenditure to use (typically an in-game meter that is filled by attacking, defending, or taking hits and is emptied to perform the "super"), and have slightly more complex inputs than normal, but do considerable damage and can turn around a match if they connect. In *SF4* there are two types of such moves, "supers" and "ultras." In many matches, merely performing one was enough to evoke a crowd response. During exhibition matches on day one, a player using the character Zangief attempted his "Final Atomic Buster" ultra move against the opposite player. He didn't connect, but the crowd still responded with an "ohhhh!" to acknowledge its use. At the GUTS tournament in 2013, one player of *SF4* character T. Hawk garnered a similar reaction for using a similar move, with a buildup from the crowd of an expectant "ohhhh!" to either a triumphant cheer at the move's success, or a disappointed/consoling "awwww!" if it missed.

On the flip side, the opponent in the Zangief match just mentioned, playing as Dhalsim, interrupted a string of attacks with his own ultra, prompting an "oooh!" response. Of course, the spelling out of the vocalizations strips them of their tone and inflection; the players were clearly expressing something like sympathy to the Zangief player—the "ohhh!" had the sound of, for example, a crowd responding to a near miss of the hole in golf, or missing a spare in bowling. Conversely, the "oooh!" for Dhalsim was more a sound of appreciation and congratulations.

However, technical play need not be flashy to garner crowd response. This was particularly true during the finals on day three in games such as

Street Fighter 3: Third Strike, *Soul Calibur 4*, and *SF4*. What was noticeable in the way participants played those games was a similarity to fencing; rather than going brutally all out to overwhelm the other player, those players instead seemed to trade a series of opening moves, feints, and forays intended to test the opponent's defenses and create an opening. This is actually a marked difference from the more frenetic style of play I observed for *Marvel vs. Capcom 2* and *Guilty Gear XX* at EVO, or *Marvel vs. Capcom 3* at GUTS; those games instead seem to involve a whirlwind of action and attacks rather than the slower pace of the previously mentioned games.

In the former type of game, the crowd responded to sudden changes in momentum. During the back and forth of testing attacks and defensive maneuvers, little was said. On the other hand, when one player's defenses were open and the other took advantage of it, the action and the crowd response changed considerably. In that situation, the attacking player with the advantage has the opportunity to perform a long string of attacks known as a "combo" (short for "combination"), with no chance for the victim to defend him/herself. During said combos, the audience shows their appreciation through cheering: "oooh!"s, "ahh!"s, and the like. Even if the combo was simply a straightforward series of normal attacks, the fact that the momentum of the match had shifted drew in the crowd. Likewise, a potential combo victim who saves him/herself at the last moment through a sudden defensive maneuver would likewise evoke a response.

What seems to be at play in these scenarios is drama. The more technical the play, the more fantastic the footwork, and the more close the shave, the greater the crowd's sense of drama and enjoyment. Consider by comparison the (very rare) occasion that a player in a match managed to defeat his/her opponent without taking any damage whatsoever, known in fighting game circles as a "perfect." While they were rare in tournament play—among the matches I observed, there were no more than five out of nearly 100—they did occur. Yet the crowd's response to them was generally lukewarm, even during the finals, where presumably the most skilled players were on display. I found that response curious until I considered it against this idea of drama: A perfect victory is, more or less, a fait accompli. The match tends to be shorter than normal, as one player dominates the field. Such fights lack drama; there is no tension, no instability in the outcome. As a result, it seemed as if players reacted less well to those situations. This is why a Zangief player who *misses* with his ultra (by all accounts a really unfortunate technical play which leaves him open to counterattack) can still get a response from the crowd: they appreciate the sense of drama that this flashy move presents.

Beyond that, there are other considerations that arise from this comparison of the perfect fait accompli to the dramatic. The first is that while technical play is obviously valorized, it has to be within a particular context in order to be recognized as such. Consider that the player who obtains a perfect victory must have at least some degree of technical skill, particularly at the highest levels such as the finals on day three. This is not to say there is no recognition—a player in the *GGXX* finals managed a perfect twice in a row, which did get some applause, and in fact an observer behind me yelled "Double fucking perfect!" as well—but that recognition is typically lower key. One potential reason is that dramatic play seems to involve both players; cheering would often escalate when one player gained momentum, and then his/her opponent suddenly turned the tables and made a comeback.

This was especially apparent in the *SF4* finals between Justin Wong and Daigo Umehara, whose matches were so close and so full of sudden reversals that they extended the entire affair by nearly an hour in order to play enough matches to determine a victor. To call the crowd's response to those matches explosive would be an understatement; the *SF4* finals being the capstone event to EVO 2009, the room was full nearly to capacity and the audience's visceral response was deafening. In such a case, the dramatic matches bring the decision to the wire, enable more matches (and more chances for displays of technical excellence), and generally create a feeling of tension. The perfect win, by contrast, shuts down play; it moves things forward too quickly, creates no tension, and provides fewer chances for players to show their skills.

On suspense at sporting events, Bryant, Rockwell, and Owens (1994) mention that when fans had a positive emotional investment in one of the winners, then suspense about the outcome made the entire experience more enjoyable. Their focus was on identification; the idea is that if a spectator has an emotional connection to one of the participants then suspense about the outcome has actual meaning; in other words, if they don't care who wins or loses, then there's no chance for suspense to build in the first place. Gan et al. (1997) had similar findings in regards to suspense, where identifying with the winning team was a contributor to enjoying the game.

Taken in context of Killian's remarks about the personas of the community—"We have heroes and villains here"—this doesn't seem surprising. A rapidly seesawing match with dramatic shifts of tempo and advantage creates suspense over the winner; when it's not clear who will be the victor, the crowd will get more into it. One possibility, however, is that the reactions of the crowd observed over the space of the entire tournament suggest that investment in one player or "side" alone might not be required; it could be that these attendees are so invested in the activity itself—in "serious fighting games"—that this alone creates the necessary suspense, and makes them less responsive to situations where there is little to no suspense, such as perfect wins.

On that note, the crowd is clearly important to fighting gamers; Evan describes his first encounter with a massive crowd around a *Street Fighter 2* machine as "the greatest thing I ever saw," and Gene notes that it was wanting to be "that good player in the middle of the crowd" that drew him to play in the arcades rather than at home on consoles. The crowds at EVO were no different; during the finals the announcers whipped them into a cheering frenzy for many of the final matches, and during the *MvC2* finals, the additional commentary by IFC Yipes (a well-known *Marvel* player with a unique, game-specific lingo; see Chapter 6 for more details) produced some of the strongest crowd reactions of them all. This notion of a highly engaged, enthusiastic crowd being central to the experience is also something Stein (2013) observed in the development of indie sports games, a genre and community that share considerable overlap with the fighting game culture.

What's also noticeable here is a focus on play rather than winning. This type of crowd reaction is clearly predicated on the actual play of the matches being the focus, rather than who wins or loses. In a sense this is perfectly understandable; as observers rather than players, the crowd hopes to see more play. This is also not to say that who wins or who loses is entirely unimportant, either; when French *SC4* player Malek finished his match in the tournament, a number of friends and fans in the crowd rushed the stage to hug him, congratulate him, and otherwise acknowledge him. This happened to a lesser extent to the winners of the other final tournaments as well. However, while winners are acknowledged, it is reasonably clear that the process leading to that point was more important to the crowd, overall, than the result.

WHAT NOT TO DO: PROSCRIBED PLAY

Conversely, instances at EVO of proscribed play—modes of play that engendered obvious social disapproval—were exceedingly rare. The reason for this isn't clear; it may be that attending the event represents a tacit agreement to a social contract where politeness dictates not being overt about displays of disapproval. Even among the pool matches and bring-your-own-console area games—more informal, smaller-scale instances of play away from the notoriety and visibility of the big screen—I observed no significant moments where players expressed their displeasure, got into arguments, or otherwise gave an indicator that proscribed play was occurring. That being said, my relative inexperience with the community and my incomplete knowledge of deep fighting game mechanics means that there may be instances of such that were not readily apparent, particularly if those who would express their displeasure had some sort of incentive not to do so: not wanting to interrupt the match, make a scene, or simply not wanting to confront the player using a proscribed tactic.

However, there was one major and extremely notable instance of attendee reaction to proscribed play that needs mentioning in extensive detail. It occurred across the *Soul Calibur 4* finals in matches featuring a character named Hilde. Unlike the other games featured at EVO, *SC4* is a 3D fighting game; the action takes place in a 3D zone rather than a two-dimensional flat plane, allowing for more directions of movement and adding an additional level of complexity to landing attacks. One common feature of 3D fighting games is the concept of the "ring out": most stages have outside edges, and if one player can force the opponent's character off the edge, the opponent (typically) instantly loses the match, regardless of their remaining health points. The feature is so common that, at one point, a nearby attendee with whom I was watching the matches said, "It's not 3D if there's no ring outs."

In *Soul Calibur 4*, the character Hilde appears to have, judging from the instances of play I saw at EVO, a certain combination of moves that sends the opponent flying a considerable horizontal distance if it connects fully. Thus it's relatively easy for a Hilde player to aim for a ring out win, rather than a more traditional fight where each opponent wears down the other's health. The other characters in the *SC4* matches I saw exhibited the same capability, and of the matches involving Hilde between the semi-finals on day two and the finals on day three, a significant number ended in ring out wins.

What's interesting about this situation is that the crowd's response to the use of Hilde, particularly during the finals, was intensely negative. Booing and shouted comments were almost always part of matches where Hilde was used. In some cases the negative reaction started before the match even *began*; as players moved around the character selection screen, the crowd would often boo and hiss at a Hilde player the second s/he selected Hilde as his/her character. I had initially wondered if this reaction involved a particular player that the community viewed as a villain of sorts, but these reactions continued regardless of who was fighting. As each game's final bracket began on day three, the EVO staff prepared intro movies featuring play from each game; the mere appearance of Hilde's ring out combo[1] sparked a rash of boos from the crowd. In short, even the suggestion or out-of-game display of Hilde and her ring out combo would result in an instant and intense booing.

Beyond the simple negative visceral reaction there were a number of ancillary ones as well. One thing that was notable about the finals on day three compared to the previous two days was the introduction of an announcer, likely due to the aforementioned concept that the final day is for "watching" rather than "playing." Although there is not necessarily any promise of impartiality on the part of the announcer, I found myself taken aback when, during the *SC4* finals, the announcer was among the people who booed Hilde players. At one point, when an opponent defeated a Hilde player, the announcer commented over the PA, "No cheap finish today!" In this sense, "cheap" refers to a technique or ability that offers great power or utility at relatively little risk.

During these matches, players in the audience would also shout counter-Hilde strategies in addition to booing, suggesting that the opponent move in a certain way, or defend in a certain way, to shut down this rote combination of attacks that resulted in (apparently easy) ring outs. In a slightly more complex way of showing their opinion on Hilde, the crowd in general reacted very positively to situations where Hilde's ring out combo, or Hilde play in general, was "shut down." Other players, using different characters such as Cassandra and Ivy, were able to defeat Hilde users to much greater applause. In particular, one Ivy player—Malek, who would go on to win the championship—managed to ring out Hilde herself with a throw in one of his matches. Crowd response to that particular win was ecstatic and vibrant, with lots of cheering; one assumes that the combination of the "cheap" ring out combo being defeated with the ironic twist of a victory by ring out played to both sides of the drama coin. It was also technically savvy and flashy, and thus popular, as previously discussed. It seems that adding the aspect of proscribed play made the crowd all the more enthusiastic.

In a similar vein, at one point a competitor in the *SC4* finals who had been to that point using a different character and playing on an arcade stick, suddenly switched to a console control pad after losing a match. Since arcade sticks had to that point been the norm at the event, this struck me as odd. That impression was confirmed, however, by the sudden explosive booing that occurred when the crowd noticed it. Confused, I turned to nearby attendees who were also watching the finals, and asked why the crowd had suddenly turned against this player. One of them responded that Hilde's ring out combination is easier to do on a console pad than an arcade stick. Sure enough, that player went on to pick Hilde—prompting more negative reaction from the crowd—and the combination did indeed make an appearance. Aaron noted in his interview that this is due to the ability to "macro[2]" on pads compared to arcade sticks, where unused buttons on the pad can be set to combinations of button presses. Since Hilde's "doom combo" involves attacks that use multiple combined button presses, the pad makes performing it easier.

These incidents stand out for two reasons: their intensity, and the fact that such responses were so uncommon outside this context. The question that remains is why this particular combination is so proscribed. In considering that question I was drawn back to my conversation with Seth Killian, who noted that EVO strives to impart as few hard and fast rules as possible, preferring that modes of play emerge from fighting gamers playing against each other. What this suggests is that the proscription[3] of the Hilde ring out combo arose out of the community. Why? Answering that question provides insight into values of play that the community embraces.

In the context of the previous discussion on what makes a match appealing, it may be that the use of Hilde and her "cheap" or "easy" ring out constitutes the same principle as a "perfect" win lacking drama or tension. Rather than enabling a dramatic match, it presents one player with a simple tactic for victory. This is quite similar to what Consalvo (2007) describes with certain uses of cheating in games; she cites Aarseth's (1997) discussion of aporia and epiphany, where finding a resolution to a game challenge is part of the enjoyment of it. Cheating removes that moment of epiphany, creating a "hollow win" (Consalvo, 2007, p. 91). Since the crowd relishes the back and forth of dramatic play compared to a decisive and one-sided victory, the choice of Hilde—which, it should be noted, almost universally meant the consequent use of her ring out combo—was strongly discouraged and proscribed. What this does not account for is the frequency or intensity comparative to perfect wins as the other example. Attendees were lukewarm to perfects, but not hostile; they might clap politely or less enthusiastically than for a dramatic finish, but they still showed some approval.

Hilde, by contrast, got nothing but vitriol. One possible explanation may simply be that the perfect win is emergent, but the Hilde choice is not; while a close match is more desirable, a perfect win can still happen in a satisfying match. Choosing Hilde up front, on the other hand, is almost the promise of a "cheap" and short match, one that's unbalanced. In that sense, the fans seem to be exhibiting the ideal that Killian mentioned; the tournament valorizes emergent events, and by extension, play rather than outcomes. Foregone conclusions and fait accompli go against the social grain. More importantly, the perception that Hilde is "cheap" or "broken"—and thus the community's disapproval of her—speaks to a core assumption regarding play in the fighting game culture: that these games are skill-based competitions, and anything that throws off that balance is, if not outright banned, then at least disapproved of highly.

THE LEVEL PLAYING FIELD

The concept of a fighting game match deciding who has the greater level of skill is an important idea in this culture, and it illustrates a both pervasive and divisive argument among its members. The idea of fighting games as being about skill rather than randomness, about control and execution rather than dumb luck, is a powerful and widespread normative idea in play practice. It touches on everything from specific use of technologies to debating which characters are favored or even usable at all in a competitive setting.

In his discussion of types of play and games, Roger Caillois (1958) presents a four-part typology: alea (games of chance), mimicry (games of illusion or simulation), agon (games of competition), and ilinx (games of vertigo). It is primarily the contrast between the last two—ilinx and agon—that is relevant to the idea of video games as a skill challenge. His brief definition of agon draws heavily on the structured competition of sports (p. 14), while he describes the vertigo-seeking games of ilinx as those that "consist of an attempt to momentarily destroy the stability of perception and inflict a kind of voluptuous panic upon an otherwise lucid mind" (p. 23). In vertigo, the pleasure of play comes from being shocked, surprised, or overwhelmed. But for Caillois, agon and vertigo are fundamentally incompatible: He claims that vertigo "destroys the conditions that define agon, i.e. the efficacious resort to skill, power, and calculation, and self-control; respect for rules; the desire to test oneself under conditions of equality; prior submission to the decision of a referee; an obligation, agreed to in advance, to circumscribe the conflict within set limits, etc. Nothing is left." (pp. 72–3).

Thus the goal of ilinx—to lose oneself in the unpredictable obliteration of the moment and the confusion of our senses—is at cross purposes with the structured, skill-focused, competitive nature of agon. Even a cursory look at fighting games as they've been described here thus far places them firmly in the realm of agon; thus, these qualities of vertigo that destroy agon are also things that would hinder competitive fighting game play as well.

Christopher Paul, in his book *Wordplay and the Discourse of Video Games* (2012), spends considerable time looking at the notion of "balance" in the realm of digital games, both as something conceptual and as something that is exhibited in gameplay practice. Much of what he talks about is directly applicable to the fighting game community's desire to create—or perhaps more accurately, insistence upon—a level playing field. In fact, in discussing the relationship between game design and balance, Paul refers to fighting games specifically, referencing game designer and fighting game enthusiast David Sirlin:

"[o]ne game designer, who works predominantly on fighting games, argues that proper game balance requires both a variety of viable options and an overarching fairness in the game that allows 'players of equal skill [to] have an equal chance at winning even though they might *start the game* [emphasis original] with different sets of options/moves/characters/resources/etc." (p. 149)

Thus the ideal state for balanced games (and Sirlin's wording in the quoted passage strongly suggests he means fighting games in particular) is a state where skill is the major match determinant, yet there has to be room for players to express a personal style through gameplay choices. Consider that an illogical but effective way to balance a one-on-one game of competitive combat is to give both players the exact same core resources with no real selectable options; a version of *Street Fighter IV* where only Ryu is playable, for example. Competition in that situation would certainly be more about skill than about what gameplay affordances a different character might offer as alternatives, but it would also be relatively boring for both player and audience. The range of potential outcomes is incredibly limited in that scenario, and as I noted, part of the enjoyable drama of these matches for the spectators is the uncertainty and range of potential outcomes.

It's critical to note, however, that the "level playing field" is not something that comes solely from actual game design constraints and affordances, nor is literal gameplay the only way in which they influence the culture.

The "ideograph" of balance and meritocracy that Paul describes happens in the culture of practice that surrounds these games as well. Chapter 6 highlights situations where the drumbeat of meritocratic participation that comes from balance can have a negative impact on the culture, particularly in how it creates barriers for female players.

Elements from previous discussions are relevant here as well. In the last chapter, for example, I discussed how important a particular piece of technology—the arcade stick—is to fighting game culture. As is noted there, these controllers are preferred by fighting gamers in part because they create a comfortable feel reminiscent of the arcade. However, they also provide a technical advantage that's related to the idea of "feel." Using the controller that feels the most comfortable for you allows skill to shine forth, working under the assumption that using an unfamiliar or uncomfortable interface creates potential problems. Likewise, the discussion of display lag on an LCD monitor and its possible effects on a match are similar. As Jordan emphasized about both arcade sticks and monitors, the idea is that "the technology needs to facilitate the match." Part of the goal of the comfortable play environment is to remove outside factors that would inhibit the perfect agon: the test of skill and cleverness that Caillois describes.

Of course, one might wonder: How is "fairness" defined? How, when, and by whom is the notion of something being fair or broken constructed? One example of that process in action is the conflicting opinions of many fighting gamers about Nintendo's *Super Smash Bros.* series of games, and the specific limitations and affordances of the *Smash* games that make them so divisive among competitive players.

SOCIALLY CONSTRUCTING FAIRNESS: CASUAL VS. HARDCORE IN *SUPER SMASH BROS.*

In his book *A Casual Revolution*, Jesper Juul (2010) discusses at length the rising casual gamer market, and in so doing makes a number of major comparisons between the "traditional" hardcore or dedicated gamer, and the more casual player. His discussion ranges from issues based on the code of the game—ways in which some games are more inclined to support casual players versus hardcore ones—to more social issues, such as the different desires each type of player has for the game experience. Although Juul does not frame the differences between the two player types as particularly antagonistic toward each other, the two styles of play and sets of expectations about what a game provides are quite different in scope. Within the community of serious fighting game fans, however, they appear to be almost entirely incompatible. Players with whom I spoke described very different scenarios for casual play versus serious play, and the valuing of one as "authentic" over the other was very clear cut.

Perhaps the biggest example of this in action is in the conflict surrounding the play of the *Smash Bros.* series of games, particularly the tournament scene for *Super Smash Bros. Brawl* (*SSBB* or simply *Brawl*). In a multi-tiered way, there is conflict among *Smash* players about how the game should be played, and then conflict between "Smashers" and the rest of the fighting game community—particularly the fans at Shoryuken.com (SRK)—about if *Brawl* or the *Smash* games in general are even fighting games in the first place.

I asked Matthew—the only *Smash* player among the cohort of interview respondents—about the Internet meme mentioned earlier that describes the popular image of the competitive *Smash* player: the "Fox only, Final Destination, no items" meme where players of competitive *Smash* are said to go totally overboard in their restrictiveness playing the game, knocking the many possibilities the game offers down to one character (Fox), one stage (Final Destination), and no items. In discussing the potential roots of that meme, he identified a rift within the *Smash* community:

> Matthew: Well, yes. That's . . . I can't speak from any surefire experience, this is purely my theorizing, is I think that meme started because of the casual vs. competitive *Smash* rift there is. I think it started on the casual side as someone once off-handedly remarked, "I don't wanna play competitive *Smash* because all they do is play Fox only, Final Destination, no items," and I think it just started spreading like that. Purely a theory behind the meme, but that's what I'd say. Especially . . .
>
> Todd: It's interesting. Do you know the site TV Tropes?
>
> Matthew: Yes, actually, I do.
>
> Todd: The TV Tropes entry which discusses Fox only, Final Destination, no items, is titled "No Having Fun Guys." And of course the gist of the trope is that the Fox only, Final Destination, no items person is not about having fun, but about something else. And again, trope, meme, these are things that are more cultural constructs than they are realities, I'm sure.
>
> Matthew: Yeah.
>
> Todd: But I'm interested in this casual vs. hardc . . . sorry.
>
> Matthew: Versus hardcore rift?
>
> Todd: I didn't mean to say hardcore, but . . .
>
> Matthew: Hardcore and competitive, to me, are synonymous. They mean the exact same thing so I take no offense. But it's . . . a lot of people argue, they're like, "Well, *Smash* is a party game, you should play it with items and four-person free-for-alls," and then other people are like, "Well, yeah, that's fun, but I have more fun doing this," and then the casuals are like "Well I have more fun doing this, so therefore

you're wrong," and then the competitive players are like "Well you don't know enough about the game so you're stupid," and then the casual players are like "No, you're stupid 'cause you're taking it to this level and it's not supposed to be there," and it's just a big . . . there's a big rift of people who think Smash should be competitive and those who think it shouldn't be. In the end, I have a lot of fun playing with items. If I'm playing for fun I sometimes put on items, like, if I'm with my little brother or something, give him a fighting chance to try and beat me, but in an actual competitive environment, I'm not gonna trust my luck. I'm trying to factor that out of the equation in everything I do.

What's clearly at stake here is a discussion of what purpose the game even serves. Hardcore or serious *Smash* players, in accordance with their playstyle, are not interested in the game's potential as a "party game" solely for a given external definition of fun. To them, the challenge of the fight is the primary source of enjoyment, not the random wackiness that erratic factors such as items involve. It is these beliefs that contribute to the wider idea of fighting games as a skill challenge and the conflation of that belief with more "serious," competitive play.

As Matthew observes it, casual players are the opposite end of that spectrum. To them the primary enjoyment of *Smash* has little to do with the challenge of testing skill against another player. It seems plausible that casual players of *Smash*, frustrated by the differing ideals of serious or hardcore Smashers, would develop a meme that lampoons what they would see as an overly-restrictive, even joyless way of playing the game. Interestingly enough, however, Hilary Kolos' (2010) research on a social gaming group that arose in a university dorm describes a group of casual players—she defines their motivations as "playfully socializing" (p. 73)—who specifically turned items off because of their effect on the match. Perhaps what is critical in both cases is that what the game code affords or does not afford is effectively set. Characters and stages can be chosen or not chosen; items can be turned on or off. The major difference in the "sides" of this conflict is that both view normative methods of play in differing ways. The result is that each is playing a version of the game that is effectively incompatible with the other primarily due to communal play practice, though the group in Kolos' study suggests that even within casual or hardcore groups, there is a certain variability to the playstyle, just as the labeling of practice, non-tournament matches in the Shoryuken. com community as "casuals" or "friendlies" does. The critical issue is that in either situation, the rules of the game have to fit the social goals of the playing group.

Interestingly enough, this is also at the root of the conflict between non-*Smash* fighting gamers and *Smash* itself. Although most of the fighting gamers I spoke to were not particularly hostile to the *Smash* games, one in particular—Gene—was vehemently against them as fighting games. Although he couched his objections in an admittance of his being an "elitist," Gene went so far as to assert, when I mentioned I was speaking to fighting game fans including *Smash* players, that I shouldn't bother with them, since *Smash* isn't a fighting game in the first place.

His objection centered around the idea of "house rules": normative ideas of play that particular groups of players might institute at a particular location or setting that are socially enforced, rather than being part of the affordances or limitations of the game code. For Gene, house rules were a part of his early arcade fighting game experience, until he played against fighters from a different locality with their own set of norms:

> Yeah, yes, yeah. I believe it was true, because at cert . . . at certain points back in the day, because we were a mall arcade and we got a ton of casual people and with casual people . . . makes, like, you know . . . house rules and arcade rules come into effect a lot, which is the antithesis of SRK, which is "play to win" versus stuff like . . . at the beginning of our arcade it was always like . . . you try not to throw the guy and other things that you try not to be cheap about, thinking that that's like, an honorable way to play or anything. So there was stuff that we had to get over at some point, especially with *Marvel*, 'cause *Marvel* . . . like, *Marvel vs. Capcom 1*, you'd be like "Oh, we're not gonna use helpers, helpers are cheap," but in *Marvel vs. Capcom 2* the game is about helpers, so when we were continuing to try and play it without helpers, you know, someone from Fayetteville could come in and just destroy everybody because they were using, you know, Storm, Sentinel, whatever. So. When we all got on SRK, it stepped our games up a huge amount just because we started playing differently. Like, we started playing the way it should be played and it kinda went from there.

This is a very telling anecdote, especially since it spells out quite clearly what the effect of meeting these other players was. The new players introduce a new norm—thoroughly beating the people at Gene's arcade in the process—and in response those players seek help to improve, leading them to a large fighting game community on SRK, who then bring those players into the institution of serious fighting gaming via gameplay norms.

The implication, of course, is that *before* any of this happened—back in the house rules days—he wasn't a serious, competitive player; he was a casual player instead. Gene does not seem to hold particular rancor toward this time as a casual player, though; he couches the house rules of not using helper characters in *Marvel vs. Capcom 2* in terms of honor and good sportsmanship, both being values that are also paramount in the serious fighting game community. The difference is more revelatory than anything else; it is as if the SRK way of playing, where playing to win may involve using tactics others see as cheap, finally led him to understand what fighting games are all about. In accepting the rules of the hardcore set, he was able to see the games themselves for what (he feels) they truly are.

This becomes even more apparent in his discussion of *Smash*, however, where he is clear about why *Smash* is not a true fighting game. The notion of house rules features into his argument; in Gene's view, the game's base code presents the game as-is (hearkening back to the idea that arcade versions and arcade play are the real fighting games) and thus going against it implies the game isn't a fighting game to begin with:

> Gene: So the whole point of . . . house rules and of the . . . the whole reason against house rules, the whole argument against house rules is, they've made the game this way for you to play it this way. Like, they put throws in the game for a reason. They're not cheap, they're coded specifically for a reason, whether that's the rock/paper/scissors analogy or whatever, you use what's in the game. *Smash Bros* . . . it's a bigger grey area. I would say . . . like, again, I haven't even played *Brawl* and *Melee*, but it seems to be that you either play the way the game is supposed to be played—without artificial house rules imposed on it—and if you can't play that way, then it's a crappy game. Then it's a broken game that there shouldn't be tournaments of in the first place, which would be their argument. Which goes back to them saying: *Smash* sucks.
>
> Todd: Gotcha. So it's a matter of . . . it seems like it's built for casuals. "Well, we can play it tournament if we turn off all this stuff," "Well if you have to turn off all this stuff then it's not tournament worthy in the first place," and you've circled all the way back to "Well, the game itself is bad."
>
> Gene: It's a casual non-fighting game, and when they tried to make it a fighting game was when people started hating, because people said "You can't turn it into a fighting game without changing all these things and all these things are not only artificial, but they also make the game stupid and boring," like you said, where . . . the story about how nobody wants to attack first, because the options are so limited now.

Gene's opinion toward *Smash* has much in common with fan attitudes toward series canon, which is both "a slippery thing" that is communally defined (Brooker, 2002, p. 106) and a perceived unbreakable norm that constrains fan and community creativeness (Markman, 2005).

The story he refers to in the final quoted paragraph is one I related to him from my interview with Matthew, who had given up *Brawl* for its predecessor in the *Smash* series, *Super Smash Bros. Melee*. For Matthew, the structure of the game in *Brawl*—the attack and defense options, even the physics engine—had led inevitably to a situation where taking the initiative and attacking first became inadvisable strategic moves. As he put it,

> [a] game where if you go for the first hit and you go to attack you're at a disadvantage is eventually gonna start becoming stalemates between two people just sitting there, hopping around, waiting for the other person to make a mistake, and unfortunately that's what's happening in *Brawl*. In *Brawl*, even the top player right now has timed people out because he's not gonna put himself at the risk of approaching because it puts him at an inherent disadvantage.

Even though Matthew is a fan of *Smash*, *Brawl* isn't satisfying to him in this situation. Considering that Matthew enjoys other, different fighting games besides *Brawl*, it's clear that a particular way of playing trumps affection for a particular game.

He's not the only *Smash* player to comment on this, either. Although he doesn't consider himself primarily a *Smash* player, Jordan has logged considerable time playing games in the series. In discussing why communities like SRK have an antipathy toward *Smash*, he also noted that the standard mode of high-level play in Smash games is to be extremely defensive, never making the first move, and that he didn't enjoy that sort of play at all:

> It's like . . . because you have to play so safe. I mean, it's a fun game if you've got four people and you're screwing around and you don't mind the randomness of it, like . . . you know, Nintendo's recent design strategy is "random is good," and so in *Smash* I've seen countless instances where you're trying to hit someone or you're mid-swing and a bomb materializes in front of you, because that's what they do, and then you hit it and it explodes and you die, and it's actually common enough that I consider it a problem, and you'll notice in *Smash* tournaments they turn off all the items and they only play on approved stages, and they ban half the characters, and blah blah blah. So *Smash* is one of those things that can be really fun and entertaining but I think that it does not engender the same kind of "hard fun," the same kind of tactical challenge that other fighting games do.

The connection here is that in casual play, this need for safety does not exist. Randomness in the form of items and stage events make the result so chaotic that the dynamic he describes for tournament play likely isn't viable. Even the goal is different; casual *Smash* involves "screwing around," randomness, and playing with friends. Hardcore *Smash* is something else entirely.

This is effectively the tension between "smashers" and "anti-smashers" that Jakobsson (2007) identified in a local community of *Smash* players in Sweden writ large, and indeed, it's likely that the tension he observed on a smaller, local level was an echo of continuing tension in the global *Smash* community. Interestingly, his work comes from 2007, and thus it predates the *Brawl* conflict described above; as his subjects were likely playing *Melee*, this suggests that this is a cycle of discontent with a great deal of history and persistence. Jakobsson describes the smashers (hardcore players) as viewing "gaming as sports," but for anti-smashers (casuals), "the joy of gaming comes from an endless stream of new games" (p. 390). The aspects of the game associated with casual play support that idea: The randomness and unpredictability of items encourages quick matches rather than long-term strategic play.

However, this notion of casual versus hardcore play and games isn't limited to just *Smash*. Earlier, Jordan had made an explicit link between party games such as *Smash Bros.* and games like the *Mortal Kombat* series, which (according to Jordan) focus on the visceral thrill of graphic violence rather than technical play: "Yeah, yeah. It's funny that I punched off your head three times. I mean . . . there is that element, and honestly, like . . . I've never met anyone who plays *Mortal Kombat* and a major goal is not just winning so you can do the fatality. I mean, that seems to be a pretty continuous major motivator."

It's worth noting that looking back on the definition of a fighting game, outlined in Chapter 1, *Mortal Kombat* fills all of those criteria: game of one-on-one melee combat, where characters have specific move sets, with quantifiable on-screen stats, that allows for multiplayer competition. However, that's only a functional, and more importantly, *technical*, definition; this attitude toward *MK* and *Smash* suggests a parallel and equally important social angle. The idea here is that while the *Mortal Kombat* games provide a certain aesthetic—heads punched off, spines ripped out, opponents exploded—from this point of view it is fundamentally a casual game at heart because it lacks the ability to support a certain style of play, regardless of its technical aspects.

As for what that style of play is, Isaac led a similar discussion about *Mortal Kombat* and its relationship to serious fighting games. He suggests at least some of the dimensions involved:

> *Street Fighter* is not about pugilism. It's not about kicking somebody in the stomach. It's not about watching . . . it's why somebody, that's why you'll find—if you've talked to enough to *Street Fighter* people—that you're not going to talk to people who like *Mortal Kombat*. It's not the gore. Not the victory. It's not ripping somebody's head off. I'd say it is the victory more than those other things, I misspoke, but it's not the . . . the appeal is not punching somebody in the face or blasting them with a fireball in itself. The appeal is knowing that you two walk up to the same arena, and you have to force the other person to make an error. You both have the same ability to block, to jump, to avoid, to . . . to advance, to retreat, to footsie, do all these things. To counter, to parry, um . . . to cross-up. It's . . . it's a give and take, it's the strategy, it's the mind games that makes [sic] all these games really similar.

For Isaac, the appeal of the game is actually independent of the code. It's about the practice of play. If a game *supports* that practice of play through its codebase, then it has the potential to be a serious fighting game. If it doesn't, then the game leaves consideration. In a somewhat ironic twist, Gene—whose distaste for *Smash* as a casual game was the entry point to this discussion—began his fighting game career as a youth by playing *Mortal Kombat* games[4].

In this conflict of the casual and the hardcore, the core issue is a merging of ideal game practice and the affordances of the code. In the case of *Mortal Kombat*, the code does not allow ideal game practice among the fans I interviewed, and so it's not really considered a true fighting game. *Smash* on the other hand occupies a more nebulous space. Fans of hardcore *Smash* argue that a particular practice of play applied to the affordances of the codebase produces the right match to satisfy hardcore play, while the prevailing view of players at communities like Shoryuken.com is that those affordances create an untenable—indeed, flat-out boring—playstyle that doesn't mesh with the ideal. Interestingly, there was no evidence either from the *Smash* players with whom I spoke, or on communities such as Smashboards, that the games favored by those at SRK weren't "real fighting games."

Thus, there are two critical issues here. One is an issue of material embodiment: what does the code of the game allow? This seems relatively clear cut, even in the case of *Smash*. What muddies the waters is conflicting notions of play practice. When opinions differ about what the gameplay experience is *supposed* to be like—normative ideas of play practice—then the viability of the game itself for serious play comes into question. In a similar vein, the previous discussion of casual versus hardcore *Smash* explored how that conflict arose and how it affects the tension between casual and hardcore players, but it did not necessarily explore *why* players of *Smash* might construct their elaborately restrictive rulesets for tournament play that so frustrate players like Gene in the first place. The specific mechanics of *Brawl*, compared to the other games that appeared at EVO in 2009, are likely the reason.

For example, in *Street Fighter 4*, the choice of which stage characters fight in has no rule-based effect on gameplay whatsoever; it is merely a visual backdrop for the action. While the stage has some bearing on matches in *Soul Calibur 4*—particularly the size and shape of the stage being more or less friendly to ring out victories—for the most part those stages were also window dressing, as far as I could observe. However, stages in *Brawl* are a different animal; many of them feature layouts with natural hazards and random events that can influence the outcome of the fight, up to and including the defeat of a player. Thus there's no reason for *Street Fighter* players to ban a stage because it would be a tournament rule built entirely for aesthetics. On the other hand, in *Brawl* banning a stage is a strategic, gameplay-oriented move, and indeed, the *Brawl* tournament I observed at EVO 2009 had a draft-style, team alternating stage ban as part of match setups.

Likewise, the issue of items is very similar. Unlike the other games in the tournament, *Brawl*'s base design involves random items which appear in stages at random intervals. These items range from the relatively harmless, to those with the potential for a major and decisive effect on the match, such as instantly knocking a player out or restoring a player's health to full. As these are mechanical aspects unique to *Brawl*'s individual structure, it stands to reason that competitive tournament play of that game would involve much greater rules that define not just the "real life" context of play, but the in-game context as well.

Items don't exist in *Street Fighter* or *Soul Calibur*, so there's no need for rules related to items in those contexts. In short, because *Brawl* has more rules to tweak than *Street Fighter 4*, it's sensible that tournament play might involve more restriction. One curious note, however: *Brawl* allows for the turning on or off not just of items wholesale, but of individual items from a list. Yet the EVO *Brawl* tournament stipulated no items of any kind. Why the dominant *Smash* culture opts for no items wholesale versus strategic bans of specific items isn't clear.

As for the overarching goal of such restrictions, *Brawl* player Matthew was both emphatic and definite on the subject, suggesting that leaving on random elements creates a "horseshoe effect":

Todd: So it's sounding like . . . mmm, hmm. How to put this. From that very brief description of items that you just gave it's seeming like their presence in competitive *Smash*—hardcore *Smash* since you said they're the same so I'm gonna run with that—items in hardcore *Smash* is a disruptive influence in terms of their randomness, or . . .?

Matthew: Yes. Their randomness is the big thing because it has been argued that using items takes skill. I support that. Using items takes a huge load of skill, to know when to use them, how to use them, when you should grab them, when you should leave them and try to trick your opponent into grabbing them . . . that's a huge aspect of skill. However, there is no control given over the items that spawn, when they spawn, and where they spawn, and a lot of items will disrupt the gameplay without you even triggering them. So like, you could be having a match. The person's going, they make a mistake, you're about to hit the kill move . . . and then a bomb spawns, and you hit the bomb instead of them, and you die. This isn't a hypothetical . . . this happens.

Todd: It's actually happened.

Matthew: This actually happens. So that's why it's been taken out of a lot of the competitive play, is because it's pure . . . like, the person was gonna get punished. They made a mistake, they

> were gonna lose the match because of it, but they won, not because of anything they did, but they apparently have a horseshoe in their back pocket.

Todd: And the whole point of competitive *Smash* is not to find who has the horseshoe . . .

Matthew: It's to find who can punish.

Todd: Who has the strongest competitive game.

In short: it isn't necessarily that items themselves are the problem; he admits that using items properly takes skill. However, the issue is that the lack of control over their impact on the match—and interestingly, their ability to seemingly, at random, destroy the positive effects of perfect (and, importantly, *skillful*) execution of game controls—is so disruptive that the game is no longer about skill. Instead, it's about luck: Who benefits the most from the vagaries of chance? As he summed up shortly after, "The fun of competitive gaming is from the competition itself. Not so much the game, but more the players. Being able to beat them is what the fun is. Knowing that it was skill that led you to that victory."

Thus considered in the context of this tension between agon and ilinx and the creation of the skill challenge environment, the reasons for these tournament restrictions become clearer. The earlier discussion of how ilinx is incompatible with agon should sound familiar after analyzing casual vs. hardcore/tournament *Smash*: "casual *Smash*" with its random items and focus on the unpredictable is much more compatible with ilinx. Comparatively, if this example is any indicator, fighting games as the hardcore player understands and supports them are agon: rule-bounded competitions, tests of skill and cleverness, incompatible with the whimsy of randomness.

Perhaps what's most interesting is that both the hardcore *Smash* competitive community and the culture of competitive *Street Fighter* or *Marvel vs. Capcom* both embrace this notion of skill-bounded agon, where a level playing field is required in order to determine, through combat, which contestant has the higher level of ability and skill. Yet because of social and game code factors, the latter group sometimes views the former—and their game of choice—with disdain. The relationship between broad philosophical views on balance, what the code of each game affords, and what individual players view the purpose and effect are of each, creates a complex network of interactions regarding these games.

BROKEN CHARACTERS AND BALANCE

Another useful angle for examining the collision of game rules and social play practice and the drive for balance/fairness is the point at which players will start to consider an option "broken." While I earlier defined broken broadly as meaning "unfair/unbalanced," in the fighting game community the word has a number of different definitions and connotations. Generally speaking, when something is "broken," it presents a perception of the broken element as unfair or giving too much of an advantage to one player or the other. Particularly powerful characters, special attacks that are powerful but incur little risk when used, and strategies that shut down entire avenues of play are just some of the examples that came up when exploring the idea of something being broken. Because these elements are so unfair, they "break" the game.

Alongside other factors, discussions of what constitutes fair technical play versus an unfair advantage drive home the point that the ideal fighting game match takes place on a level playing field, or more specifically, that it is an arena where skill, rather than external factors, is the determinant of a winner or loser. Remember, too, the earlier discussion of Consalvo and Aarseth on the subject of cheating and the hollow win. Beyond the issue of the lack of aporia making the match boring, there's a very real possibility that the *perception* of brokenness—a character granting an unfair advantage—constitutes flat-out cheating. However, much as the players in Consalvo's work have varying social constructions of when cheating is appropriate, fighting gamers have varying definitions of what exactly gives a character an unfair advantage.

So what does "broken" mean? To the fighting game players I interviewed, the definitions varied. Garrett framed broken characters as those who make it "impossible to win." Both Garrett and Nicholas used the character of Akuma in *Super Street Fighter 2 Turbo* as an example of a broken character, with Nicholas specifically using the phrase "he doesn't work like he's supposed to," implying that the very function of the character is damaged. It should be noted that "fixing" Akuma was one of the goals of David Sirlin, as he attempted to rebalance *Street Fighter 2 Turbo* in the creation of *SF2T: HD Remix* (Killian & Sirlin, 2007).Yet in spite of the claim in the initial FAQ on the rebalancing that he would be balanced, Akuma is banned in tournament play of both games.

Jeff's discussion of brokenness was more socially situated; rather than giving me a strict definition either way, he recounted a story of online *Marvel vs. Capcom 2* play where his opponent—who Jeff was beating over and over—would continually shout into his microphone that Jeff was picking "broken" characters. This suggests that for the person he was playing, "broken" simply meant "unfairly powerful"; Jeff's retort was that he was using admittedly powerful ("high tier") characters, but that it was the skill of his opponent that was the problem. Thus for Jeff, the characters weren't overpowered, but to the person he was fighting, Jeff's superior skill combined with the understanding of the characters he was using created the *perception* that they were "broken." Of course, this is predicated on the notion that both Jeff and his opponent have the same definition of "broken" to begin with.

Among those players who had exposure to *Soul Calibur 4*, the potential brokenness of the aforementioned Hilde was a thorny topic indeed. The respondents I spoke to were quite emphatic that her moveset—her list of attacks and their properties—is quite strong, regardless of any other considerations. Even Ibrahim, who had a relatively moderate stand on Hilde's place in the *SC4* cosmos, put it thusly, when I asked about the EVO crowd's intense negative reaction to Hilde being picked during the finals:

Todd: Yeah. Well, I was wondering about that. I mean, is there kind of a . . . because it seems like the crowd was indicating that there's this backlash against . . . which my untrained eye kind of told me was this regulation, five or six hit combination that's done every time and you do it until they fall off the edge of the ring.

Ibrahim: Absolutely. That's why she is so powerful. She has built into her character the ability to ring you out from almost anywhere. She can just walk you to an edge and push you out. No other character has that kind of ability, and . . . no matter how much damage it actually does—but it does half life even if you don't get rung out—a ring out is an instant death and no other character can do that. So, she's just so much more powerful than every other character in the game for that mechanic.

Earlier in the interview, he noted that he didn't think "the developers intended it to be that way, but that's the way it ended up." Players discovered this combination of attacks that rings out almost instantly—earning an immediate win regardless of how much "life" the opponent has—and so in the process, Hilde leapt up in the rankings of character power[5].

Garret agreed with Ibrahim's sentiments about Hilde's level of power, but he was quick to point out that Hilde is neither indestructible nor unbeatable. If anything, his frustration with Hilde seemed to involve the idea that the appearance of being unbeatable would make players who encounter Hilde unlikely to come back to the game after repeated losses:

I know the people that started the fervor, and . . . the bad thing about Hilde is that people don't realize how beatable she is. Like, she has one of the most powerful things I've ever seen in a fighting game, but it's only one thing. Like, that's her shot, and if you really put, like, effort into knowing how to beat it, like . . . she doesn't have anything else. If you shut that off, the match is over for her. The whole match is over for her. She doesn't have any other fallbacks; she has nothing, and um . . . but . . . the issue with Hilde is that when new players come to learn the game and someone uses Hilde on them, what am I supposed to say to you? Like, when someone says, when someone asks me "Does that happen even if you know how to beat it?" Uh, yeah, it does. I don't know how many people have turned away from the game because of this broken-looking character.

This followed earlier statements about how Hilde, in spite of her powerful tools, is beatable, an example Garret mentioned to explain that superior skill can and will beat out in-game mechanical advantage. When I suggested that the various aspects of counterpicking—choosing a character that is strong where your opponent is weak—were similar to rock/paper/scissors, he replied, "In a way, but the better player's gonna win." Counterpicking is not always safe; for example, it may mean playing a character with whom the player isn't familiar, putting him/her at a disadvantage.

It's important to understanding the concept of counterpicking because it represents an orientation toward play intended to encourage or restore this idea of perfect balance in competitive situations. In a counterpick, a player chooses a character whose in-game affordances are believed to balance out/negate/counter the strengths of his/her opponent. The usefulness of counterpicking is a subject of debate. David Sirlin, discussing *Street Fighter 4*'s online multiplayer mode, argued that the fact that the game does not hide the character of the first player to choose allows the opponent to consistently counterpick, a weakness of the game (Sirlin, 2009). Discussion of counterpicking on Shoryuken.com ("Counter Picking.. Your thoughts?", 2009) ranged from feeling it was "cheap" to arguing that people who counterpick only do so because they have no actual skill, to arguing that it's simply a part of play one should come to accept. By contrast, discussion of counterpicking in the *Smash* community seems to encourage it as a part of the play of the game ("Counterpicking made easy", 2008; "The important of counter picking", 2010). Ultimately, the decision is left to the player. As many posters in the SRK thread mention, counterpicking isn't always a smart move, particularly if the player who counterpicks doesn't have training or skill with the countering character they choose. Whatever the level of expectation there is about its use, it doesn't rise to the level of a ban in tournament rules. As an interesting aside, David Sirlin participated in the *SF2 HD Remix* finals at EVO 2009 and was the only player to ask for a blind pick scenario, where the first player whispers their choice to a tournament organizer, and then is beholden to pick that character once their opponent has chosen. In almost every other scenario, players chose simultaneously, even if it opened them to counterpick.

However, not all counterpick situations play out similarly. In the *Guilty Gear XX Accent Core* finals between Martin "Marn" Phan and Peter "FlashMetroid" Susini, Phan lost his first game playing as the character Jam Kuradoberi, and then in the second round changed to the character Eddie. He then went on to win, and so continued to play Eddie. Even at the highest level of play—Justin Wong and Daigo Umehara in the *SF4* finals—there was no small degree of character switching, with Justin Wong starting as the character Abel, then moving to Rufus, until finally settling on Balrog. Switching characters did not seem to rankle with the crowd or create problems unless it seemed specifically that the player was falling back onto some perceived technical advantage, as was the case with many Hilde players; and in those instances, the switch seems to have been as much about changing the circumstances of play—such as moving from a stick to a pad—as it was about choosing an individual character. Not only was the player picking the despised Hilde, he was *also* creating a circumstance of play where performing the combination of moves that made her despised in the first place would be easier.

This view on play is actually quite resonant with the comments Seth Killian made to me at EVO, particularly on the difference between restrictive and emergent philosophies on play. The emergent way of doing things—which seemed evident in many of the responses from people I interviewed—suggests that rather than restricting a character for being "broken," it be left to the players of the game to determine how to beat this seemingly game-unbalancing situation. One thread ("Wreaking Havoc in Wolfkrone: The anti-Hilde thread", 2009) on *SC4*-focused forum 8 Way Run is a particularly interesting example of this. The thread's very first line indicates that it is a follow up to Hilde not being banned, and focuses on developing anti-Hilde strategies. It goes on for quite some time with a number of players—even one or two self-identified and dedicated Hilde players!—contributing their thoughts on what moves and strategies work well against Hilde, particularly what they refer to as the "doom combo," or the series of moves mentioned above that have massive ring-out potential (and thus contribute to her being considered high tier).

The predominant idea in this situation is that skill, more than anything else, is the real determinant when it comes to a match in these games. Characters such as Hilde might be exceptionally powerful, but the thrust of both the responses I received in interviews and read on community forums is that if a serious player makes an effort to learn the powerful character's weaknesses, then s/he cannot be truly "broken." One 8WR thread about the future of powerful characters like Hilde ("The future of Algol, Hilde and Star Wars", 2009) has responses that point to one interesting metric: Since none of the top placers in 2009 at tournaments such as EVO or Nationals were using Hilde, that is evidence that she isn't broken.

Presumably, the logic here is that if Hilde were broken—that is to say, so powerful that she disrupts the natural play of the game—she would be represented among the winners out of necessity. Another read is that if Hilde did appear in these tournaments (and she did at EVO, multiple times) then by virtue of being broken she would confer such a massive advantage that anyone playing her would reach the winners' circle on the power of her character alone. Since neither of these appear to be true, she therefore cannot be broken.

The flip side of the Hilde coin is a character in *Super Smash Bros. Brawl* named Metaknight. Although I was only able to speak with one *Brawl* player, he did have interesting insights to share on a debate in the community about whether or not Metaknight should be banned. Matthew described himself as initially being against the idea of banning, but that over time he's become uncertain, particularly based on some tournament results:

> Matthew: Um . . . if you would have asked me, like, honestly, like, maybe two weeks ago since the game came out [e.g. from the game's release until two weeks prior to the interview], I would have said no, and it would have been a resounding no, but it's starting to become . . . I'm on the fence, now, because I'm starting to see some data that's been brought up, just of pure domination in the tournaments.
>
> Todd: On the Metaknight front?
>
> Matthew: Yeah. Like, I know every game has its best character, it's just I'm starting to wonder if Metaknight's too much "the best." Then again, local tournaments and the past, like, four major tournaments, he's only won one of them. So. As of right now it's a no, but it's a no that could easily change.

He went on to indicate that the argument over whether Metaknight should be banned was highly fractious in the *Smash* community: "He's such a polarizing force, a lot of people feel the community is going to tear itself in half soon." Also interesting, however, is the idea that significant data collection on tournament results goes into these decisions about who is broken, powerful, or weak; for more on that topic, see the discussion of "tier lists" in Chapter 5.

Interestingly enough, that statement has resonance with one made by Ibrahim about the *Soul Calibur* community after the release of *Soul Calibur 3* on the Playstation2 console. According to him, a large number of bugs in the game code gave considerable advantage to some characters, "breaking" the game. However, due to limitations on the PS2, the game could not be patched or fixed on its own, "so all those bugs just became part of the game, and there was sort of a split in the community of players on whether or not we should try to ban these bugs in tournament play, or let them go, and let them go prevailed, and I was on the other camp, so I just quit playing it." The community decision as he describes it was that many of the bugs could not be tracked or even noticed in order to be banned, so there was little choice but to let them go unchecked[6].

Even a cursory glance at Smashboards, the preeminent *Smash Bros.* online community, certainly seems to support Matthew's claims of intense debate and fractiousness. The moderators, in an attempt to control the spread of new threads on the topic, condensed the arguments into one thread ("Official Metaknight Discussion", 2010) which then grew to over 800 pages and over twelve thousand posts, though not all of these are on topic and the discussion seems to have grown into a wider analysis of top tier characters in *Brawl*. They also include links to two threads summarizing the pro-ban ("Why we can't wait to ban Metaknight", 2010) and anti-ban ("Chill out. Metaknight won't ever be banned.", 2010) arguments. The pro-ban stance focuses on Metaknight's tournament dominance and lack of counter-picks (e.g. characters that are strong against his weaknesses), while the anti-ban stance argues that all fighting games will have a "best" character, and that removing Metaknight from the situation does little, if anything, to improve it.

What's interesting about these two scenarios is that they are effectively opposite ends of the same line. The aim of both of these perspectives—the 8WR thread suggesting ways to defeat Hilde, and the ongoing discussion of banning Metaknight—have the same relative aim in mind: providing a game space where it's the skill of the players rather than the mechanical advantage of the characters played, the stages played upon, or other random events that decides the outcome. Again, there is considerable resonance here with Jordan's comment about technology and arcade sticks, noted in Chapter 2: the idea that the technology should facilitate play, rather than interfere with it. Character balance is perhaps not "technological" on the same level as an interface point like an arcade stick, but it is part of the game code.

AT THE INTERSECTION OF CODE AND DISCOURSE

So, what picture of fighting games do we get from observing the practice of play? Certainly, we find a love of competition, with all the drama and uncertainty that it can bring, much like spectating more traditional physical sports. A fighting game match presents an open possibility space, slightly bounded, where the emergence of an outcome through the auspice of the competitors is the primary joy. However, the appearance of unfairness or imbalance has a significant negative effect on that joy. Close matches where ability is on display, where players move skillfully within that possibility space to create opportunities and defeat their opponents, are the highest good.

What all these examples highlight—other than these persistent, dominant ideas about balance, skill, and fairness in the fighting game community—are various ways in which game code and mechanics intersect and intertwine with the culture's views on play. To these fans, fighting games present an opportunity for Caillois' agon: a competition between two fighters, where all things being equal, the competition will bear out who has the greater skill when that player achieves victory. Of course, that phrase "all things being equal" is the rub. Issues of noise, balance, and fairness are centered around this idea that it is not only desirable, but *necessary* to eliminate those outside forces which would interfere with the skill competition.

Disagreements about just how that should go down do happen, and the comparative views of *Smash* and *Mortal Kombat* point to where those roads can lead. But even those disagreements make clear that the games that fighting fans love are not just defined by their code. The actual experience of play, and the social mores toward play that they embrace, are just as important and just as valid in defining them.

NOTES

1. You can see this combo in action at http://www.youtube.com/watch?v=dhn8HxE43_4#t=00m36s; interestingly, this particular video is a pre-made introduction that was shown to the crowd at the event before the *SC4* finals began.
2. In this sense, "macro" refers to the ability to set up a controller button to act as if multiple buttons were pressed at the same time. The *Soul* series typically has four base buttons: horizontal attack, vertical attack, guard, and kick. Since a typical controller has more than four buttons, the game allows players to map combinations to the unused buttons, making moves that require pressing multiple buttons at once easier.
3. I want to emphasize that I don't use proscription here in the strictest sense; there is no hard-and-fast rule. However, the behavior of players at EVO and the sentiments I read on forums like 8 Way Run suggest that her use, and the use of that combination, are at minimum decidedly frowned upon. Perhaps, interestingly, because it's among a small list of characters and moves that is associated with "newbie" behavior and a focus on winning rather than skill.
4. Interestingly enough, later incarnations of the *Mortal Kombat* series have made appearances as featured tournaments at EVO in 2011, 2012, and 2013, suggesting that over time, the game has acquired some of the qualities that the fighting game community would consider "tournament-worthy." The game *Injustice: Gods Among Us*, which shares a development pedigree with the newer *Mortal Kombat* games, was a featured game at the GUTS 2 tournament held in Boston in June 2013 as well.
5. And, now that the series has moved on to the next game, *Soul Calibur 5*, Hilde appears to have both lost her "doom combo" and dropped in the rankings. Easy come, easy go. For more information on how these rankings, called "tier lists," are constructed, refer to Chapter 5.
6. This is an issue that is partially solved by online-capable consoles, where bugs and game balance issues can be patched by downloadable content. Most of Capcom's newest releases—*Street Fighter 4* and *Marvel vs. Capcom 3*—have routinely used patches to re-tune and re-balance the game system for tournament play. The PlayStation 2, however, did not have a reliable and constant Internet connection to enable this sort of patching, and so the situation Ibrahim describes emerged.

4   Playing Together, Online and Off

In reading so far you may have noticed there's not much discussion in this book of people playing fighting games by themselves, except perhaps in the context of practicing. It's certainly *possible* to play fighting games alone, versus a computer-controlled opponent, a mode frequently and interestingly titled "arcade mode" or "story mode." This is how I played these games growing up, since I didn't have regular access to an arcade and didn't have many friends who shared my interest in the genre. Of course, when such friends *were* around, playing against each other was the preferred mode, and when I could make it to an arcade, play against other human beings was more or less inevitable. That happened even if I wasn't interested in doing so, in fact, because part of the arcade experience is surrendering yourself to the unpredictable nature of play in a public space. You never know who's going to step up, throw down a quarter, and gleefully intone that they "got next."

The reason for this lack of discussion is also the focus of this chapter: social play. Think back to the qualities of a fighting game discussed in Chapter 1: fighting games are competitive, and they allow for multiplayer competition. For the community of hardcore fighting game fans, these are perhaps the most critical definitions of the genre and the games within it. This one core value shared across the interview respondents had resonance in almost all of the themes and topics I pulled from speaking with them. The play situations that the respondents described to me overwhelmingly involved playing fighting games against other human opponents.

This isn't to say there weren't mentions of playing alone; Nicholas, for example, talked about playing against the CPU on his home console, and Jordan also said he enjoyed playing against the computer. However, the context in which these quotes are presented suggests they aren't the norm. When Nicholas was mentioning playing this way, it was in the context of his very earliest days as a gamer, well before his entry into fighting game culture, and while he sometimes played alone, he just as often played with friends or siblings. Likewise, Jordan indicated that he plays against the computer mostly for fun and to relieve stress, since he doesn't have enough time to devote to multiplayer practice anymore; when I asked point blank if multiplayer was his preferred mode, he responded, "Yeah, totally." Among the other interviewees, there was almost no mention of solo play at all, with the possible exception of passing remarks about using training or practice modes—a mode in the game where the player can attack an unresisting, unplayed CPU opponent—to improve and practice.

Naturally, social play was the norm at EVO 2009, considering the event's purpose as both a social gathering and a tournament. However, even taking that into account, certain events suggested social play was the desirable norm. One instance in particular stands out; on the first day, I spent some time observing Capcom's demo stations for the then-unreleased *Tatsunoko vs. Capcom*. Since people were filing out of the convention space, some stations had no players at them, and one had a single player at it, practicing combos and playing against the computer. I was content to watch him play for a while, as well as those around him; that player, however, made frequent attempts to pull me into the game. At first, it's likely that my standing nearby was taken as an indicator that I *did* want to play. However, in the end he asked multiple times, clearly trying to draw me in to playing despite having the console to himself. Across all three days at various open stations for play at EVO, this drawing in of others—or inserting of oneself into an open space—was the norm.

It is difficult to say if this is a foundation stone upon which other aspects of the phenomena noted in this chapter are laid, or if it is a byproduct of a particular normative attitude toward the experience. However, it is important to note that in the following discussion of social gaming behavior, the assumption made by the respondents, and by extension the fighting game community, is that fighting games are ideally played not against a computer, but against another person controlling the other character.

This chapter examines a few of the ways in which gameplay and socializing/being a social actor intersect. For example, if the ideal of play is in an arcade-like setting (if not a literal arcade) against another person, how do fighting game matchups play out in a world where home versions played on Internet-capable consoles like the Xbox 360 or PlayStation 3 are the norm? Considering the "casual/hardcore" rift discussed back in Chapter 3, are there different social situations where fighting game fans move between different playstyles, or are they "always on"? Finally, tournament events such as EVO are naturally about competition and play, but they're also chances for players to interact as fans/enthusiasts in a social setting *dedicated* to their interests. Examining the non-play-specific interactions and elements of those scenarios sheds light on different aspects of fighting game culture that looking solely at gameplay could not.

PLAYERS AS SOCIAL ACTORS

A game is nothing without players, the participants who make it happen. It is no mistake that both Caillois and Juul[1] mention, as part of their very definitions of play and games, that it is something shaped by the actions of the participants, who have an interest in the eventual outcome. In the age of digital games—particularly an era where the massively multiplayer online (MMO) game is so popular—the play of games must also be considered in terms of how players function as social actors during play.

Some of the earliest work on how gamers play socially comes from Gary Alan Fine, whose *Shared Fantasy: Role-playing Games as Social Worlds* (1983) examined players of pen and paper role-playing games (RPGs) in the Minneapolis area. Fine was interested in examining how players came to engage the role-playing experience. Fine's analysis drew heavily on Goffman, particularly *Frame Analysis* (1974). Goffman argues that life experience and activity are understood through frames: organizing principles that bring together different experiences, actions, and beliefs, and "govern events—at least social ones—and our subjective involvement with them" (pp. 10–11). Goffman describes a scenario where social interaction helps to define for us what the world is like; he draws on a number of metaphors related to both the theatre and games themselves to make his point, particularly the ideas that our perception of what is real has variability depending on both context and social activity, and that certain behaviors or cues—which he calls "keys" (p. 45)—signal social actors to shift their frame of reference.

As Fine puts it, a player managing these multiple frames is in the "real" frame of everyday life, the frame of being a player involved in a game, and the frame of being the character s/he is playing inside the narrative of the game world. His findings suggest that players move freely between these frames during play, depending on the needs of the moment. The magic circle as imagined by Huizinga is much less in evidence here. While the players in Fine's study are clearly in a demarcated space—quite literally, as his analysis takes place in a gaming-specific physical venue—with its own rulesets, the players he observes do not necessarily enter into that venue and leave the everyday world behind. Rather, at any given moment a player can adjust his/her salient frames depending on the social context at the time:

> The possibility of the rapid oscillation of frames suggests that frame stability and change should be conceptualized as an interactional achievement of members rather than as a function of stable situated meaning. Since participants commonly and cooperatively shift frames in the same situation, frames are not merely a shared individual schema that is triggered by the objective properties of a situation; rather, they are part of a dynamic consensus that can be bracketed, altered, or restored through the collective action of the participants. (pp. 203–4).

One such example is the concept of metagame knowledge; he recounts an example from play where a player wanted to act on knowledge that he had as a player (the "reality" frame) but which his character did not. The game master (GM), as referee of the rules and a sort of informal activity leader, had to shut this down for the sake of the game. Another similar example is in another GM allowing a player who had rolled (on a die) a failing result, and who had consistently been rolling poorly, to re-roll the attempt. Although this was "cheating"—against the rules—the GM felt that part of the social contract of gaming allowed for the breaking of the rules so that everyone could continue to enjoy themselves.

While not all of Fine's various frames are of relevance to fighting game fans—in particular, they tend to see individual characters as assemblages of in-game affordances first and narrative/aesthetic designs second—it's clear that there are analogs between Fine's roleplayers and arcade-going fighting gamers. Two competitors having a match in a public space like a tournament or arcade are moving between frames of engagement at any given moment: the literal frame of "player" focused on the game, of "competitor" or "good sport" engaging the social rules/mores of the game culture, and possibly even a "performer" frame where they acknowledge the public performance of gameplay and alter their in-game and out-of-game behaviors to please or work the crowd. The key is that in social play, a player is never only inhabiting one part of the experience; s/he is moving between elements of play and socialization as they become more or less salient.

Part of Jesper Juul's discussion of casual games (2010) focuses on social meaning and social goals, and his analysis also presents a scenario where movement between frames is part of the social game experience. He analyzes multiplayer games in order to uncover how mimetic interface games, such as *Wii Sports*, came to be such a success among casual players, particularly in social play. In so doing, he argues that multiplayer games take on meaning through a shared understanding of the goal of the process. Juul suggests there are three frames of play when it comes to a particular player's actions in a multiplayer scenario: goal orientation (the desire to win), game experience (wanting playing the game to be fun, interesting, or satisfying), and social management (understanding the effect of gameplay decisions on the social experience of multiplayer play). As he puts it, "[t]he nominal description of a game will tell you to focus on the first consideration [e.g. game experience], but the other two repeatedly come into play" (p. 127). Thus management of the social situation can and does have an effect on play. A desire to fulfill a certain social imperative—for example, not wanting to beat a child and allowing him/her to win, or competing particularly hard against an annoying player in order to beat him/her and take them down a peg—ends up influencing the interaction with the game. In this instance, the links to play behaviors in the fighting game community—particularly gameplay norms, per Chapter 3—should be obvious.

Consalvo (2007), in *Cheating: Gaining Advantage in Videogames*, explores how cheating, as an activity, intersects with a number of player factors, and her work is a good example of how even in single player situations, the notion of shared social goals for gameplay can have an impact on play practice and socialization. In general, she finds that ideas about cheating—breaking the rules of a game—vary, and more to the point that even those players who agree that a particular act is cheating can vary in when they feel that performing said act is appropriate or not. Much like the keying of frames for Fine's players, Consalvo argues that cheating is an activity that takes on a different character depending on the situation of the player and the game: "We need to see cheating as an important part of those practices and spaces, but not as a static 'thing' or core trait. Besides, that would be impossible, for just as games and gameplay practices change, what we consider cheating and how we respond to it have changed over time as well" (p.128). This is yet another example of how the context of play has an impact on play decisions. One of the philosophies of cheating Consalvo identifies is "you can't cheat a GameCube"; effectively, that when playing a single-player game, cheating is acceptable, but once other players—social play—enter the equation, the various forms of cheating become unacceptable.

A related and critical concept to Consalvo's argument is the idea of "gaming capital," derived in part from Bordieu's concept of cultural capital. As Consalvo puts it,

> Along those lines, I have reworked the term into gaming capital, as mentioned earlier, to capture how being a member of game culture is about more than playing games or even playing them well. It's being knowledgeable about game releases and secrets, and passing that information on to others. It's having opinions about which game magazines are better and the best sites for walkthroughs on the Internet. (p. 18)

Thus, while puissant skill with games is likely to garner gaming capital for a player, in this case it is more than that. Engagement in the culture is just as much a necessity for obtaining that sort of currency in the community.

She draws in the notion of paratext as well, suggesting that acts and texts that may seem peripheral to actual gameplay—walkthroughs, cheat codes, Easter Eggs, tip websites, etc.—are really a vital part of the gameplay experience themselves. The idea of paratext was originally put forth by Genette (1997). He used the term to describe a sort of "threshold" between the most basic level of the text on the inside, and discourse in the world about the text on the outside: "[m]ore than a boundary or a sealed border, the paratext is, rather, a *threshold*, or—a word Borges used apropos of a preface—a 'vestibule' that offers the world at large the possibility of either stepping inside or turning back" (pp. 1–2, emphasis original). Genette's focus was on the written work, and the ways in which things like author dedications, prefaces, and other intertexts created a context for the consumption of the "core" text to which they were linked and subservient.

According to Consalvo, Lunenfeld (1999) then took that idea and updated it for a transmedia world. He argues that as the barriers between media break down and synergy and cross-promotion become the norm, the potential range of paratexts explodes. Those paratexts can then become fascinating texts in their own right, rather than being ultimately subservient to the "original" as Genette argued. In other words, if one wants to consider the meanings made from digital games, one cannot simply look at the isolated act of play; it must be situated in a social context and a cloud of paratexts related to it. Cheating—in many ways, a core ethical play value and certainly an orientation toward game rules—is one highly illustrative example of that principle at work.

Juul and Consalvo aren't alone in thinking that shared goals/mores and social gameplay go hand in hand. "Enjoying themselves" is the expressed primary goal of the university student players researched by Kolos (2010). In her study, she examines regular social game play in a dormitory floor lounge, exploring their motivations, actions, and the ways in which the group has become "inclusive," ranging across skill levels, backgrounds with gaming, and gender to become diverse. She argues that rather than focusing on "games"—close-ended, goal-oriented competitions—research on social play is better served by a focus on play. For the students she interviewed— and even played with—their "shared goal . . . to take part in a playful social activity, influenced the standards they used to accept new players. The social barriers to entry and the interpersonal stakes were almost always low" (p. 128). In that sort of setting, players of various skill levels and backgrounds regarding games can come together harmoniously by a social agreement for a group goal: having fun together.

Remember too earlier discussion of Jakobsson's (2007) examination of a gaming club in Sweden focused around *Super Smash Bros. Melee.* His argument is that beyond the matter of the literal rules of the game code, in the club's play of *Smash* the social rules of play had a major impact on the actual game experience. He describes a conflict between two types of players—"smashers" and "anti-smashers"—whose differing ideas about certain game elements led them to play and interact with the game (and each other) in differing ways. Though the social group Kolos observed was perhaps a little more harmonious, in both cases, it's evident that social play involving multiple people brings another dimension to consider into focus. As both Kolos and Jakobsson argue, analysis of gaming in a social context must take into account the effects of that context on the experience of play.

The findings of Jansz and Martens (2005) regarding players at a LAN event also speak to scenarios where the social aspect of play and gamer culture is more critical than the ludic. While they initially expected that a desire to compete—a motive consistent with the public image of hardcore gamers—would be the highest expressed motive for attending the event, what they found was that "[t]he possibility to game in each other's presence at a LAN event was the foremost gratifying property of LAN gaming; the social motive obtained the highest score among the motives found" (p. 349).

Though they note that a desire not to contribute to the stereotype of violent hypercompetitive gamers may have had an effect on what they uncovered, their findings suggest that in the context of a massive, social gaming event, it's the social experience and opportunity that's guiding participation and play, rather than a sole desire for heavy competition.

What all of these works speak to is a relationship between the formative rules of a game and gameplay's place in a player's social actions. For Fine and Juul this means players consistently moving between the frame of the real and the frame of the game as social interaction and convention dictate. Kolos and Jakobsson both examine scenarios where a shared social understanding of the activity has a transformative aspect on social play. Finally, according to Consalvo, the MMO player who purchases in-game gold through real money trade companies may be just another player to some, and an unethical cheater to others, depending on not only their normative feelings toward the rules, but also the type of gaming capital they wish to reflect and gather.

ONLINE VS. OFFLINE: THE AFFORDANCES, LIMITATIONS, AND "NOISE" OF ONLINE PLAY

One might wonder, if the arcade is dying out and a core value in the fighting game culture is that their games are intended to be played against people, then why do arcade spaces and tournaments still happen? It's possible to buy a copy of *Marvel vs. Capcom 3*, take it home, put it in your PlayStation, and get into a match with a random stranger living anywhere from Tokyo, Japan to Tupelo, Mississippi. In such a world, doesn't the arcade seem even more obsolete? The answer is, yes and no. As has already been discussed, the physical arcade space has its own particular emotional, nostalgic, and affective draw for much of the fighting game community. Certainly, while consoles add their own expense and thus socioeconomic class-related dimensions to access, online play adds on the digital divide-oriented issue of network access as well, whereas local co-op requires only the console.

However, there are more telling and informative reasons for why online play is not the dominant mode in the fighting game community, and those reasons primarily involve the technology and cultural context of online play. Respondents identified that competitive fighting game play moves at a very quick pace, and that the speed of various in-game moves and techniques is measured in "frames," as in the number of animation frames the motion takes up on-screen. Online play involves a certain degree of inherent lag time, even with high-speed broadband connections; in an online match, information about what players do in the game has to be relayed to both participants in a way that makes the connection feel as seamless as possible. This lag can cause controller inputs to be lost, delayed, or otherwise mistimed, resulting in a less satisfying experience. Ibrahim described it thusly:

Todd: Do you play online, too? At least in terms of like, matches on Xbox Live or PlayStation Network, stuff like that?

Ibrahim: Uh, I don't play *Calibur* online. I do play other games that I don't take quite as seriously online.

Todd: That's an interesting phrase. Is it . . . well, no, I mean, I wanna ask about that. Is there something about the online experience that makes playing a game you take seriously like *Soul Calibur 4* distasteful, compared to . . .

Ibrahim: Not distasteful, but like I was saying, the frames make a difference, and fighting games online inherently will lose a couple of frames just sending information back and forth. So, the timing required to play online is different from the timing required to play offline, so if I get acclimated to that online laggy type of play, when I try to transition back to offline to play at tournaments, I will get destroyed.

Aaron described the online play experience in his favored game, *Tatsunoko vs. Capcom*, as if he were "playing against the system, not the other player" because of (at the time) serious lag problems with the game's online modes. The general feeling in these scenarios isn't necessarily that playing online is terribly onerous, but that the way the technology works has an adverse effect on the experience. Lag and dropped frames are a problem, working against the notion of a "level playing field" that is so critical in this culture; if one player has heavy lag, s/he is at a disadvantage due to inability to properly react, and thus a crack develops in the possibility that the match accurately and equally measures which player has higher skill through competition. Put simply, the concern is that in a situation where precise timing is required, any negative impact on that is a risk.

However, concerns about online play stretch beyond simple technology issues. Some respondents noted that there is a substantial difference in behavior between many of the players they meet in online games compared to the opponents they find in "real life" venues. These negative experiences online involved players who were poor losers, poor sports, and generally used the semi-anonymity of Internet play in order to break a code of good sportsmanship that the respondents typically embrace.

Certainly, this isn't a new thing in online competition or social gaming; Ian Shanahan (2004) describes a situation where not only was another player patently racist and offensive in the context of online anonymous play, but also did it to gain a tactical advantage in a *Star Wars*-themed lightsaber duel game. Tracy Kennedy (2009), writing about the effect of social play and harassment on female Xbox Live gamers, cites a number of unnerving stories where the online environment led to poor sportsmanship based on gender perception. One of her participants describes a game of *Halo 2* where a player, having been identified as a woman when she spoke up in voice chat, was then systematically "camped"—singled out and repeatedly killed—by a male player with whom she had previously had a more equitable playing relationship.

Jeff in particular had a number of stories about his experiences playing *Marvel vs. Capcom 2* over Microsoft's Xbox Live service. He described scenarios where his opponents were openly hostile over voice chat; Xbox Live includes a feature where if both players have compatible headsets (included with the console), they can talk while playing. The other player, who was losing, became openly hostile and attacked Jeff verbally:

> Todd: And, uh, you had said he was kind of being . . . was he being a jerk? Like, you'd said that he was sounding really mad because he was losing, but.
>
> Jeff: He . . . he was getting very upset; the term—I'll borrow it from *World of Warcraft*—they call it "nerdrage." Just where someone is just getting extremely upset over a video game, and <coughing> excuse me, sorry. To his credit, he kept coming back two or three times before he quit, which is good. I mean, that's showing that he's . . . maybe not even, I don't know what his reason was, but I hope it's 'cause he was trying to get better, but he was just screaming at me the whole time, and, you know . . . "You're garbage!", "You're trash, man, you're terrible!", "Like, that was terrible!" and I'm like "Dude . . . I'm terrible but I'm winning. What does that mean you are? I don't understand. Like, are you trying to hurt my feelings, or . . .?" The amount of stuff that he was saying was really amusing.

Isaac described similar experiences while playing online, mentioning that he encountered his share of sore losers and hate mail as well, though he brushed off the idea that this presents a serious issue: "Now I'm polite, when I play against people, and you know, when I lose, I lose, and I'm gracious about it, and the people who are sore losers, well, all they're gonna do is send me a nasty message, right? Big deal . . . and if they live in China or they live in Wisconsin, who knows where they are, and they don't know who I am."

Interestingly, neither of these players seemed to shy away from online play because of the behavior of other players. Jeff, Isaac, and Garrett expressed that they've had some encouraging and fun play over XBox Live. Their descriptions of their encounters with sore losers seem to be less about explaining their distaste for online play than about their dislike for sore losers who use the relative anonymity of online play to lambaste their opponents. In some cases, dislike is less accurate than "outright amusement";

Jeff's tone especially conveyed that he was telling funny stories about people he sees as silly or foolish.

Issues of lag are presented as considerably more serious barriers to on-line play than bad behavior from anonymous opponents. Consalvo (2009b) identifies lag as one of three types of "noise" that affects communication in online play, the other two being more linguistic, such as language and jargon barriers. Specifically, she refers to the ability of lag to disrupt tem-porality, so that different people experience events that are expected to be simultaneous at different times and speeds. The effect on an online fighting game match is more or less the same; rather than experiencing the event as continuous and smooth, it becomes choppy and disjointed, and as was previously mentioned, the potential effect this has on game balance makes it less appealing[2].

However, the suggestion is that while online play is flawed—either tech-nologically or socially—it's better than nothing at all. What this points to is the existence of a preferred context for the social fighting game experience, and considering what online play does and does not offer gives us insight into what makes up that preferred context. The reservations considered here point to some of the things that players desire, but do not get, out of online play: smooth, uninterrupted control of the game, being in the physical pres-ence of your opponent, and having a sense of good sportsmanship rather than being a sore loser.

Conversely, what are some of the benefits of online play that make it worth enduring these shortcomings? Isaac, continuing from his comment above, has something to say on this topic: In his words, online play "satisfies my requirement for fighting people who play better than I do . . . and more importantly, what the online feature has much more than arcades do, is that you're guaranteed to run into a much more variety of players [sic]." Nicho-las described a situation in where he was able, thanks to online play, to fight against a player he might never have a chance to face off against in person:

> Nicholas: And so I ran into [a *Street Fighter 2 Super Turbo*] game [on XBox Live], and then I went to Dhalsim, and then the loading screen showed me I was fighting against a Dictator player, and I had heard about . . . there's this guy named Yuu Vega in Japan, and he's one of the top Dictator players, M. Bison players . . . he's known as M. Bison in the USA but we just call him Dictator[3].
>
> Todd: Right.
>
> Nicholas: Yeah, he's a Dictator player in Japan, and it's first of three rounds and so, what happened was, I got him dizzy in the first round, but you know that . . . Dhalsim has the Yoga Flame trap on Dictator in ST, and my execution was off just a little bit, so he was able to get out and kill me, and second round I managed to get him in the corner again but my ex-

ecution was off again and so he got out and killed me, and the third round he perfected me. He did Psycho Magic in the corner and Touch of Death and I was done.

Todd: So you were . . . you were actually fighting this top-ranked player from Japan.

Nicholas: Yeah.

Todd: What was that experience like? Was it any different for you? Did you see his name and go "OMG!" and then just kind of . . .

Nicholas: [laughs] Actually, yeah, that is kind of what happened.

Todd: [laughs]

Nicholas: I was like . . . I lost, but I was really happy about it. Like, I might never get that opportunity in my life, to go play Yuu Vega, and it was really him, I could tell. I might have caught him off guard at first but he just totally wrecked me. In Japan, the tournament standard is best of one game, so . . . they have to be on point every time or otherwise that's it.

Thus for all its flaws, online play in this instance was worth it. It provided the opportunity for a match that otherwise would likely never have happened; much as Ryder & Wilson (1996) suggest about Internet technology and education, the online capability offers a set of affordances that offline play doesn't, enabling certain opportunities that might otherwise be missed. What this suggests—in Nicholas' case, at least—is that these rare opportunities to fight challenging and experienced opponents are worth putting up with the inherent flaws. Though the *ideal* would be to face them outside that context, the opportunity is enough to make it tolerable or even desirable.

In a different vein, online play also provided opportunities for some players to attempt to bring players "into the fold," so to speak. Jeff described a situation where he was actually able to turn a sore loser around by reaching out to him:

Last night another guy I played against, I picked Sentinel, Cable, and . . . someone else, and right away he's on the mic complaining, he's all "Oh, you're picking Sentinel. Oh, I'm so surprised," and I was like "Alright, dude, whatever," and then later on in the match I hit him with this combo with Cable that should have been really easy to block, if you know what you're doing, and I told him, I said, "Hey, dude, I know you got a mic so you can hear me. I'm not trying to be a dick, but, if you ever see a Cable jump like that, just keep holding block for two more seconds, otherwise he's gonna get a free hit on you, and that's why I hit you then," and he actually turned it around and said "Oh, you know what, I didn't know that," you know, "Thanks for telling me." So it's kind of like, we connected, and hopefully I bettered his play and that's gonna make the fighting game community better as a whole.

From his point of view, Jeff saw this not as a reason to abandon online play, but to help bring a player into the "real" fighting game culture. The ideal fighting game player isn't a sore loser, and doesn't blame his losses on the characters that are chosen. Instead, s/he learns from mistakes and helps others to overcome theirs, even if it means s/he might end up losing future matches. The phrase "gonna make the fighting game community as a whole" combined with "bettered his play" is very telling in that regard.

Thus what we see in looking at online play versus offline play is a venue with potential that is both defined and limited by the technology that makes it possible. Being able to play with people worldwide from the comfort of one's home (and remember, a "comfortable space" for play is important to many fighting gamers) and to potentially have those people be world-famous players is a draw for some. Plus, if the physical venues of the arcade or tournament spaces aren't feasible, then online play may be your *only* option for playing against others. That said, engaging with the game in that space means accepting the potential for an "unbalanced" match due to lag, and being exposed to some very poor sportsmanship indeed, courtesy of the online space's nebulous ability to make people accountable to "real life" identities.

BEING ON OR BEING OFF: MOVING BETWEEN
PLAY MODES AND SOCIAL SCENARIOS

Consider the following scenarios: a hypothetical player is a fan of a fighting game like *Street Fighter 4*. On day one, that player's friend, who is also a fan, comes over and wants to play a few matches. The next day, s/he's asked to babysit a younger cousin who would like to play video games, but who isn't exactly a competitive *SF4* player. Presumably, these hypothetical situations would play out differently because they represent two specific contexts. Day one will likely (though not necessarily) involve more serious play, as the two participants are both part of the shared fighting game culture. But the young child on day two isn't, and so our hypothetical player will likely (though again, not necessarily) "go easy" on the young cousin. Alternately, in that situation the player may opt to not engage fighting games at all, perhaps choosing a title in a different genre that's more appropriate for playing alongside a young and inexperienced competitor/partner.

The principle here is the idea that social context can and does have an influence on how players approach and execute gameplay. Although many—if not all—of the fighting gamers I spoke to are dedicated to fighting game play in specific, they are all also gamers in general. A number spoke to me about playing other non-fighting video games, or at the very least mentioned having played them in the past. Others talked about the difference between playing their "main" game—the one on which they focus their energy—and how they play other fighting games that may or may not be related. What became clear from examining those narratives is that these players can and do move between playstyles and sometimes even social behavior when it comes to different games.

One example of this principal at work comes from my interview with *Smash* player Matthew. We had been discussing the various games that he enjoyed playing in the context of his being a "hardcore gamer;" I asked him if, while playing *Wii Sports* with friends, his highly analytical and competitive *Smash* mindset appeared while he was playing a more friendly, casual game. He responded,

> Matthew: They're pretty discrete, because I only really get into that mode if I'm playing to win, or playing to learn as an amendment to that. So if I'm playing Wii bowling—a game where like, to be honest, the outcome of me winning or me losing has no bearing on almost anything—I'm not gonna get competitive about it. It's just gonna be fun for me, you know? Throw the ball, just . . . yeah. Even though competition is inherent in, like, bowling, because . . . you know, you are trying to get a better score than the other person, I don't take it seriously. So. I dunno . . . it's just, in a game, if you're gonna play to win, yeah, there's a different mindset to take into it.
>
> Todd: So it's not necessarily that you're . . . it's not necessarily that you're doing different things between friendly game of Wii bowling and competitive game of *Smash Bros. Melee,* but that *Smash Bros. Melee* is a very high-investment activity for you, and you're throwing, you know, throwing more of yourself into it, and the Wii bowling experience is kind of "Well, I'm Wii bowling."
>
> Matthew: (laughs) Yeah.

He went on to elaborate that his competitive or casual mindsets were not so much about the nature of the games themselves, but about his level of investment. For Matthew, playing competitive fighting games is a high-investment activity in terms of time, effort, and energy. When he plays those games, he adopts a more serious playstyle. A friendly game of *Wii Sports* bowling, by contrast, doesn't require that, and he relaxes many of the norms that affect not just his playstyle, but even his mood, in a competitive fighting game.

Ibrahim, a *Soul Calibur 4* player, noted that even within his favored game there is a more focused, hardcore tournament playstyle and a less regimented, almost teasing style he uses for casual matches:

> Todd: So whether or not the game is casual doesn't have a lot of bearing on [which character] it is you pick [to use].

Ibrahim: Yeah. Not who I pick, but I might play slightly differently in a casual game than I would in a tournament game.

Todd: How so?

Ibrahim: Um, I might . . . I won't go for absolutely every trick in the book in a casual game. In a tournament game I have to be unpredictable and keep my opponent off their game, so I will play, like, a more varied game in a tournament game, but in casual it's . . . too difficult to try and keep up with that, so I'll just, you know, do the same move over and over until it wins.

Todd: Do you ever do, kind of like . . . when you're playing casual, do you do stuff that you know is stupid but you don't care because you're playing casually?

Ibrahim: Yeah, absolutely. Yeah. All the time. Or I will make it a point that I must do a certain move in a casual game; something very slow and flashy and stupid, and if it hits it becomes a moral victory.

This quote is interesting because Ibrahim admits to playing in a style that—though perhaps not outright mean or antagonistic—is certainly not consistent with the ideal observed at EVO, or even described by the other interviewees. This sort of moment was rare among the players I interviewed, who for the most part did not relate stories of their own "bad behavior."

In both of these cases, there's a casual mode, and a hardcore mode. Matthew swaps between them based on the game he's playing: *Wii Sports* bowling is low-investment casual play, *Smash Bros.* is high-investment hardcore play. Ibrahim moves between playstyles based not so much on game as on his perception of what the match is for. In a tournament game he has to bring a particular playstyle to be competitive, but in a more casual match he can "spam" (repeatedly perform) a special move or artificially limit his play (e.g. "I must hit with [x] move this match") and be satisfied with the result, despite that being incongruent with his typical competitive style.

The idea here is that what shifts in these scenarios is less the games themselves, but more the sorts of goals for play that come out of them. As noted above, Juul describes a critical element of multiplayer gaming being a shared understanding of goals. Games themselves, social situations, and context of play can all alter what this shared understanding of the goal of the enterprise is. When Ibrahim says he has to be "unpredictable" in a serious game, this is because the expectation about the goal of the game is that it's a skill test to determine a winner between challengers. The shared goal demands a certain play performance. The behavior of online players who are bad losers is likely attributable to the same thing: the serious player might—as many of the interviewees did—view a casual match as a way to improve and practice. The bad loser, on the other hand, is playing specifically to obtain a victory.

In this situation there is no shared understanding of goals, and the inevitable result is social conflict.

Certainly, shared goals of play were important to the players Kolos (2010) observed, and in her conclusion she argues persuasively that a focus on play rather than the game—on what people are doing and why—may be a useful critical tool for studying social play. For the players in her study, the important thing was that they viewed fun, casual, social play as their collective goal. As a result, the group was able to accommodate a wide variety of playstyles, personalities, and backgrounds. Even players who would otherwise be considered more hardcore or serious gamers shifted their play somewhat in the context of gaming as a group.

SOCIAL PLAY AND THE TOURNAMENT SCENE: EVO AND GUTS

At the EVO tournament, play is certainly the sun that the event orbits; the socialization that takes place *on the convention floor* is surrounded by and takes place inside the context of fighting game play. However, it is also a time for enthusiasts to be around other enthusiasts, and to engage in the activity that they love as a social group. There is a significant comparison between EVO and an event such as Campzone 2 (Jansz and Martens, 2005) or DreamHack (Taylor and Witkowski, 2010). Each case is a large-scale social event taking place in the context of a shared pastime or interest involving gaming technology.

Many of the observations that those scholars made at the events they studied carry over to EVO, particularly the demographics of the attendees. I was struck by how few women were in attendance; only a handful caught my notice, and of the even fewer with whom I had a chance to speak, none were actually attending EVO to play. One was a supportive girlfriend who had come to watch her boyfriend compete; another two were the mother and sister of a competitor who had traveled from California to support their son/brother in the tournament. That said, I did observe some women players carrying arcade sticks and wearing convention badges, identifying them as probable participants in the tournament itself. However, as the event progressed (and potential fighters were eliminated from the brackets in the pool matches), these sightings dwindled to effectively nothing; on the last day, all competitors in the finals for each game were male.

As one might expect of an event with global reach, there were a wide variety of ethnicities in attendance at EVO. In terms of broad groups, Caucasians, Africans or African-Americans, Latinos, and a number of different Asian cultures were represented over the course of three days. Attendees from the United States came from all over; interestingly enough, the proof of this is that many who came to EVO brought t-shirts or other clothes that identified their region or even city of origin, typically advertising a gaming group from that locale. Washington (Seattle), Texas, New York, and a number from California were the most numerous. During the finals it became clear that there were competitors from as far away as France (the *Soul Calibur 4* champion, Malek) and Japan (fighting game icon Daigo Umehara, who would go on to win the *Street Fighter 4* tournament).

Chapter 6 has more discussion on some potential factors for this paucity of female attendees, and the influence of ethnicity and race on the culture, but it is worth noting that the following discussion of these spaces should be considered with these contextual demographic factors in mind.

That said, it's important to discuss the ways in which attendees—particularly those simply playing together on the demo stations and bring-your-own-console (BYOC) floor compared to the tournament matches—played socially. During the first few days of the tournament, the majority of the space was taken up by elimination pools: tables with a monitor and a single console system (in almost every case, a PlayStation 3) for the playing of placement matches. A full half of the convention hall was devoted to those stations, with the Smashboards-run *Brawl* tournament taking up a full third of the remaining BYOC space on the south half of the room. As the need for the existing technology at the elimination pool tables dwindled—via the progression of the tournament—these tables were eventually co-opted by casual players who would gather in small groups to play there, though they were limited to whatever game had been played during the elimination pool at that station.

On the BYOC floor, the range of games being played was quite high. Some stations involved people playing then-recent releases like *Street Fighter 4*. Perhaps more interesting were those few stations where attendees brought not just games and televisions or monitors, but entire wooden arcade *frames* they had constructed themselves to house hardware and give the impression one was playing on an authentic arcade cabinet (see Figure 4.1).

Over the course of the event, there were two such places. One involved someone set up near the north entrance doors to play the original *Street Fighter 2*. Another was at the far southern corner of the room and was a collection of two to three red-painted cabinets containing a wide variety of games, from old Neo-Geo arcade selections to a version of the *X-Men* arcade game made by Konami in 1992, notable because it is not a typical fighting game per EVO's focus, but rather a member of the related side-scrolling "beat 'em up" genre instead. Gamers moved between these areas as their interest drew them.

For the most part, socialization at EVO seemed to center in small groups with actual gameplay—or more specifically, the displays and monitors on which gameplay took place—as an organizing space. This isn't to say all socialization was necessarily based around play. To echo earlier statements, not all participation was play-based; on the third day, most participation involved watching and cheering for matches in the finals. However, particularly on days one and two, when the elimination pools were still filled with

Figure 4.1   A pair of wooden fan-built arcade frames made in the image of arcade cabinets, EVO 2009. Photo by author.

competitors playing through their matches, the relatively intimate setting of the pool booths—a table no more than a person height across with a TV and enough room for two side-by-side chairs—gave rise to batches of small groups together.

Similarly, the bring-your-own-console spaces and even the booths for both Capcom and Namco-Bandai to feature their upcoming and current games were roughly the same: a TV and enough space for a few people to stand close together around it, connected in sequence. These close gathering points, with a small cloud of onlookers centered around the two people playing the game, have considerable resonance with the crowds one might find at an American game arcade. In the BYOC and test booth areas, even the "I've got next" practice, where the next player in line indicates that they will play the winner of the current match, was commonly seen.

Because much of the observed socialization at EVO was in a play context, many of the behaviors I observed did involve play in some form. Perhaps the most common was the practice of good sportsmanship. The pre- and post-bout handshake was so ubiquitous that there were very few times it *didn't* happen; after three days it became very jarring to not see it. One such instance occurred in an elimination pool match of *Street Fighter 3* where one player performed a "full-parry." In *SF3* it is possible, with quick and precise timing, to "parry" an incoming attack, rendering it ineffective and actually giving an advantage to the defender to counterattack (hence the reference to a similar maneuver in fencing). However, an attack that hits multiple times must be parried for each hit, so someone who parries every hit of a multi-hit attack has "full-parried" it; the popularity of the oft-mentioned Daigo Umehara's EVO 2004 full-parry of a move by Justin Wong[4] goes a long way to emphasizing both the rarity of such an event, and the skill required to pull it off. When the match I observed was over, interestingly, there was no handshake involved.

That said, however, gestures suggesting good sportsmanship were the norm. The handshake is perhaps the most common, but there were a number of other ways in which it manifested itself. The "fist bump" (touching of fists at the knuckles) was one of them; vocalized thanks and congratulations like "Good fight" and "Thanks for the match" were also common, as were exhortations to the crowd to give both competitors applause during the day three finals. This was observable in the BYOC areas as well. The general trend is that at the end of a fight—win or lose—there should be some acknowledgment of the other player, with whom one spent those 30–90 seconds (the length of a usual match, based on the in-game match timer).

The notion of good sportsmanship extended outward to other instances as well. One noticeable moment of camaraderie and cooperation among players was at Capcom's demonstration booth for the (then-unreleased) *Tatsunoko vs. Capcom*. The company representatives, using the Japanese full version of the game, created a contest to see who could do the most damage/get the highest hit count in practice mode. Despite the competitive nature that "contest" implies, over the course of the day I saw numerous players huddled together near the *TvC* booth, commiserating about which attacks and techniques might be most useful. One player asked, of a character being used, "Would light kick be faster?" Others would enter the conversation, suggesting entirely new permutations of moves in combination to try, even other characters; when the contest first began a small group were experimenting with the character Hakushon Daimaou[5], but by the time I next made my way to the booth, fragments of the original group plus new members had moved on to trying a different character, Roll. They compared notes, tried new combinations, evaluated the results, and in the end came to a community decision on the best way to proceed despite it being, nominally, a "contest."

Interestingly, this seems to stand in contrast to the booing behavior observed during the finals, and in fact even the announcers got into the act when it came to the crowd's booing of unpopular *Soul Calibur 4* character Hilde on day three; recall that at one point, the commentator during the *SC4* finals informed a Hilde player there'd be "no cheap win today" after he lost a round. During one of the aforementioned *Guilty Gear* finals featuring the well-known player Martin "Marn" Phan, an observer sitting two seats to my right and one row back shouted, quite loudly, "You suck, Marn!" I blinked in surprise and turned to look, catching the attention of someone sitting nearby, who offered an explanation: "I know [Marn]. He's a cool guy but he goes out of his way to be an asshole." This was resonant with another instance a few days earlier during the *Street Fighter 3* pool eliminations, where during a doubles match—teams of two who would alternate to play one-on-one matches—one of the inactive players suddenly shouted "You suck, man!" after an in-game event. Thus, it's not clear to what extent these sorts of comments are more considered an acceptable level of "trash talk" or friendly ribbing rather than actual expressions of disapproval. Certainly, they were more isolated and, in an affective way, felt different in character than the mass booing responses to Hilde players.

As a point of comparison, I attended a second fighting game tournament in 2013, the "Game Underground Tournament Spectacular" or GUTS tournament. Hosted by Boston-area gaming store Game Underground, the GUTS tourney[6] took place on the Massachusetts Institute of Technology campus in late June. As a researcher at the MIT Game Lab, which helped sponsor the event, I had a high level of access to the venue and tournament, and was able to observe various parts of the event over two of the three days it was held.

Naturally, there are some obvious differences between the two events. Being a smaller local event, the use and nature of the venue—university classrooms versus hotel conference ballrooms—and other organizational elements were smaller in scale. As a national-level tournament with multiple big corporate sponsors, EVO obviously has more resources with which to work[7]. However, despite this change in scale, the GUTS tournament was on its most fundamental levels highly similar to EVO. Their tournament structure—a double elimination style bracket where losers can fight their way back in—was consistent with EVO's, and the chronological structure was also the same. The first two days of GUTS were devoted to pool matches, where the third day was primarily devoted to "main stage" finals for a handful of featured games. One major difference was that rather than being in one room, GUTS had a central main stage in a lecture hall, and breakout rooms in nearby MIT buildings for both casual/BYOC space and pools for some tournaments.

One interesting note of comparison between EVO and GUTS is the stream commentators. Both tournaments employed live streaming of matches on the Internet, a practice which has been steadily growing in the online gaming world, particularly e-sports (see Taylor, 2012). However, EVO's final day of matches involved live commentary which was also played locally so that the live audience could hear it. Comparatively, GUTS did not give their commentators live mics, though they were clearly commenting on the accompanying livestream.

In summary, the social aspects of the tournament were consistent with the sorts of events described by Jansz and Martens and Taylor and Witkowski above: gaming (or technology) enthusiasts from various backgrounds coming together in celebration of their hobby. Good sportsmanship and collaboration provide a social context surrounding the game play that the participants have come to enjoy. In this sense, the rules of the game are part of the scenario, but not all of it; like the players of *Smash* noted by Jakobsson (2007), the experience is as much about being in the context of that play, sharing expertise and a feeling of being among other enthusiasts, as it is about the literal rules of play. The behaviors and trappings of the people attending EVO, much like the attendees of DreamHack, strode an interesting line between showing their personal identity and cultural affiliations and engaging in large group activities as a cultural collective. Certainly, attendees were fans of different games, from different locations, and from the discussions and matches overheard and seen had differing ideas of what ideal play should be like. However, in the end, what was critical was that they were there, together, to be in the presence of play and among other lovers of the same *types* of play.

ICONOGRAPHY, CLOTHING, AND OTHER BADGES OF THE CULTURE

The issue of the clothing and iconography I observed at EVO extends the discussion into another dimension: The attendees as fans not just of fighting games, but of video games in general. Scattered throughout the tournament were shirts and even neckties that built on various memes and icons from video gaming. Among these were a stylized Mario (of *Super Mario Bros.* fame) labeled "Thug Mario," someone wearing a necktie with a screenprint of *Blazblue* character Arakune, Pac-Man shirts, and a shirt featuring the character Bub from the 1980's-era game *Bubble Bobble*. Many similar shirts were observed beyond these specific instances as well. One attendee on the first day even came in full costume as a *Street Fighter* character, though his M. Bison[8] outfit was the only example of such costuming ("cosplay") observed.

The ubiquitous arcade sticks also served to identify a certain gamer chic; these controllers are often housed in quite large wooden boxes, and while some players left their stick boxes unadorned, others decorated them. Prints of fighting game characters were common observances for decorated boxes, though there were also characters identifiable as being from current Japanese anime series (the most common being at least two representations of protagonist Ichigo Kurosaki from the anime/manga series *Bleach*). The decoration of the arcade stick seems to be twofold in such a case. Firstly, it helps to identify the owner's interest in games, anime, or both; secondly, it creates a distinctive art that points to the owner specifically and his/her interests as well. In the case of interviewee Evan, whose favored game is the anime art-inspired *Arcana Heart*, his most treasured arcade stick is decorated with artwork of his favorite two characters—Konoha and Mei-Fang— from the game.

These emblems and badges—both the sticks themselves and the ways they are decorated—are very much props in the front stage performance of identity that Goffman (1959) discusses, working on many simultaneous tiers. Even having an arcade stick in the first place says "I play fighting games in a particular way"; decorating it with decals of characters as Evan did may indicate a number of additional things. In the interview, it was clear that he chose those decorations because he enjoys playing those characters, but we also discussed that his choice of character reflected his preferred playstyle in the game as well. It may be that having Konoha on his arcade stick indicates his love of *Arcana Heart* and Konoha, his love of characters that play *like* Konoha does, his appreciation of the art style, his adoption of the arcade stick norm, or many other things. Comparatively, there were arcade sticks at EVO that were simply undecorated, plain wood: what messages might those send? What's important to recognize here is that the various props and decorations favored by these players may contribute to a wide variety of performed identities.

It is also worth considering these badges of gamer and fan identity in the context of Taylor and Witkowski's discussion of personalized spaces and public activity at DreamHack in Sweden. As they note, "[t]he range of performances on show pushes the sense that, for these participants, gaming is a meaningful leisure activity and that participation in this activity can be very many different things" (2010, p. 5). They also cite Simon (2007) on case mods; his notion that visual modifications are tied to instrumental modifications for more useful hardware can likely be applied to arcade sticks as well. Players use arcade sticks for their greater level of control and precision; the need to decorate them as a badge and flag extends outward from that.

SOMEWHERE BETWEEN SOCIALIZING AND PLAYING

As most of these examples show, the ways in which playing the game, participating in the culture of play, and simply interacting with others socially "around" the game play out in the fighting game community are complex and varied. There are influences on multiple levels here. The technology angle is quite prevalent; be it the contribution of lag and the erasure of physical distance of online play or the ubiquitous arcade stick pulling double duty as interface and emblem, the apparatus of control and display which one might think is purely an interface element taking on entirely different meanings refracted through the context of social play. And that's just one area of interest; there are plenty more examples here of how these various elements come together.

Usefully, this highlights the ways in which play is in many ways separated from the artifact, and not limited to engagement with it. Instead, play represents a network of actions and beliefs, some of which extend temporally well past the actual moment of picking up a controller and—in the fighting game context—throwing your first virtual punch. Fighting game culture presents scenarios where even *watching* is play and participation, after all. Most importantly, the way this culture plays and views play is a critical element in how individuals in that culture interact with each other. To be a serious fighting game fan isn't just a matter of knowing mechanics; it's about codes of sportsmanship, knowing when to be serious, when to have fun, and more.

NOTES

1. Here I refer specifically to his book *Half-Real*, which is in many ways a discussion about the game form that attempts to reconcile the early-life divide in game studies between games-as-narrative and games-as-mechanics.
2. To put this in the context of non-digital sports competition, imagine a fencing match where one contestant sees everything a second after it happens, and their reactions occur a second after they actually make them. Considering that the base unit of time in fighting games is the animation frame—a fractional part of a second—this is how a lag-filled match feels.
3. This is due to a complex problem involving character names in the original *Street Fighter 2*. The game features three distinct "boss" characters: a massive boxer, a lithe acrobat wearing a claw for a weapon, and a man dressed in high-ranking military costume. In Japan, the boxer's name is "M. Bison," the acrobat is "Balrog," and the military man is "Vega." When the game came to the United States, Capcom was concerned that the boxer's name would be seen as, among other things, an attack/slander on boxer Mike Tyson. Thus, they shuffled the name of these characters: The acrobat became Vega, the boxer became Balrog, and the military man became M. Bison. To avoid confusion in a global fighting game culture, these are often simply called "Boxer," "Dictator," and "Claw."
4. See Chapter 1, note 1.
5. Interestingly, for a number of reasons, this character wasn't included in the American release of the game; Capcom's booth provided Japanese copies, as well as test builds of the American release.
6. More accurately the GUTS 2 tourney, this being the second time it had been held.
7. GUTS still had sponsors, even some of the same sponsors that one might find at EVO, as well as the involvement of noted fighting game event streamers Team Spooky. However, unlike EVO, none of the companies that make the games, such as Capcom or Namco-Bandai, were involved.
8. Refer to note 3, this chapter; the cosplayer was dressed as the "Dictator."

5   Online Fighting Game Communities

As we have already discussed, one way that serious fighting game fans disseminate information, find each other for play, and (generally speaking) acculturate new blood is through physical meet ups. These happen often in
arcade or tournament spaces, be they smaller local events or big international affairs like EVO. However, these physical spaces are just one part of
the picture. In the last chapter, we discussed the social aspects of how fighting game fans play online and off; this chapter discusses the impact of how
these players congregate online in communities dedicated to fighting games,
typically in the form of asynchronous online message boards.

While the EVO tournament is a major fixture in fighting game culture in
its own right, it is also in many ways an outgrowth of a particular online
forum called Shoryuken.com (SRK), named after one of the signature moves
of *Street Fighter* character Ryu. It is not the only community of its kind by
a long mile; most fighting games with a wide enough user base and a competitive tournament scene have their own similar online communities. Fans
of Namco-Bandai's *Tekken* and *Soul Calibur* series have Tekken Zaibatsu
and 8 Way Run.com (aka 8WR) respectively; players of the *Guilty Gear*
and *Blazblue* series congregate at Dustloop.com, and there is a large and
active community of *Smash* players at the Smash World Forums (also called
Smashboards). Adequately covering every online fighting game forum and
community would be a considerable challenge, as they range from small sites
with only a handful of close-knit active participants to massive, multiple-
thousands-of-users affairs. Here we'll be speaking mostly about two of the
larger forums: SRK and Smashboards.

Why these two communities? Aside from their large user base and popularity, both SRK and Smashboards highlight a critical function online
communities play in the fighting game culture: they're clearinghouses for
knowledge about the community's standards for play, and a central location
for the acculturation of new members at a distance, meant to complement
and enhance the experience of meeting and playing in person. These are
forums where more experienced players congregate to socialize and talk
about play, but they're also where new players who want to become involved come to learn how that's possible. Of course, this means the new

and old sometimes clash, and the results aren't always pretty; this chapter describes how one such situation erupted on Shoryuken.com. However, understanding how these communities operate provides useful insight into both the formal and informal rules of fighting game communities, as well as how those rules are disseminated among the members.

ONLINE GAMING COMMUNITIES

There is a fairly robust amount of research dealing with online communities, as well as work that looks specifically at the role of online communities in gaming cultures. One of the most well-known of these is Celia Pearce's *Communities of Play: Emergent Cultures in Multiplayer Games and Virtual Worlds* (2009). Pearce—and her avatar Artemisia—engaged in an ethnographic examination of the *"Uru* Diaspora:" the migration of players of the online game *Uru* to other online spaces once the original game closed. Pearce describes a scenario where these players used online forums outside of the game as a way to anchor their relationships and their community even when the virtual space they inhabited fell away. In many ways, forums like Shoryuken.com do the same, though the distance that the community bridges is more physical than the virtual diaspora that Pearce describes. Disconnected into various social groups across the globe, each with a particular local identity and sometimes even a local playstyle, spaces like SRK provide a way for those groups to unite.

Pearce calls such communities "communities of play" (p. 5), constructing them as a "deliberate counterpoint" to communities of practice. She draws the distinction primarily because of the idea that while play is a form of practice (and thus a community of play can be considered a community of practice), play and play spaces are different enough to warrant their own specific considerations. The key difference between the community that Pearce observed and the fighting game community may be in the fact that Pearce's *Uru* diaspora primarily interacted in virtual worlds and spaces, like MMORPGs and *Second Life*. Fighting games, by comparison, are not necessarily virtual worlds, and there is very little to suggest that fighting gamers "inhabit" those spaces during play in quite the same way[1]. Still, many of the book's observations about gaming communities apply to the fighting game culture.

For example, the "ludisphere" is a concept Pearce introduces to describe the ecosystem in which communities of play operate, one which pulls in game factors, social factors, and technological factors, among others:

> One observation we can make is quite simply that emergence happens, regardless of where the world falls along the fixed synthetic/co-created, ludic/paidiaic spectrum. . . . As play communities migrate between these ecosystems, traversing magic circles, they adapt to accommodate the ecosystem, and the ecosystem also adapts and mutates

> to accommodate them. The larger sphere of virtual worlds and sup-
> porting technologies (forums, chat, voice over IP, etc.) between which
> players migrate can also be viewed as a kind of metaecosystem, a web
> of complex relationships between these more bounded networked play
> spaces. (pp. 33–4)

This web of relationships is the "ludisphere," the spaces and contexts in which player culture forms and operates. Forums, online game statistics and match-finding services, even the ubiquity of the arcade stick—these are all influences that come together to create fighting game culture, and thus elements of the fighting game culture's ludisphere.

A number of other scholars, looking at the MMO space and games such as *World of Warcraft*, have spoken to something very similar to Pearce's ludisphere. Both Mark Chen (2008) and Alex Golub (2010) have, through ethnographic research of *WoW* players, identified how important the social aspect of play is in that context. Golub examined "mediumcore raiders"—players who engaged in difficult group play but not at a particularly extreme level (thus the comparison to "hardcore")—and in his findings, communication technology outside the game (online forums, voice chat software) provided "another context in which the life of the guild, anchored in in-game raiding, occurs outside of the game" (p. 39). In examining a different set of raiders,[2] Chen noted that the ability to reflect on their play as a group—via elements like the ones Golub mentions, such as forums—was critical to the survival and cohesion of that community. That said, Chen's later auto-ethnographic analysis of that same raiding guild's rise and fall (*Leet Noobs: the Life and Death of an Expert Player Group in World of Warcraft*, 2012) observes that these extra-ludic elements can destroy a community just as easily as they can build it up. As gameplay and social elements both inside and outside the game changed over time, players were forced to reevaluate their commitment to a certain type of practice; if that commitment wavered due to any of a number of potential influences, the possibility existed for the community to splinter or dissolve entirely.

One way that gaming communities often function in this context is in the public, collaborative construction and dissemination of game knowledge. In the MMO space, this is frequently encountered as "theorycrafting:" an attempt by players to make understandable the various algorithmic systems—visible or no—that are involved in a game. This is very much the sort of behavior that Taylor (2006) calls "instrumental play," the domain of "powergamers." Wenz (2012) refers to theorycrafting as the group application of scientific method to the systems of a game, or rather, "the scientification of gameplay." However, both Wenz and Taylor (2008) are cautious about the possibilities for surveillance that elements like popular add-on technologies or commonly used "mods" bring into the equation. Such surveillance may be passive—add-ons that record data without the knowledge of other players—or they may be more participatory. Theorycrafting, for example, often contributes to the notion of a "right" or "wrong" way to play, which feeds into community standards of how a game should be played (and surveillance to ensure that others are following that model).

The natural end of this sort of thinking are communities based on theory-crafting that then have a possibly negative impact on the broader community of play for a given game. Christopher Paul's (2009; 2011) work on Elitist Jerks (EJ), a forum and community for players interested in theorycraft for high-level *WoW* play, highlights the potential impacts that the existence of such a group can have on the wider community. The Elitist Jerks—in speaking on his research, Paul noted "they live up to the name"—are dedicated to producing information on best practices for efficient play, again hearkening back to Taylor's instrumental player approach.

Paul argues that, for good or for ill, the existence of such a discursive community outside the game can nevertheless have repercussions inside it:

> This fundamentally changes the way WoW works. . . . Although this may not be a change felt by every player and some could even resist dominant norms, all are impacted when getting into certain groups requires specific choices or when game design is altered in order to please the vocal contingent of theorycrafters. (2011)

Put simply, the existence of this theorycrafting community outside of (but parallel to) *WoW* can have an impact on any player of the game, whether or not they participate with or buy into the specific style and approach that the Elitist Jerks community does. For example, if a group is forming to tackle multiplayer content, and the leader of that group buys into the Elitist Jerks mindset, then s/he will "enforce" it through selection or rejection of teammates and approaches to play.

In short, what this research points to is a very powerful link between gameplay and the communities that surround that gameplay. These communities are where players engage one another about normative practices, strategies, and other elements of the play experience. They are part of a network of gaming paratexts where social and gaming capital (see Consalvo, 2007) is earned and spent and knowledge is both distributed and produced. However, the impact these communities have is not always positive, nor is it always limited solely to the participants in that specific community. As you'll see with the following examples from the fighting game culture, these online communities can often have a wide-ranging impact.

SHORYUKEN.COM, ACCULTURATION, AND KNOWLEDGE PRODUCTION

Almost everyone I interviewed, when asked how they got into fighting games, would eventually bring the discussion back to online forums. Garrett mentioned discovering 8WR after looking online for tips on *Soul Calibur 2* play, while Ibrahim was pointed to it by people he met in an arcade. Evan described meeting players from out of state at a local tournament who were SRK regulars, and—after being struck by their skilled and (to him) new and different style of play—was compelled to go online and join the community. Gene tells a similar story, where SRK regulars from another arcade came to his regular playing space and demonstrated the "SRK playstyle" (recall the various elements of practice from Chapter 3) through numerous wins; he "came around" their style of play, which led him back to SRK to learn more. Jeff came back to fighting games after a long absence by participating in a local *Street Fighter 4* tournament, and another entrant saw his play and directed him to SRK . . . and so on, and so on. Clearly, though these meetings were happening in an offline space, they are notable for consistently bringing people to one online fighting game forum or another, the common thread that links them all.

It's worth noting that for many of these stories, the entry into the online forum is also the entry into serious fighting game play, and a landmark moment of departure from engaging in more casual play. Gene and Evan's stories in particular are excellent examples of this, in that it was observing (and being beaten by!) the playstyle used by SRK regulars from another geographic location that led them to make the leap, giving a relatively clear delineation between "who I was before" and "who I am now." Take, for example, Gene's description of the process:

> People from other cities started coming to our places because people want more competition and they started beating us because they were kind of doing all the tricks, and so that got us to, you know, kind of drop what we thought the game was supposed to be played like and kind of play it like it was *really* [vocal emphasis his] supposed to be played like.

That last sentence is very telling; it suggests that however he played before—whatever his "style" happened to be—was the "wrong" way to do things. Garrett's whole reason for joining such a community in the first place was to expand his knowledge of the game. Nicholas, interestingly, came to SRK because of the 2004 Daigo Umehara/Justin Wong EVO match where the now-famous parry video[3] was made; being exposed to that level of skilled play, he "wanted to see what the community was like."

Of course, given that these respondents were also *recruited* for this study primarily via online fighting game communities, it isn't surprising that so many of them have histories where entry into such an online community figures prominently. Still, that fact alone says something about the link between serious players and community membership. Even Isaac and Jordan, who are relatively casual players despite being serious fighting game fans, regularly read and post on SRK. The community is both a source of knowledge and a beacon to those who seek it out, and in the process, new visitors are welcomed into the fold and exposed to a playstyle that they often come to embrace. Jeff described his experience playing *Marvel vs. Capcom* 2 in the post-SRK-join era as "almost like you're playing two different games."

Beyond serving as a gateway to the rules and mores of serious social fighting game play, such forums also serve a more mundane matchmaking function. Remember that the ideal for fighting games is that they are played against other people, and as previously discussed, online play presents certain opportunities but also has a number of drawbacks that make it less than ideal for some players. How sites like SRK, 8WR, and the like fill that void is by allocating space for "matchmaking," where players can post invitations to play or requests for opponents inside a geographic area in the hopes of meeting new people to play against in person. This covers almost every type of meet up, from tiny three-to-four person fight nights at a local player's living room to local tournaments featuring hundreds of players.

Shoryuken's matchmaking forum is quite large and very active, consisting of nine separate subforums: seven for various regions of the United States, one for Canada, and one for "World" (presumably: everything else). 8WR has three subforums for the United States, one for the rest of "the Americas," and a fifth for "Europe, Asia, & Australia." Smashboards focuses on tournament listings, both those held online and those held offline, including a number of regional subforums for various parts of the world. This is merely a surface-level cataloging of available forum spaces; inside each forum there are even greater subdivisions, with threads for states and even individual cities in some cases.

When it comes to those interviewees who play in local social groups, a number mentioned that they came upon those groups via online forums. Ibrahim, Jordan, Jeff, Gene, and Nicholas all described situations where they created social connections with people they could regularly play against—either friends, in Nicholas' case, or groups and local events for the others—via matchmaking at an online forum. At the time of the interviews Jeff played regularly with a group at the University of Maryland—Baltimore, for example, and while he no longer has the time to devote to it, when Jordan first moved to Boston he spent time regularly playing with a handful of friends he met on SRK.

Nicholas is an interesting case, in that he also is a common user of other matchmaking online than forums. Because he is a fan of an older generation game, *Street Fighter 2 Turbo*, he often plays on a matchmaking service called GGPO[4], developed by Tony Cannon, an EVO founder and SRK moderator. GGPO allows players to connect via PC to play emulations of arcade fighting games, and Nicholas was a longtime GGPO player before he eventually moved to consoles with the release of *SF2T: HD Remix*.

In these cases, what the online framework—be it forums or a service like GGPO—provides is an opportunity to connect with like-minded strangers for play opportunities. Since the culture of online fighting game forums suggests that most frequent users are serious fighting game fans, the matchmaking forum is a place where one can satisfy a desire to play in-person (or even online) against other serious players to provide a new challenge. While much of the play that is arranged on the matchmaking forums is either at events in public spaces or online via services such as Xbox Live or PlayStation Network, it's worth restating that a number are also simply at the homes of forum members, who make the information available to interested parties through private message via the forums.

Thus online forums in the fighting game community serve two parallel purposes when it comes to bringing new individuals into the fold. As a repository of expertise and information, it first serves as a gateway for new players to be drawn into the serious fighting game way of life. Effectively, it is both a recruiting tool and an acculturation effort. Once the player becomes invested in the culture, the matchmaking services are a way for players to engage in the activity the way it's "supposed" to be done: one-on-one competitions with other skilled players, be it (primarily) in offline social groups and events, or sometimes through online play. However, there is also a potential downside to such an arrangement, especially in a scenario where a community used to being seen as niche suddenly leaps into the public eye.

IMMIGRATION IN FIGHTING GAME-LAND: SHORYUKEN.COM AND THE '09ERS

When the time came to recruit participants for interviews, doing so proved to be more challenging than I expected it would be. Since the first phase of the study had focused on the EVO tournament, Shoryuken.com seemed like a natural first place to go. However, interest was very scattered; my initial recruiting thread focused on EVO attendees and low response there prompted expanding that search to any fighting game fan. In the end it was word of mouth from respondents—and in one case, an endorsement from an interviewee on my second SRK thread—that was most effective. While recruiting interviewees is always a challenge, in this case it seemed particularly difficult, and I began to wonder if there was something particular to this context that was hindering me.

As I progressed with the interviews, a phenomenon often came up in discussion that suggested events in the fighting game culture—particularly as they applied to Shoryuken.com—might have contributed to the community being reticent to speak to me. As Jordan relayed, there is a term among longtime SRK users for someone with a 2009 forum join date who appears to know very little about fighting games: an "'09er." The dislike of '09ers stems from the sudden surge in popularity for fighting games after the 2009 release of *Street Fighter 4*, and the consequent effects that had on many fighting game online communities, particularly one that is as strongly associated with the *SF* series as SRK.

When *SF4* came out in early 2009, there had not been a major fighting game release from Capcom in a very long while; *Marvel vs. Capcom 2* was the closest in 2000, leaving nearly a decade of gap, as both Jordan and Nicholas discussed when giving me background on the phenomenon. By that time, the SRK userbase—which had been a smaller, relatively tight-knit group of high-level players—had already solidified into social equilibrium, with no real mass influx of new posters. Jordan described SRK as "a highly insular, very specialized community that's used to being discarded" in the pre-2009 days, and being for the most part "highly knit, tightly wound." In truth, that description could likely apply to the fighting game scene in general during that period as well.

Once *SF4* was released, everything changed. Suddenly not only were fans experiencing a renewed interest in fighting games—particularly *Street Fighter* series games—but gaming media and other mass media were also pointing to Shoryuken.com as the place to go for information. As a result, massive amounts of new users suddenly poured into SRK, and the resulting effect on the existing userbase was, as Jordan describes it, just shy of catastrophic:

> And so the . . . the forums were crashing constantly. Like, it really sucked. I remember I was in the middle of a couple, like, trades, and trying to like . . . buying and selling things, and you know, I like to go here to hang out and I can't, 'cause there's a million people showing up on the forums and so the site was tanking all the time, and . . . and then you just get constant . . . and so these newcomers are just constantly making the threads I talked about, right? They're just these stupid speculation threads, they're like "Oh my god, in *Street Fighter 4*, Akuma should be able to throw *three* fireballs because that's awesome and Akuma's awesome!" and that's like . . .that's what it was like all the time, and . . . you'll notice that after the site upgrade they no longer show the join dates, because there's such prejudice against the '09ers, but it used to be it would show when someone joined, so you'd say "Oh look, this person joined the month that *Street Fighter 4* was announced like everyone else, there's no reason to take them seriously. In fact I want them to go away because they're disrupting my life."

As he describes it, the SRK regulars were suddenly on the defensive. New users with no knowledge of or appreciation for the culture that the long-time userbase had developed were suddenly breaking all the social rules and mores, posting "like 20 different threads about the same thing . . . when there's already probably one big thread that's stickied that says, that answers

like, 90 percent of your questions" as Nicholas put it. Jeff described a similar situation with the *Marvel vs. Capcom 2* forums. The clutter and traf-
fic negatively impacted the servers, which crashed repeatedly, depriving the
normal userbase of their online space and communication altogether.

This is almost exactly what Celia Pearce describes happening as various *Uru* players made their way to *There.com* as part of their diaspora.
As those players moved in, there was a demonstrable effect not just on the
community as a social space, but on the actual technological performance
of *There.com*: "For a small and growing virtual society like *There.com*, the
sudden onslaught of a large group of players en masse placed a significant
burden on the system. Once again, the clients and servers were overworked"
(p. 98). The result was aggressive behavior ("griefing") on the part of *There.
com*'s existing users, although Pearce doesn't specify if the various griefing
behaviors were intended as retribution or as an attempt to drive the *Uru*
players away, though she does mention that some *There.com* users went as
far as to complain to the management.

That the established users of the community went on the defensive is not
a surprise; their territory was being threatened on multiple levels and so they
reacted against it. Jordan and Nicholas both noted a potential good side:
more players. As discussed above, more players equates to more challengers,
more play, and presumably a growth in the community, provided they're
players who follow the proper model of play. On the other hand, consider
this quote from Jordan:

> . . . there's a little bit of a pride issue, right? Like, when you've been on
> the site . . . like, I only joined in '06. If you've been on the site since 2000
> and people are showing up and saying "Oh, I'm hardcore, I've played
> all these games, blah blah blah" and then you want to be like "Well
> where have you been for all this time? Why do you only care now that
> there's a new, shiny toy?"

The dilemma, of course, is identifying the potential "good" new members
from what must have felt like a horde of "bad" ones.

Interestingly enough, a thread on SRK dated early February of 2009
("Message to Newcomers who Feel Unwelcome", 2009) is an attempt by
one SRK user to elaborate to new members why it is they might be made to
feel unwelcome by SRK regulars. His argument echoes many of the sentiments and ideas Jordan suggested above; on the subject of posts with simple
questions that are already answered on the forum, the original poster—username "eoneo"—made the following analogy: "[emphasis original] *it's a bit
like going on a chess forum and complaining that the knight's movements
are too confusing*. Can you imagine how much shit you'd get?" (para. 10).
The poster argues that SRK is "[emphasis original] **first and foremost a
forum for high level discussion about fighting games**," and thus constant
"newbie" questions are out of place. His hope is that new users will use

permanent ("sticky") threads and reading to answer their questions, rather than create new topics that clutter the forum.

There is a significant link between the type of behavior toward the '09ers described here, and some of what goes on at the *World of Warcraft* community. As previously noted, Christopher Paul's work on Elitist Jerks is an example of a community of theorycrafters interested in maintaining "best practices" for play. Paul notes that the problem of numerous threads about "stipulations of who is right and who is wrong with little to support one's point" is "solved on EJ because of the high level of moderation on their boards; they are notorious for deleting posts and banning users" (2009, pp. 19–20). The userbase of Elitist Jerks has an expectation of serious attention to the site's theorycrafting model, which produces a certain standard of forum behavior that is then enforced vigorously by their moderation team. Expertise is valued, and posts that show serious thought and expertise remain; those that don't, are cut.

It's reasonable to argue that the userbase on Shoryuken was doing something highly similar, but in a less regimented way. While each individual subforum (as well as the overall site) does have a moderation team that steps in for extreme cases, locking or moving threads as necessary, the userbase also heavily relies on social pressure and unfriendly communication to discourage new members that don't follow the social rules of the community. The social stigma against people with a 2009 join date is a defense mechanism designed to keep the social structure of SRK itself intact, and in the process, it defines publically which values the site considers important. Foremost among them is a slightly more cynical echo of the ideal mentioned above, where willingness to learn is valorized. New users who keep their heads low and learn the ropes are likely to be left alone; those who break the social rules face swift social retribution.

This illustrates some understandable but contradictory rhetorics about the community itself when it comes to who can become part of it. Interviewees spoke of a pervasive belief that the more people the community has, the greater the base of potential players and challengers. It's an inclusive rhetoric that seeks to draw other people in to the activity; the root of why, for example, someone playing online might take the effort to bring an opponent playing in a way outside the ideal performance into the fold. Yet at the same time, there was/is this powerful negative reaction to the '09ers at SRK, though in fairness, SRK is only one community among many. It's not clear if the players I spoke to were aware of this contradiction, or even if they would see it as one; a story from Gene about southern California's fighting game culture suggests that there are contexts where the community doesn't feel the need to bring in every possible new player, just those who exhibit great potential.

It may be that the users at Shoryuken were particularly on the defensive because their space was being literally threatened as the flood of new users crashed the site and new forum threads crowded out "legitimate" discussion, and this made reinforcing the borders a bigger priority than bringing in new blood. What this illustrates is that the community does embrace an inclusive rhetoric, but that contextual factors influence when that rhetoric comes into play. A sign of adhering to the existing norms that make up the community—as inferred by the forum post on feeling unwelcome described above—could go far to helping a potential new community member make inroads.

FORUMS AND COMMUNAL INFORMATION: TIER LISTS, "OFFICIAL THREADS," AND FRAME DATA

Beyond their social function, online fighting game forums are also a place for the dissemination and even creation of information about play. One example of that at work is "tier lists": lists of in-game playable characters ranked in accordance with their capabilities and strengths. Two players of *Smash Bros. Brawl* constructed an argument for the existence of tiers on the *Smash* wiki (Kirschner & Schumacher, 2008); while they center primarily on the *Smash* series, the existence of tiers in other games is prevalent, even to the point where one forum has been created solely to retroactively creating tier listings for fighting games that predate their popularity in the community (http://www.gdlkgame.com/forum).

To explain tier lists simply, a character that ranks high in a tier listing is expected to have a better chance of winning a given match based on the in-game attributes of that character, irrespective of player skill or other circumstances. Thus Cammy, who is considered "high tier"[5] for *Street Fighter 4*, has a greater expectation of victory than a "low tier" character from the same game (for example, *SF4* 's Hakan), based solely on the capabilities, affordances, and limitations of those characters. Tiers are constructions of the fighting game community that are based on various factors—Kirschner and Schmuacher state they "must be decided by a very large sample of data under very controlled tournament conditions" (2008, para. 8)—and even within a game, various sources for tier listings may differ depending on the ways in which they are determined. One tier listings thread for *SF4* at Shoryuken.com, for example, includes a comparative listing of multiple sources and cross-analysis ("Character Ranking Notes (Tier lists + more)", 2009).

Considering that she became an almost iconic example of this phenomenon in action, I was interested in where Hilde of *Soul Calibur 4* fit into the tier listings for that game. Definitive results were difficult to find, especially given that, as previously noted, tier listings are not top down, developer-provided lists, but something constructed by the community. To that end, I looked for promising threads on tier listings at 8WayRun.com, a large and popular *SC* series forum. One well-discussed thread places Hilde in the highest tier, noting that "Hilde is just amazing, and everyone can agree that she is top tier" ("Official SC4 Tier List And Character Guides", 2009, para. 8) for various technical reasons. Interestingly, the same forums also contained a thread from a potential Hilde player who was interested in her tier standings without the ring out combination observed at EVO: "We all know she's S-Tier. But what if she didn't have the Doom Combos?" ("Hilde's Tier w/o Combo?", 2009, para. 1). The thread (which was not heavy on discussion) varied between those who argued for a considerably lower tier without the use of that combo, and those who feel her problems were either other technical aspects of the character, or endemic to the game itself[6].

This was resonant with something Seth Killian had mentioned in passing: that the people in this community know the tiers, but that they also enjoy "rooting for the underdog." In that sense, it may be that the choice of a low tier character creates its own degree of drama or tension; will the player of the supposedly weaker character have enough skill to make up the difference? Can s/he overcome an inherent deficiency created by the game rules to pull out a victory? Ibrahim mentioned that "if you pick [a low tier character], you will instantly *garner* respect from other players because he's known as a low-tier character and you've decided to choose that character because you're trying to show your skill rather than how powerful your character actually is, with or without you." He goes on to note that "[i]n Korea they actually have a title for people who pick low tier characters . . . it's like an honorific title they'll give you for choosing that character. You're a hero to them." Interestingly, the focus there seems to be less on the inherent can or can't of the character, or even on winning or losing, but on what that particular player's skill can "bring out" from the low tier character's capabilities.

However, tier lists can also be a force of orthodoxy in the community and in the tournament scene. This was readily apparent at EVO 2009 during the *Marvel vs. Capcom 2* finals. At that point, *MvC2* was a game with a long, long history; almost a decade at that point, giving the community plenty of time to do the collective work of data gathering, analysis, and testing that goes into the construction of tiers. By 2009, those tiers were fairly well cemented, and the number of characters that appeared in the day three finals for *MvC2* bears that out: the game has over 50 playable characters, but in the finals players used no more than 12–14 of them. In addition, the ones that did get used were a consistent mix of the same characters that make up the "Top Tourney Teams" listed for the game on its Shoryuken.com-hosted wiki ("Marvel vs Capcom 2/Tiers," 2012).

Thus the *MvC2* situation reveals a play context that is more or less calcified: the characters at the top of the tier lists have been established, and using characters outside of those lists is not just untenable but virtually unthinkable. However, two caveats on this example: First, the "main stage" tournament represents a different context than everyday play, and second, I didn't have a chance to observe elimination pool matches for *Marvel*. It's possible—indeed, likely—that outside the specific context of pro-level competition there is a wider range of used characters. That being said, the pro context is also the idealized and normative context when it comes to the hardcore fighting game community, and so the adherence to/persistence of high-tier character usage there is still quite telling about the power tier lists have in the community.

Tier lists aren't the only way that these communities come together for the purposes of research and dissemination of information, though. Another way that this manifests itself is in the collection and posting of "frame data" for various characters in fighting games. Remember from the earlier discussion of technology in fighting games that the base unit of action in these games is the frame of animation; hence the search for lag-free LCD monitors/TVs for tournaments and the preference for offline versus online matches. Consider that any given fighting game character is defined primarily by their attacks: the list of moves they can use to damage the opponent. These moves and techniques are measured in terms of speed by their animation frames, as well as what mechanical properties the character has during those animation frames. A sheet of frame data for a given character collates this information for everything that character can do.

This is a highly complex way of thinking about in-game characters and affordances, especially for the uninitiated, so consider an example. SRK's series of online fighting game wikis includes a page for Ryu[7] of *Street Fighter* fame for *Street Fighter 4*. The various column headers describe the properties each move can have: its name, whether it needs to be defended against "high," "low," or both, how much damage it deals, how much "super meter" it grants when used, and the number of frames of animation for various states of the attack. So for, say, Ryu's Medium Punch, there are three frames of windup once the button has been pressed ("startup" frames). The attack is then capable of hitting the opponent for three frames (the "active" frames), and then Ryu is vulnerable for 21 frames ("recovery") once the active frames are done. Of course, if the attack hits or is defended against, these numbers can change. And that's just a few features of one attack!

If your head is swimming trying to comprehend this, fear not. Even writing this attempt at a simpler example was a considerable challenge. These sets of information are incredibly dense, complex, and specialized. In a way they don't even feel "meant" for the lay individual, who likely doesn't have the context to make use of them. Certainly, they highlight a persistent truth about competitive fighting game play that this research bore out: reflexes and physical execution are only the beginning. That being said, the important thing to note here is that high level players can and do make use of these sheets of data, and they are both tremendously important and, like tier lists, community-produced and collected. Shoryuken's various wiki pages for different games—everything from *Street Fighter 4* to *Marvel vs. Capcom 3* to *King of Fighters XIII*—present page after page of highly detailed information about the mechanical affordances of characters. Some include frame data; others are detailed analyses of attacks that are less mathematical, but all of them represent communal gameplay knowledge codified and made public for players to use. Forums like 8 Way Run and Dustloop are no different, with similar offerings for the games on which those communities focus.

Something similar but perhaps a little more accessible to the non-hardcore player is the notion of the "official thread" for a character or game. These are frequently sticky (i.e. not deleted over time) forum threads that serve as collections of basic information about a character or game. They most frequently happen at the character level; sites like SRK and Smash Boards often devote specific sub-forums for each individual character in a game so that fans and users of those characters have a dedicated space to discuss that character. Looking through these various sub-forums across various sites produces threads like "The Emilie de Rochefort (Lili) Thread" (*Street Fighter x Tekken*), "Smokin' Sick Style! The Dante General Discussion Thread!" (*Marvel vs. Capcom 3*), "Tira General Discussion / Q&A" (*Soul Calibur V*), and more.

The general thrust of these threads is similar to a frame data sheet but is considerably less complex. The standard format seems to be a brief description of the character, an image, and then some basic information: that character's special moves and the motions to accomplish them, and then some additional data, usually a list of basic attack combinations or a brief analysis of the character's strengths and weaknesses. As replies are made and the thread grows, the original poster of the thread usually will return to the original post and update it with key information. Since these threads can often pre-date the release of a game in the United States, this process often involves posting known information and then communally separating speculation from fact so that this single thread becomes a clearinghouse of known, reliable information. Since being made "sticky"/permanent is often a sign of tacit approval in asynchronous forms, these threads then take on the character of being "the" place to go for valid information, which in turn can urge those maintaining it to keep up strict standards for verifying what the community produces. Hence the branding of this style of thread as "official."

What is happening in all three of these scenarios—tier list construction, frame data posts, and "official" info threads—is the use of the online space to consolidate, disseminate, and in many ways control information about the game that contributes to play. This happens with differing degrees of officiousness, but the key tenet appears to be making sure that this information is tested and reliable, since pro-level players (and those who aspire to pro-level play) use it to formulate gameplay strategy and tactics. Recall Jordan's comment that the '09er crowd at Shoryuken.com were frequently taken to task for loading up forums and threads with irrelevant, speculative, or false information; part of the community's negative reaction may have been because of this central role the online fighting game spaces provide. Because of the importance of that role, quality control—and policing— become high priority activities.

It's also important to note that this centrality of information has a direct impact on play. Tier lists are the big example, since they can have ramifications outside of tournament play. A character being perceived as high or low tier can have an impact on how often that character is chosen, or even how people react to that character being chosen before a game is even played (see the discussion of Hilde in Chapter 3, this volume). But frame data and even "official" threads can have similar effects. In many ways this info is the fighting game community's version of theorycrafting: identifying strong, useful, efficient ways of play that are oriented toward victory. However, like theorycrafting in the MMO world, this act causes ripples throughout fighting game-dom, even for those who don't engage in it.

ORGANIZERS VS. OLIGARCHS: THE PEOPLE BEHIND RULES AND NORMATIVE PLAY

Up to now this chapter has considered the ways in which online spaces are used to structure play. However, one question is yet unanswered: Who ultimately decides all of this? How is it that these normative rules of play get created and established? Are they community efforts constructed entirely out of social play, or is there a central group that the community as a whole can look to, in the aims of creating norms about play practice in a democratic way? Essentially, how much of this is "democratic"—a forum of peers—and how much comes from "on high?" In the end, it varies, but the approaches observed in this research suggest much about the role of normative play in the fighting game experience.

The *Smash* community provides perhaps the most detailed example. Matthew describes a group of people who make the suggested Smash tournament ruleset—the "*Smash* Backroom" (SBR) or "*Brawl* Back Room" (BBR)—as an "oligarchy" who read tournament results, view community input, and then produce a set of rules and community standards for play. A number of threads on Smash Boards support this, particularly the BBR's public information thread ("Information and Updates from the Brawl Back Room", 2010) and their suggested ruleset for tournament play ("BBR Recommended Rule List v2.0", 2010). The ruleset in particular is illustrative not only in how specific it is about match conditions, but for the broad and quite complex method of choosing the stage (combat environment) of each tournament round. I observed this method at EVO as well, and the representative of the tournament organizer for the *Smash* event taking place there—which was not tied to the main EVO tournament itself—spent considerable time explaining it to me.

Yet at the same time, Matthew also pointed out that the BBR has no "official" power, per se, and that their recommended set of tourney rules is only a guideline:

> However, that ruleset actually has absolutely no bearing on pretty much anything in *Smash*. Everything in *Smash* is up to the individual T.O.'s . . . the tournament organizers, I should be more specific. They're the ones who have the final say to say, "You know what, I support this rule," or "I don't support this rule," or "I support this level," and they're more of a representative of the community that they come from, so really, the *Smash* Back Room is only like—and they even say— "These are just our guidelines, these are what we think it should be," but the power is really in the tournament organizer's hands. So that's where most of the decisions come from.

Of course, this isn't to say that *Smash* tournaments across the globe have wildly varying rules. I presented Matthew with a hypothetical: what if a tournament organizer (T.O.) was dearly in love with *Smash* that had more casual rules; for example, what if s/he left on items? Would s/he be able to attract players to tournaments and events? His response: "Generally, people who agree with that sentiment will show up, and people who disagree won't, and then he has to make a decision, is he gonna keep playing with his belief that items are awesome and the group of friends and group of players that go there? Is he gonna build, shape the community for them, or is he gonna try and get more people to show up by modifying his rules?" In short, while a given tournament organizer has *theoretical* power to alter play norms, in practice that power is likely very limited depending on the audience the T.O. is attempting to attract. One who prefers casual *Smash* will no doubt attract players who prefer items and fewer restrictions; one who prefers hardcore *Smash* will consequently attract a different sort of playerbase. In effect, the organizer only has the power to alter play norms within the limits of the type of play s/he valorizes.

However, *Smash* is a different animal than the other games and communities described here in many ways. For starters, their method of ensuring the level playing field is primarily *restrictive* in nature. While the central goal remains the same—creating an environment for the skill challenge between players—their method is to systematically eliminate elements which would interfere with the process. Thus the extensive ruleset created by the *Brawl* Back Room, which were also related to me in brief at EVO by the T.O. there. Those rules not only call for the turning off of items, but also for detailed lists of stages into various categories (Starter, Starter/Counter, Counter, Counter/Banned, and Banned), ways to resolve conflicts ranging from who chooses characters first to who gets what controller port on the Wii running the game in the first place. Beyond banned stages, there is also one actual mechanic ban of note: while Metaknight himself is not banned, his "Infinite Cape Glitch" is. According to its entry in the *Smash Bros.* wiki, the glitch allows a Metaknight player who can execute it to walk through a match effectively invulnerable to attacks by other players ("Infinite Dimensional Cape", 2010).

The general ruleset for EVO matches, by comparison, is somewhat different, particularly since it encompasses not just one game, but the entire range of them played at the tournament in the first place ("Evo Championship Series >> Tournament Rules", 2009). A small subset of the rules deals with the actual play of the game, in three ways: who chooses what controller port on the console (which is similar to the BBR ruleset's method), the way characters are chosen, and the rules that go into effect once the match has begun. The remainder of the ruleset deals not with the actual conditions of play, so much as with the way players move through the tournament (brackets and tournament etiquette/rule violations). For example, there is a discussion of "yellow cards" and "red cards" for disqualification, but only one of the potential violations involves anything close to actual gameplay: the description of "excessive stalling" involves "repeatedly 'accidentally' picking the wrong character." Interestingly, starting in 2013, wireless PlayStation controllers are now also banned ("EVO Reminder: Wireless Dualshock 3 Controllers Are Banned!", 2013) because the way the controllers sync with the PS3 units used for elimination pools means a player whose match is over can interfere with the next match on that console, accidentally or otherwise. The philosophy behind the EVO ruleset is best summed up in a quote from the rules themselves: "These rules are an attempt to insure that the tournament runs fairly and as smoothly as possible." They are not structural rules for gameplay so much as procedural and technological rules for running a large-scale tournament.

Yet within the specific rulesets for each *individual game*, there are examples of restriction similar to the *Brawl* Back Room, though typically smaller in scope. In *SF2: HD Remix*, Akuma is banned. The rules for *Marvel vs. Capcom 2* describe a number of glitches that are illegal for use in play, and both the *MvC2* and *SF4* rulesets give specific scenarios where in-game options—assist characters, ultra techniques, and other in-game choices—can be switched between matches. In *Melty Blood: Actress Again*, Archetype: Earth (a character) is banned. Considering the idea—mentioned many times above—that EVO prefers to adopt an emergent style for tournament rules, these regulations seem, at first glance, contradictory. Aren't they in the same class as the long list of banned stages and the removal of items in *Smash*?

The answer to this question isn't immediately apparent, and it is the fact that the goal of both rulesets is to ensure a fair match that muddies the water. According to Seth Killian, EVO's logic is emergent rather than restrictive; as styles of play that are considered "cheap" arise in the community, players develop tactics to counteract those techniques through experimentation and play. He considered this attitude a "social collective" view, where a cycle of powerful playstyle discovery followed by counter tactics emerging continues over and over. Yet at the same time, it is clear that repeated play and testing is also how the *Brawl* players reached their set of rules in the first place. To call one "emergent" and the other "restrictive" suggests value judgments one way or the other on just how far an organizing body has to go before they're viewed as restricting play. From the standpoint of an outside observer, both groups use emergent gameplay to construct normative ideas of play to the same general end: the level playing field.

Thus the rhetoric in which both communities define themselves publically might be construed not as one community being "emergent" and the other being "restrictive," but rather a commentary on the nature of fighting games to begin with. In other words, the competing definitions end up being a sort of territory war between two imagined interpretive communities (see Zelizer, 1993, for an example of journalists doing something very similar), both formed from normative ideas about play. The conflict between the hardcore *Smash* community and not only other fighting game communities, but even *within Smash players*, highlights this. What's at stake in each case is the definition of what a fighting game is in the first place, and the ways in which those boundaries are described are in methods of play.

The intra-game community split in the *Smash* community is quite telling, since in their case, the two groups don't even appear to be playing the same *game* anymore thanks to their differences in normative play ideals. A similar situation in sports might be the difference between competitive basketball and a small two-on-two pickup game. Both of these activities involve the same *physical apparatus*—a basketball, a hoop—but fundamentally they are different games, with different contexts, outcomes, and rules of play. Casual *Smash* players and hardcore ones alike are using the same literal physical apparatus, the basic code of the *Smash* games. The difference comes in their normative ideas toward play. Each faction—and then on a larger scale, *Smash* players versus other serious fighting game players—is striving for the discursive space to claim legitimacy for their style of play. In short, they're competing for the power to define what fighting games are in the first place.

Returning to the question at the start of this section—is this a democracy or a dictatorship?—the answer is that it's a little of both. It's worth noting that the top-down parts of the culture, places where specific rulesets are written by a small group and then rigidly enforced, are primarily tournament spaces where this sort of thing is necessary for the smooth running of an event. The enforcement of polite, sportsmanlike behavior and the banning of technology that might interfere with matches is a more or less functional-level way of restricting play. In truth the power to make these decisions occurs at the event level: an event organizer can structure their tournament however they wish, but as Matthew said of *Smash* T.O.s who might run a tournament with items on, this power is not absolute. Without an agreeable base of participating players, the change in rules is mostly rhetorical. Certainly, while the directors of the EVO tournament make the ultimate decisions, they are also attuned to the culture at Shoryuken.com, with which the tournament is deeply affiliated.

Thus by and large, when it comes to restricting choices in characters, special moves, or other in-game issues, these restrictions are socially-built and softly enforced, which is where other structures discussed in this chapter and beyond come into play. Hilde is a little too powerful in *Soul Calibur 4*, but banning her outright doesn't sit well with that community, and so they don't ban her, but they *do* boo her when she appears. Some games feature downloadable content characters which cost money or are platform-specific, and so they are sometimes banned, not for being too powerful, but because not every player has equal access to using them. On the other hand, while Phoenix in *Marvel vs. Capcom 3* has a game-changing, powerful ability to come back from being knocked out, the community hasn't banned her; instead, they focus on building strategies for defeating her. While event hosts can exert some force to shape how tournaments or meet ups will go, that power is strongest when dealing with formal event issues, and weakest dealing with actual gameplay; in the latter case, community approval and buy-in seems particularly needed.

THE FIGHTING GAME LUDISPHERE

Consider that in the early days of the fighting game culture—indeed, of games culture period—this exchange of information, the acculturation of new players and the communal development of play strategy, took place in literal physical spaces. The arcade was necessary because it was one of the only ways to regularly keep in touch with other people playing these games. As is the case with many other cultures, though, the introduction of online spaces, and the continuing increase in access to those spaces, changed this. Now sites like Shoryuken.com and Dustloop and even game info/hint sites like GameFAQs provide a way for players across physical and temporal borders to share, discuss, and collaborate when it comes to their passion for fighting games.

Yet this is not a situation without certain potential drawbacks. The more durable and popular certain ways of playing become over time, the more entrenched they also become within the community, competitive or not. Ease of access to this information means that players can easily acculturate new blood to the mores and norms of the culture, and as was noted about Shoryuken.com and the '09ers in particular, if that new blood doesn't adapt fast they'll find themselves decidedly unwelcome. The result is a community that leverages online spaces to make their way of playing, and the tools they use to play, widely available. However, this also seems to generate, in some, an expectation that this ease of access creates an *obligation* to internalize it.

What's undeniable is that these online communal spaces—forums, wikis—are a critical part of the fighting game ludisphere. As information clearinghouses, venues for interacting with other players, and spaces where the work of acculturation is done, places like Shoryuken.com surround and inform the play of fighting games.

NOTES

1. In truth, there's every indication that fighting game players are highly instrumentalist when it comes to issues of the fiction of fighting games, seeing each individual avatar/fighter primarily as an assemblage of in-game capabilities before anything else. This isn't to say they ignore the fiction, but rather that it is of relatively low importance to them.
2. According to Chen, this specific group of raiders went from being initially social to embracing certain elements of hardcore raiding, elements that eventually contributed to the group's dissolution.
3. See Chapter 1, note 1; as you can probably guess, this iconic video's impact is wide-ranging indeed!
4. The name is an acronym for "Good Game, Peace Out," a common thing to hear in the arcade and online fighting game world. Interestingly, companies like Capcom have gone on to use GGPO's online architecture as the basis for online play modes both in fighting games and other online multiplayer scenarios, such as cooperative brawlers/beat-em-ups.
5. As of this writing, at any rate; reference http://forums.shoryuken.com/discussion/173987/ssf4-ae-2012-tier-list-thread-op-last-updated-may-2013 for the SRK community tier list. It's worth noting that as the "metagame" develops and different strategies emerge, tier lists have a degree of fluidity to them.
6. And of course, see Chapter 3, note 5: once the sequel *Soul Calibur 5* rolled around, Hilde lost her "doom combo" and her tier ranking suffered as a result.
7. Viewable online at http://wiki.shoryuken.com/Super_Street_Fighter_IV_AE/Ryu#Frame_Data.

6 "Asian Hands" and Women's Invitationals

So far, we've considered what it means to be participate in fighting game culture from a number of different angles: material/technological and historical influences from the arcade, community standards and gameplay practices, and the social spaces where these fans come together to communicate about games, play them together, or sometimes both. Now, however, we'll explore something a little different: ways in which aspects of players' "real life"—a common term I use with some skepticism—identities can influence, and be influenced by, their identities as members of the fighting game community. Specifically, here we'll be looking at how ethnicity, nationality, and particularly gender, intertwine with and refract gameplay norms and social play in the fighting game space.

In terms of the theoretical grounding for this research, this chapter is about the idea of intersectionality: the ways in which differing identities and identity categories can influence and affect one another in various contexts. While some aspects of an individual's identity may be more or less salient in a given social context, as social actors the other parts of their identity can and do inform others' understanding of the person. As the term intersectionality is used in feminist discourse, it primarily deals with systems of power and inequalities. For example, Kimberle Crenshaw (1991), writing on identity politics in social justice, noted that part of the problem with identity politics is "that it frequently conflates or ignores intragroup differences" (p. 1242). She discusses how violence against women of color is often not just about the victim's race *or* her gender, but both her race *and* her gender (among other factors, like social class). More importantly, Crenshaw argues that discourses about the experiences of women of color that are victims of violence are often excluded from anti-violence narratives that are not intersectional and lump all victims together.

While intersectionality has had a strong influence on research using feminist approaches, it is a complex issue that a number of scholars have explored in depth, considering some of the more thorny issues that the approach brings up. Leslie McCall (2005) discusses the relationship of intersectionality to the researcher's approach to categories; she describes *anticategorical* intersectionality, which claims that lived experience is too messy and complex to warrant considering different intersecting identities as categories, and *intercategorical* intersectionality, which takes existing categorical definitions of identity as a structural starting point for analysis.

Kathy Davis (2008, p. 79) believes that the somewhat muddy definition of what intersectionality even *is* happens to be, ironically, one of the approach's strengths: "It does not provide written-in-stone guidelines for doing feminist research. Rather, it stimulates our creativity in looking for new and often unorthodox ways of doing feminist analysis . . . it encourages each feminist scholar to engage critically with her own assumptions in the interests of reflexive, critical, and accountable feminist inquiry." In short, intersectionality is useful not because it gives us a to-do list for producing "good" feminist work, but because it encourages researchers to reflect on how systems interconnect and to devise approaches for research that take those interconnecting systems into account.

The aim of this chapter is to identify some of the intersectional moments of being a fighting gamer and participating in the fighting game culture. I've chosen specific, illustrative moments that, when I was analyzing what I had seen and heard, highlighted how the influence of ethnicity or gender suddenly changed the tenor of the moment, making certain assumptions, practices, and beliefs in the fighting game community more apparent than they might normally be. These narratives—a player who wishes for "Asian hands," the public sexual harassment of a woman player and its aftershocks in the community, and more—make it clear that the fighting game community experience is not necessarily universal and, indeed, for some players who fall outside an imagined norm, can be quite difficult.

ETHNICITY, RACE, AND VIDEO GAMES

Issues of race and ethnicity have a thorny history with video games. David Leonard has written extensively on how video games further negative and hegemonic portrayals of Blackness, offering up games like the *Grand Theft Auto* series as bell hooks-like examples of "consuming the other" safely through a protagonist of color (2003; 2009). Anthony Sze-Fai Shiu compares the games *Duke Nukem 3D* and *Shadow Warrior* as examples of how Asian cultures, and the Asian body itself, are co-opted and parodied for an assumed predominantly White audience. In general, video games have a very poor record of handling issues of racial representation in their content, as these pieces of research exemplify. And indeed, a cursory look at popular fighting game titles finds they are often no exception. The standard-setting *Street Fighter 2*'s cast of "World Warriors" is almost exclusively a parade of cultural and ethnic stereotypes: the Chinese woman acrobat, the massive sumo wrestler, the burly (and, through association with narrative trappings, thoroughly Communist[1]) bear-wrestling Siberian, and the unusual Indian yogi with supernatural abilities.

However, race also features quite prominently in the relationship between players and gaming culture. Betsy DiSalvo and Amy Bruckman (2010), coming from a technology education standpoint, were interested in the motivations young African-American men had for playing games. In particular, they noted intersections between gaming interests, ethnicity, and gender. They found that the men in their study played games primarily as a way to interact socially offline; they didn't view online social interactions as necessarily being "with people," a standpoint that is in many ways echoed by the fighting game community's focus on "in person" as being the true way to play. Further, a sense of competition and joking around/teasing with friends during that play was also important, which is again echoed in the community's arcade-inherited culture. Perhaps more interestingly, it reflects the boisterous, commentary-oriented approach to spectatorship for games like *Marvel vs. Capcom 2* that I observed at EVO, and that were embodied by fan favorite Michael "IFC Yipes" Mendoza.[2]

In discussing the relationship between ethnicity and professional competitive gaming, T. L. Taylor—who also cites DiSalvo et al.'s work with African-American youth and gaming—notes an important factor that is specific to fighting games: They're by and large a console-oriented, rather than a home computer-based, culture:

> That the fighting game scene originates in the arcades, and is not centered around the home PC, is crucial. It also transitioned into a console scene, a second key factor in situating its more heterogeneous configuration of player opportunities and identities. Consoles, especially those that are a generation old or purchased used, have been an important point of entry for people who can't otherwise afford computational technology. (2012, p. 131)

As Taylor says, consoles are more accessible than home PCs (if, as she later points out, less "mod-able"), and the arcades that consoles have largely replaced are even more accessible yet. Inequities in access to home PCs across ethnic and socioeconomic lines mean that the culture of fighting games arose, in part, from which groups had access to which technologies. Different access—especially salient in an age where the digital divide is alive, well, and dovetails with ethnic and social class power and capital inequities—thus has a direct impact on who has access to the culture and, beyond that, how the culture builds itself from the ground up.

One of the things I found pleasantly surprising about EVO in 2009 was that it appeared to be a relatively diverse crowd. Far from the public imaginary of adolescent/early 20s white males filling the expo hall, there were a large number of players of color evident among the attendees. Mind, this is a surface examination of the situation; for reasons one might expect, I didn't attempt much casual conversation with attendees about their ethnic background. It's also worth noting that EVO is a major, international event; players there represent not just the US fighting game scene, but players from all over the globe that had come to compete. Still, at least in terms of apparent racial diversity, EVO as an event—and as a meeting space emblematic of the wider culture—was host to a wide range of players. Of course, almost universally, those players and spectators were male, and the issue of gender is one we'll return to later in this chapter.

This isn't to say that in terms of race or ethnicity, everything is rosy and perfect in the fighting game community. A casual skimming of threads on Shoryuken.com provides numerous examples of racialized language, slang, and sometimes even slurs as being the norm for communication in that space. Granted, in an online community it's difficult to identify the ethnicity of the "speaker." It may be that these are examples of reclamation or retaking and repurposing problematic slang. Indeed, one memory of a (now sadly vanished) Shoryuken.com thread for *Marvel vs. Capcom 3* suggests that latter case, where players of color are re-using or reclaiming slang. *MvC3* includes a mechanic called "X-Factor Cancelling," which had been abbreviated to "XFC." However, SRK poster BullDancer referred to it accidentally (and jokingly) as "KFC," even adding "fuck me for being black" and invoking a particular stereotype of African-Americans. Though the advent of *Ultimate Marvel vs. Capcom 3* precipitated deleting the original thread, a discussion of the KFC joke's history—including a screenshot of the original statement by BullDancer—can still be found on the Shoryuken.com *Marvel* forum ("So You Wanna Go For a Ride?: Syke and Windy's MvC3 Basics Thread," 2011).

Interestingly, some of the community adopted "KFC" (instead of the expected "XFC") for a time, but it was far from universal. A look at the Shoryuken.com forum rules thread for both *MvC3* and *Ultimate MvC3* ("READ ME FIRST: MVC3 FORUM RULES," 2012) shows that the forum moderators will now deliver infractions for the use of the "KFC" joke. That said, the expressed reasoning for these infractions is not necessarily that the term has a racial connotation—though a simple Web search provides numerous threads discussing that very point both on and off SRK—but rather that it's potentially confusing to new players coming to the forum for information. To quote forum admin "trag": "We don't need another made-up term like 'BBQ' [referring to shorthand for a mechanic in another game] for the sake of being cute. It's not only confusing to new players . . . it's just outright stupid. It actually derails the conversation when you have to explain what it is." It's difficult to say if the moderators are unwilling to engage the racial dimension or the joke, or simply feel that appealing to a more practical reason for attempting to eliminate its use is more effective. In either case, however, this is just one example of gaming slang with a possible racial origin that, once it made an appearance in the culture, mutated as it passed through different uses.

Along similar lines, the aforementioned Michael Mendoza/"Yipes" is famous in the fighting game community for his exuberant, slang-filled, high-energy commentary on fighting matches, particularly those in the *Marvel vs. Capcom* franchise. During EVO 2009, one of the final years in which long-appearing game *Marvel vs. Capcom 2* would be played at the tournament, Yipes was given a mic during the *MvC2* finals on day three. This in and of itself was not unusual; the other finals also included voiced commentary from various community members. However, the character of Yipes' commentary itself was quite different. Where a *Street Fighter* match might have a commentator mentioning a skillful use of technique, or excitedly mentioning that one competitor or another had just seized a rare opening in their enemy's defenses[3], Yipes frequently gave such shouts as "And here we go, another America's Favorite," "Scoops! Scoops!", or "Make it rain!" His most well-known piece of such slang comes from a compilation video on YouTube of his *Marvel* commentary[4] where he makes numerous references to "Pringles" and "curly moustache" (in reference to the Pringles logo of a man with a distinctive curled moustache).

Bear in mind that as I sat in the crowd at EVO, I was in a strange "between" space regarding the culture and its emblems and icons. I enjoy fighting games, but I don't compete; I knew of Yipes's various famous comments, but I didn't know where they came from. However, I did observe a marked difference in not just how the crowd reacted, but in my own personal reaction, when Yipes took up the mic. While an EVO crowd at finals is always boisterous, during the *Marvel* finals they were particularly vocal, reacting not just to on-screen play but to Mendoza's commentary. And in truth, I was more excited, too; there was a degree of showmanship, of working the crowd, in Mendoza's performance that I didn't experience with other commentators at the event.

Without knowing more about Mendoza's particular background, it's hard to say what particular influences went into his personal commentary style. One can speculate, though, that the locales where Mendoza played/plays in public, and the cultural influences at those locales, would have an influence on this style. As such, this is certainly an area that deserves more in-depth research. To what extent do the divergent crowd and commentary styles of the (comparatively) reserved *Street Fighter* community and the boisterous, high-energy *Marvel* community reflect different local cultures? Does the "East Coast" culture—arcades in the Philadelphia and New York City areas where *Marvel* is more popular and where commentators like Yipes operate—contribute to that particularly flamboyant style?

"ASIAN HANDS" AND THE EAST VS. WEST "DIVIDE"

Another way in which ethnicity really comes into play in the fighting game community is a persistent privileging of Asian background as a marker of innate skill. A very telling example of how some in the fighting game community feel about the perceived dominance of Asian players—particularly Japanese players—comes from my interview with Jeff:

> Todd: Like I just don't have the experience playing, I don't have the reflexes either, but that's neither here nor there. But like . . .
>
> Jeff: You don't have Asian hands?
>
> Todd: Ha! Is that a . . .
>
> Jeff: You don't have Asian hands.
>
> Todd: Is that a common way of saying it?
>
> Jeff: Oh yeah. I didn't . . . I've certainly been upset that I'm not Asian at certain points, when I just can't, when I *can't* hit a move, I'll throw up my hands and go "Ahh! If only I could have Asian hands!" and I've heard other people say it too, because you just see, like the Korean players and the Japanese players, they're just like "Whatever! Got it first try!" and it's like, "Aaaah! Give me your fingers!"

This came during a moment where I explained my own lack of skill with fighting games and what contributed to it. Jeff's response was joking, but it speaks to a larger context where Asian players are considered to be just naturally, automatically better than their American counterparts.

Not all such references are necessarily about some sort of essential quality that sets Asian players apart, however. As was mentioned in the discussion of arcades, in Japan the arcade scene is alive and well compared to its decline in the United States. Many interview respondents were quick to mention that greater access to arcades contributes to a wider range of players and access to more skilled training opponents, both of which give Japanese players a competitive edge. Evan describes a scenario where a known player in the US scene, Arturo Sanchez, went to Japan to play: "He could beat everybody in America, at that time he would go over there and send back reports of him losing for like an entire day, so. It's just like, he'd go into an arcade and there'd be like 20 people in there, and he couldn't beat any of 'em, or he'd go to a tournament every week and lose first round every week, so." Evan is speaking about the strength of the arcade scene in Japan, but there is also a note of "even one of our best isn't at the level of their average player" in the story he tells.

Thus Asia—and particularly Japan—is both a heated rival and a sort of ideal motherland, where the arcade still exists and the players are top notch. The tension becomes a sort of love–hate relationship; figures like Daigo Umehara win championship after championship, making it look easy—even *claiming* that it takes very little effort (Ashcraft, 2008)—and are considered heroes for their puissant skill. At the same time, they're also considered rivals to be defeated, and in their own weird way are just "better" than us. Gene encapsulates a bit of the Daigo effect particularly well:

> Gene: Yeah. I mean . . . yes. Daigo is . . . Daigo has always been Daigo, and he's from Japan, and obviously the Japan players, quote-unquote have a "mystique," and since this is a culture that overlaps very much with kind of the Japan-ophiles or however you call them, that people instantly like and respect the Japanese players, because they . . . they have such a great arcade culture that we, that people like us have always wanted, and they still have an arcade culture while we don't have an arcade culture anymore, really, so people are obviously going to like Daigo and root for Daigo because A.) He's the best, he's the Japanese player, people like the Japanese players, he's not the most colorful Japanese player, he's not, you know, like, he's not Mago or Kindevu or, you know, guys who climb around, he's . . .
>
> Todd: He struck me as kind of reserved, yeah.
>
> Gene: He's a force of nature in the game. He is what everyone measures against.

Yet those same players who like and respect Daigo for being such an icon would probably be thrilled if an American player were to best him for the championship at EVO. Recall that at EVO 2009, national pride played an interesting tug of war with the crowd's opinion on broken characters in the *Soul Calibur 4* tournament. A crowd chanted "USA! USA!" as opponents took on French player "Malek," right up until an opponent picked Hilde, at which point they started cheering for Malek instead.

Constructing Asian players in this manner has echoes of Said's (1978) *Orientalism*; coming from the mysterious Orient, Asian players have their own aura—"mystique," as the quote above puts it—that makes them both exotic and unreachable at the same time. As Said put it, "[t]his cultural, temporal, and geographical distance [from the Occident] was expressed in metaphors of depth, secrecy, and sexual promise: phrases like 'The veils of an Eastern bride' or 'the inscrutable Orient' passed into the common language" (p. 222). This othering is also very similar to the sort of effects observed in the athletic world in the United States, particularly in discussions of how sportscasters and announcers deal with ethnicity, race, and gender when speaking about athletes themselves. Eastman and Billings (2001) found that Black athletes were often described in terms of their natural athletic ability and physical attributes, whereas White athletes were more frequently described as being skilled or smart players, focusing on mental attributes and effort.

The stereotyping of Asian players as being better somehow, either through circumstance (the arcade scene) or simply having "Asian Hands," resonates with that. Certainly, the fighting game community is not downplaying the skill of Asian players; however, the reasons for that skill tend not to be widely interrogated. If an Asian player is good, it's because s/he comes from the mystic land of free-flowing arcades, where the endless high-level competition has forged them into something altogether different, or, in the case of the nickname attributed to Daigo Umehara—"the Beast"—not even altogether human. This is particularly interesting, considering that phrases such as "Asian hands" suggest a sort of embodied essentialism of this *Orientalism*-esque mystique.

WOMEN'S PRESENCE IN THE FIGHTING GAME COMMUNITY

The relationship between gender and gaming is a very wide field indeed, and the history of gaming communities that exclude, degrade, or harass women that enter them is long and crowded. Tracy Kennedy (2007; 2009) has examined how one group of women gamers playing on Xbox Live— "GamerchiX"—came together to create a social support network sparked partly by the intense amount of harassment they were subject to during online play. Kishonna Gray (2013) has done some very similar work, in her ethnographic look at two "clans" of players, all women of color. Gray outlines both the hateful speech these women encounter and their survival and coping strategies in that environment, including the need to ignore or "mute" harassing male players.

In a similar vein, the backlash against Anita Sarkeesian's Kickstarter crowd-funding campaign for, and subsequent release of, her "Tropes vs. Women in Video Games" video series was so intense, widespread, and vicious that it attracted media attention worldwide ("Television Interview about Harassment in Gaming", 2012). In Sarkeesian's case, even the promise of exposing gender issues in gaming content—let alone gaming communities—made her a target for harassment and threats of violence, and while she's perhaps the most visible recent example, it's just the tip of the iceberg. In short, gaming culture's relationship with the portrayal and treatment of women has a long, problematic, thorny history.

By and large, women are definitively marginalized in the fighting game community, and when they do appear in the narratives of this research, it is typically not as competitors, but as observers or supporters. One interesting example of that at work is the few interview subjects I spoke to who either talked about an existing significant other, or a former/potential one. "Teaching your girlfriend how to play" was an infrequent but extant narrative, and it often served as a metaphor for teaching someone who doesn't know what they're doing how to play. It's not particularly seen as a negative; Jeff describes being happy about teaching his current partner to play fighting games. Yet at the same time, his description included sentences such as this: "I taught her how to do a fireball, and she can do it on purpose[5], and it's exciting to see her do a fireball on purpose 'cause she just knows it's . . . I dunno. I dunno how to describe that. It's a good feeling."

The idea being, he's happy that she's showing skill (which is valued) yet at the same time, it has the ring of teaching a child to walk: She's taken her "first steps" and it's terribly exciting. This experience reflects the findings of researchers like Walkerdine (2007), who noted that some women frequently come to gaming technology via male friends or partners.

Of course, the question remains, if he were teaching a brother, male cousin, male friend, or other male to play, would it elicit the same reaction? Judging only from his responses it's impossible to say, nor do I wish to ascribe any particular misogyny to Jeff himself, but his sentiment was echoed by Isaac and Nicholas, which—read in combination with various SRK threads discussing women players—suggests a gendered norm. The fighting game community's emphasis on skill and expertise means that it echoes a sort of geek masculinity, running parallel to hegemonic masculinity, but with a focus more on technology, knowledge, and skill than physical power and prowess (Kendall, 2000; Consalvo, 2003; Dutton, 2007). In this instance, the masculinity of these communities is not necessary focused on maintaining patriarchal/hegemonic power, but does create a context where femininity is non-ideal and women remain objectified and marginalized.

I also don't want to give the impression that there are no women players, competitive or casual, in the fighting game community. Rather the opposite; I think their relative absence from the spaces where I've observed the community playing socially is strange because of the knowledge that there are many women players out there. However, in a culture where even the best and brightest of women players are treated with disdain, hatred, and abuse, it stands to reason that many either don't make their gender public, don't "make an issue of it," or avoid the community altogether. Consider the experiences of competitive *Street Fighter* player Sola "BurnYourBra" Adesiji. In an interview with a teammate in the (now-disbanded) Dominion Method Gaming player team ("BurnYourBra discusses the difficulties of being a female gamer", 2011), Adesiji talks about some of the highs of her experiences as a woman of color in the fighting game culture, but has considerably more to say about its challenges: racial/gendered insults thrown her way, lack of respect, and in general mistreatment by her male co-competitors. One very interesting point, in line with this chapter's interest in intersectionality, is her discussion of what she calls "the look"; Adesiji speaks to her perception of men's attitudes towards women in the community:

> There is almost an invisible rule in the way male gamers see female gamers in terms of looks. I've read and I have come across a lot of individuals who think because a certain person or persons are of Asian descent that they're automatically good. Now, I will admit, Japanese players are really good, that can't be denied. But when it comes in terms of females, it feels to me like it's almost a written rule that if you aren't Asian, and if you don't have the look that fits into this beauty hierarchy, then

you're just not good. So, for me, I feel like it's a double standard that I really can't fight. I'm not Asian and I don't have the Asian Aesthetic [sic] look. I'm an African American female, so I am looked at as trash by some people.

In this quote one can see various threads converging: the aforementioned belief that Asian players are just "naturally" better, patriarchal views on women's bodies and specifically toward the bodies of women of color, and the implication that women in general lack playing skill all come together in what Adesiji sees as a damaging prevailing attitude and double standard.

GENDER AND THE FALSE MERITOCRACY OF THE FIGHTING GAME COMMUNITY

Speaking specifically to competitive gaming cultures, such as the world of e-sports, the presence and participation of women players in a space that is doubly male-coded—video games and sport—is frequently contentious, despite women's longtime presence in both arenas. Nick Taylor, Jen Jenson, and Suzanne de Castell (2009) have written about the ways in which participation in competitive gaming for women is often channeled into existing, patriarchal frameworks that sideline and diminish women's potential and place in the community. Emma Witkowski (2012), in her ethnography of high-level e-sports players (specifically, *World of Warcraft* "Arena" players), notes that in more professionalized e-sports situations, organizing institutions like Major League Gaming (MLG) provide a gendered "scaffolding" that is aimed toward replicating existing structures of "sporting masculinity": emphasis on aggressive competition and reflecting male bodies, with women sidelined. She describes the career path of one prominent woman Arena player as being a constant negotiation with the expectations a hegemonically masculine sporting culture would place on her, such as the idea that women aren't suited for competition or the assertion that something other than skill explains her victories, as women are always already less skilled than men.

In fact, the perceived relationship between gender and skill is one of the stickiest wickets in this context. In *Raising the Stakes* T. L. Taylor mentions the segregation of male and female players not just in e-sports, but in more physical sports throughout history, has been in the name of fairness. As that argument goes, because there will always been a perceived "skill gap," splitting women off into their own play space is the "fairest thing to do" (2012, p. 125). Consider that in gaming—as Christopher Paul (2012) argues—and *especially* in the fighting game community, this notion of fair play and balance is tremendously important, as previously discussed. This idea that players must be separated then splits off into two related but distinct philosophical concepts. The first is that skill is the only important thing, and thus the paucity of women players in the competitive fighting game community will end once women who have sufficient skill—again, the only important factor—appear. The second is that any attempt to support or buttress the increased participation or presence of women is "special rights" meant to buoy women who don't have the necessary skill to compete.

Naturally, both of these ways of thinking don't take into account structural or cultural factors that would impede women of any skill level from competing, and the anger and blowback that male gamers can produce in response is considerable. T.L. Taylor contextualizes some of the reasoning for this quite well:

> The frustration typically comes not from any deep-seated concern for the collective costs of gender segregation on both women *and* men, but instead from a feeling that women are getting unfair and undeserved attention and benefit. The line generally goes that women-only competitions valorize weaker play and that the women competing against each other, while admittedly better than average players, are simply not as skilled as men in the scene. The argument is typically that if they were they would either be on men's teams or competing in matches against men. As one male team captain simply stated to me, "Women just aren't good enough at *Counter-Strike* to play against men." (p. 126)

This drumbeat of "if they were good enough they'd be playing" dovetails, in the fighting game community, with repeated rhetoric about how the community is blind to ethnicity, gender, sexual orientation, or any other identity category: all that matters is skill. This puts women players in particular in an interesting double bind: unacknowledged structural and cultural barriers act to keep many (not all) women who want to compete away from the culture, yet at the same time, their *lack* of presence is used as a sort of back door justification for not just prevailing attitudes about women's lack of skill or belonging in the competitive culture, but also for the lack of women players in the first place. Women don't belong because they're unskilled, which is proven by their not competing, and so on, and so on.

This rhetoric has a strong resonance with discussions about, for example, women in the workforce, particularly regarding compensation and an equal work environment. In the patriarchal world of fighting games—just as in the patriarchal world of work in capitalist society—it is the privilege of men to insist that women reach success on male terms without addressing the influence of the power dynamic on the process. As an example of this principle in the workplace, consider Heilman's (2001; also Heilman et al., 2004) exploration of workplace scenarios where women succeeding at male-typed tasks resulted in *negative* rather than positive responses. In her research, she argues that because women aren't *supposed* to succeed at male-coded tasks—and hardcore competitive gameplay is unquestionably male-coded—when they *do* succeed at them, rather than being given credit for their success, they're disliked. It may be that if a large number of skilled women players were to emerge, their success would be attributed to something else, continuing their marginalization.

What this research articulates is that there are substantial barriers to women's participation in competitive gaming cultures. What's worse, those barriers are in many ways the result of a set of beliefs and practices that feed back into themselves, creating a cycle that is difficult to engage with or break into (or out of). Ignorance on the part of predominantly straight, cis-gendered male gamers to the barriers the culture puts in the way of women players contributes directly to this cycle, creating the illusion of a perfect skill-based meritocratic system.

An interesting example of some elements of this false meritocracy/double standard in practice occurred at EVO in 2010. That year, after considerable debate on Shoryuken.com's forums, the tournament organizers decided to hold a "women's invitational" alongside the main *Super Street Fighter 4* tournament. Access to the invitational was open to any woman player who was also registered for the standard *SSF4* tournament, though participation was not compulsory. The invitational had playoff finals, prizes for the top three places, and took place on the final day of the event with the other finals, just like the other major tournaments for EVO that year ("2010 SSF4 Women's Invitational: More Info and FAQ", 2010). In the finals, French player Marie-Laure "Kayane" Norindr took first place, beating out the previously mentioned Sola Adesiji.

The lead-up to and creation of the invitational were issues of great debate on SRK's forums, even after the event was complete ("The Role of Girls and Women in the FGC", 2010; "Would you want a women's invitational in a future Evolution Championship Series?", 2011). The many pages of these threads—and others like them—include everything from reasoned debate on not wanting to send women players to a gender ghetto to male players "trolling" by insisting female players return "to the kitchen" where they belong. The official information from the announcement thread gives the impression that part of the tournament's reason for existing is a history of "bad behavior" on the part of the SRK/EVO community and a desire to show "hey, women play these games too!" in the end.

That said, a very common discourse in the threads surrounding this event is that a tournament space *only* for women is a mistake. However, there were variations in tone on that central theme. Some did, unsurprisingly, fall into the "we don't need women playing at all" or "if they were any good they'd be in the main tournament" category. But then there are posters who argue, as did one with the tag "VirtuaFighterFour," that the existence of highly skilled women players actually was an argument *against* a women's only space: "There are good female fighting game players. Singling out women by having them ender gender specific [sic] events is MORONIC." Some players objected on the idea that a side tournament was putting the women on display for a male audience, or that a side tournament wouldn't get the coverage the players deserve: "A side tournament doesn't get put up on a stage infront [sic] of 2,000+ people and likely then streamed to the rest of the world," wrote one user, though interestingly enough, the actual event *did* do just that.

Comparatively, discussion of the benefits of such a tournament was limited, even among those users who believed it had potential or was a good idea. When the organizers announced the format, replies in the announcement thread wavered between a general (sometimes even grudging) acceptance and a continued argument that the very idea was sexist. A number of users seem to have been convinced the invitational was not a problem by the addition of the requirement that invitational participants also take part in the "normal" *SF4* tournament pool. Somewhat distressingly, an additional note in the announcement about transgender individuals being welcome if they identify as female sparked a number of body-policing and transphobic comments from the userbase. One moderator, in reference to the allowing of transwomen in the invitational in a thread discussing the future of such events at EVO, even mentioned that "traps were allowed last year," using a viciously transphobic term for transwomen.

And despite the groundswell of support, grudging or otherwise, resistance did continue to the idea, and not just from male players. One woman player, Miranda "Super_Yan" Pakozdi, articulated her objection along two lines. One is simply that fewer women play, and so the ratio of players from the entire community that will be both female and highly skilled is naturally low. Her second point, however, is more complicated:

> 99.9% of the time a guy says "Hey you're good" to a girl playing games, what he means is "Hey you're good for a girl" or "Hey I want to get in your pants" . . . I know this is true because I'm a girl and I hear it a lot (and I'm not really good at Tekken), and also because I have a lot of guy friends who have confirmed this. If someone is constantly reassured they are good at something, there isn't much incentive to push yourself to get better. Girls in Japan push themselves because they know they're expected to compete with guys, and they understand the first sentence in this paragraph. . . . Girls in America, especially the pretty ones, are given false titles of being "the best" at SFIV, Tekken, 3S, etc. when they're not even close to getting out of the scrub-league because guys love handing out compliments to girls. It's sweet and charming, but it's also ridiculous.

Taken in context of, for example, Sola Adesiji's earlier comments, this argument provides us with a lot to unpack. Pakozdi clearly finds the idea of this tournament to be in line with the condescending or even pandering behavior she finds irritating in male players. Her objection echoes some core fighting game community values, including the central "skill über alles" view where only playing ability is important. It's interesting to compare both sides of that coin. Male players use that idea to perpetuate an often unbalanced system, but it also presents an ideal that many women players might aspire to: a situation where their gender—something that is a source of trouble in the male-coded/oriented fighting game culture—really is no longer an issue, where their skills can shine through.

I had a chance to speak with Sola Adesiji at length about her experiences as a woman player, and in particular a woman of color who's part of the competitive community. What she shared with me paints a picture of a serious player who loves the games and who wants to engage them to gain mastery, rather than to be "a woman who plays games." When I asked if she had to make a particularly strong effort during her days playing in Minnesota arcades, she responded thusly:

> It depended on the person and the arcade. In the beginning I really didn't care. I didn't . . . I wasn't like, "Oh I'm a Black female playing." It didn't really dawn on me. I was just interested in the game. But as time progressed I noticed that people wouldn't give me the time of day; if I put my quarter up and I knew I was after the person playing, and someone put their quarter up, when the person was done playing I would grab my quarter and put it in knowing I'm next, and the other guy would just cut in front of me, like totally ignoring that I'm there. And then sometimes it would be on purpose, and other times it would be "Oh, I didn't know you were there," "I didn't know you were gonna play," because I'm a female. So there were times, you know, it depended . . . and I never really took it to heart. I was just like "Okay, whatever." So I mean, when I started playing, like, you know . . . they were surprised. And some guys didn't take it kindly, some guys actually accepted it, but never was I like, "Oh, I'm a female and I play." It was just like, "I love this game. If I happen to be the only female in the arcade that likes this game, so be it."

She went on to say that as she was able to prove her skill and seriousness, "Then [male players] started coming out of their comfort zones" and would offer suggestions and feedback on her play. In many ways this is an example of what the fighting game culture considers the ideal trajectory: a player who plays for love of the game becomes part of the community. However, what this experience suggests is that for women this period of "dues paying" where their seriousness and skills are in question is longer than it is for males, because there is a default assumption that women aren't interested in serious play.

That love of the game is also what helps keep Adesiji motivated to continue despite abuse and resistance she encounters; as she put it when discussing some of the abuse she encountered when she entered the tournament scene, "I'm here for the game. I had to tell myself, 'I'm here for the game.'

I'm here to play, for me. You know, there are gonna be people out there regardless of what I do that are gonna hate me. So I'm not here to please them. I'm here to please me, and the people I consider friends. And that's what I've been sticking to. And you know, it's hard, but that's my focus." While she doesn't shy away from competition and enjoys being competitive, I got the impression that Adesiji plays to master the game on her own terms. What's interesting about this attitude, however, is that it implies—along with anecdotes like the above one that she shared—that some of the abuse Adesiji has been subject to comes from the perception by male players that she is, for lack of a better word, flaunting her gender and the fact that she's a woman player, when her interiority couldn't be farther from that. We even briefly discussed the origin of her username/nickname, "BurnYourBra," which she said "has nothing to do with feminism" and was simply an old email address a friend suggested she pick, as a joke, when the name she wanted to register for Xbox Live was already taken. There is a sort of elegant justice in that this player who has no interest in being the spokesperson for all women players has a name evoking stereotyped images of feminism, images which male players read in that very stereotyped way.

As T. L. Taylor says of a parallel context in e-sports, this issue is very thorny with no clear-cut right or wrong answers. Many applauded the invitational as a chance to showcase skilled women fighters and give the mere fact that women played fighting games at all some much-needed visibility; others, like Pakozdi, decried the idea as well-intended but ultimately exploitative, creating a tournament ghetto for women players who (in her eyes) should strive to play at the level of the male competitors and let that skill speak for itself. Rather than suggest that either—or any specific—outcome is the "best" outcome, I believe it's important to examine the issue, and responses to the issue, in terms of how they highlight certain beliefs held and expressed in the community. The objections raised to the invitational, as well as the ways in which it obtained community buy-in, foreground how the issue of gender, assumptions about the relationship between skill and gender, and how a primarily male playerbase understands the role of women in its community, come together to create complicated problems without easy solutions.

CROSS ASSAULT

In early 2012, a major event occurred in the fighting game community that presents another fascinating picture of the conflicting and often harmful rhetorics about women and women players prevalent there. In order to promote the soon-to-be-released crossover fighting game *Street Fighter x Tekken* (*SFXT*, with the "x" being read as "cross"), Capcom partnered with IGN and livestreaming site TwitchTV to present *Cross Assault*, a reality-show style competition between two teams, Team *Street Fighter* and Team

Tekken (named after the two franchises that the game itself, as a crossover, featured) with the winning team receiving a cash prize (Goldfarb, 2012). The two teams would include veteran fighting game players, "experts" in both *SF* and *Tekken*.

Tom Cannon (aka "inkblot"), one of the founders of EVO and Shoryuken. com, did a detailed analysis of both teams ("Cross Assault: Introducing Team Tekken," 2012; "Cross Assault: Introducing Team Street Fighter," 2012). His analysis of the two women players in both rosters—Sherry "SherryJenix" Nhan on Team *SF* and the aforementioned Miranda "Super Yan" Pakozdi on Team *Tekken*—is quite complimentary to both, but there are elements of each that are signposts for larger issues. His description of Nhan starts by saying "[Nhan] is not gimmick or 'girl-player.' She's a legit player who can burn you if you take her for granted." Likewise, he establishes Pakozdi's credibility as a pro player right away, though he does so by invoking male players ("NorCal legends like John Choi and Ricky Ortiz") that she's played with before.

In analysis, I think what Cannon is trying to do is forestall criticism of both players as being "just girl players," doing so relatively explicitly in Nhan's case. He believes these two players to be real, viable competitors and he wants his readership to think of them that way as well. However, to do so he has to engage the rhetoric of the community, and that means making statements like the examples I cited above. Contextualizing Pakozdi in terms of the (male expert players) she's been around, "so she has seen a ton of *Street Fighter* played at the highest level," places her in a very particular light. Cannon considers her an expert, but the description also subtly places her one tier below the people he mentions. She's not a contemporary; while she's got "a fighting resume that most players would envy" she's also painted as a bright student rather than a seasoned co-competitor.

However, the more significant points that *Cross Assault* brought to the fore are issues of the fighting game community as a welcoming and safe space for women players. As the tournament progressed, Pakozdi—a member of Team *Tekken*—was subjected to steady amounts of comments and jokes from team captain Aris Bakhtanians that amounted to sexual harassment. The number of comments made on day one alone—compiled into a 13 minute video[6] by an unknown YouTube user going by the username "crossassaultharass"—is striking, and their content diverse.

In many cases Bakhtanians appears to be reading from and/or responding to live chat responses to the program (which was livestreamed via TwitchTV), including voicing suggestions that Pakozdi and Nhan should mud wrestle ("and I get the winner?!"), a moment where they ask how Miranda smells which is followed shortly by Pakozdi's voice on the audio saying "Get away!" with a slightly nervous-sounding laugh before Bakhtanians is heard saying "Not bad," and a moment where Bakhtanians asks point blank: "Miranda. They wanna know your bra size." It's interesting to note that later on in that exchange, in which Pakozdi is quite vocal about not giving him that information, Bakhtanians shouts "Come on, are we a team or not?"

As the tournament progressed, however, the situation worsened, and by day six Pakozdi appeared to have reached her limit. On the sixth day of the tournament, she appeared to forfeit a match, choosing not to play an elimination match. The list of reasons that she gives in the show's post-elimination interview[7] points very strongly to a disaffection with not just treatment by Aris (which is more implied than stated) but with the fighting game community as a whole; she discusses revising plans to attend the Final Round tournament and needing "a break" from the fighting game community. She admits that there were times when it was hard for her, but Pakozdi is clearly reluctant (as one might expect) to go into specifics about what precisely was a negative influence.

Internet and gaming media response to the situation was swift and quite varied. Many major gaming news outlets—Kotaku, Giant Bomb, Destructoid, the Penny Arcade Report, and many, many more—were quick to run stories commenting on the situation, generally supporting Pakozdi and condemning the actions of Bakhtanians. However, others were less inclined to support Miranda; as reported by Destructoid, "fighting game community leader Mike Watson called out [Pakozdi], saying 'The entire time you were giggling and enjoying the attention. Someone mentions harassment and not until then do you complain?'" (Sterling, 2012). Other attacks on Twitter and sites such as the Shoryuken.com forums were also cited. Clearly, the community was divided on the issue.

The situation was exacerbated by Bakhtanians' own additions to the discourse, where he quite strongly spelled out that he felt what he did was not only not wrong, but also a natural part of the fighting game community's practices. Both on stream of the *Cross Assault* show and in interviews and online discussions after, Bakhtanians described a scenario where the fighting game community is built on certain rowdy, male-coded behaviors and that certain forces—including movements within the community to get fighting games more involved in official e-sports events—were attempting to censor and sanitize that behavior, and thus keep the community down. One of his most infamous quotes on the situation speaks to that reluctance to become like what he saw as a very safe, sanitized e-sports community: "[t]his is a community that's, you know, 15 or 20 years old, and the sexual harassment is part of a culture, and if you remove that from the fighting game community, it's not the fighting game community—it's StarCraft" (Klepek, 2012). Bakhtanians also likens asking fighting game players to tone down or remove offensive language to asking a basketball player to play with a football instead.

Bakhtanians' continued insistence that you cannot remove the misogynist (and, by logical extension, sometimes racist and homophobic/transphobic) joking/speech from the practice of fighting game play without changing it wholesale into something else is vital in understanding the barriers that work against women fully becoming part of the fighting game community in the first place. Just as the discussion surrounding the EVO 2010 Women's Invitational deployed rhetoric of false meritocracy—the idea that there would be more women in the community if they could play on the same level as men—this discussion suggests that players who object to this treatment aren't really true players, and that if they were true players they would understand these are "just jokes" that are inherently *and inseparably* part of the game.

Also, the fact that these attacks—and there are considerably more as the video grinds on—are responses to the viewing community's ongoing discourse with the program via livestream chat is vital to understanding how problematic this situation was. It goes without saying that while some degree of trash talk or teasing from the stream was also directed at male competitors, the tone was likely quite different. It is easy to assume that harmful or silencing acts such as these come from the speaker being a racist/misogynist/homophobe, but as Blaut (1992) notes, there is a difference between racial practice—particularly "cultural racism"—and the identity marker of being "a racist"; see also Heider (2000) on institutional racism in newsrooms. Bakhtanians' behavior was harmful, but it didn't come from some place of elemental misogyny; it was a positional response within fighting game culture, mediated through his engagement with the live stream.

Along those lines, as the issue wore on, reactions from the community, and from community leaders, emerged, and a few of them present interesting looks into how the fighting game community not only views women, but how it feels such scandals relate to their group identity. One particular set of reactions highlights the internal division within the community, as well as the frustration of some of its luminaries. Tom Cannon wrote in a blog ("Back to basics, getting beyond the drama," 2012) on Shoryuken.com, within days of Pakozdi's departure from the show, that "this drama does not represent what the fighting game scene is or why it is so special. But it's a glimpse of what we could become if we don't take this week's lessons to heart." Cannon's post goes on to attempt to characterize the "real" fighting game community and culture, including an EVO 2011 highlight reel video he calls "a great cure for your post-drama hangover." The video itself is actually quite slick and professional, editing together clips of crowd reactions (typically big, cheering crowds), intense tight shots on focused players, and similar imagery to give the feel of EVO as a celebratory group event . . . and, by proxy, the fighting game community as being the same.

In commenting on sexual harassment, Cannon describes the community as "the most diverse on the planet, with players from all races, sexual orientations, and walks of life." He calls out Bakhtanians' assertion that sexual harassment and "rowdy behavior" are synonymous with the community. In summary, he calls for the community to "get back to basics," by which he means going back to the "formula that built the scene . . . [p]lay the game. Play to win. Watch what happens. That's all you need, because when you do that, amazing things happen. All the time. What does the scene need to be successful? Stick to what we've done over the past 20 years, because it's amazing." He ends the post by including a video of a favorite memory of his from the culture and calling for readers to comment and include their own.

This message of "the community's not really like this" and "let's focus on the good things" was echoed by Pakozdi herself, who provided a response to the entire affair over Twitter on March 2, 2012. In said response she takes a very similar rhetorical tack to Cannon's. For example, she emphasizes that Bakhtanians is just one person that doesn't necessarily speak for the community: "But that night, and every minute since then, I've received hundreds of comments/tweets from people both in and out of the FGC supporting me. These people outnumber Aris like 200–1." She even takes the gaming press (mentioning Kotaku specifically) to task for claiming that the problem is systemic rather than idiosyncratic: "Maybe some people (like the people who wrote the @Kotaku article) don't understand that it was just one person who did this to me." Pakozdi reasserts her love for the community and the joy she's received from being a part of it and, like Cannon (whose article she explicitly references at the start of her response), she includes an EVO highlight video from 2010 at the end of the video, with only the note "I'll just leave this here"—a particularly Internet-lingo way to imply something is self-evident—to frame it.

In both of these cases there's an incredibly strong undercurrent of "we're not like this," "don't judge everyone because of one jerk," and the like. To Cannon and Pakozdi both—and, if the response thread on SRK mentioned above is examined, many SRK users as well—the community is defined by the enjoyment it brings, not by the idiosyncratic and abusive actions of individual fighting game players. It's in many ways a direct counter to Bakhtanians' assertion that various forms of sexual assault and abusive behavior are inseparable from fighting games and that such behavior has always been a part of their practice. In short, Bakhtanians defends his actions by claiming that they are *de rigueur*, and Cannon and Pakozdi fire back that he doesn't speak for anyone but himself and the community at large isn't like that. Meanwhile, the community itself, as expressed in central community spaces like SRK, pulls in both directions.

Things escalated when, within a single day after Cannon's post on SRK calling for the community to pull back from "drama," two commentators on a fighting game web stream—Martin "Marn" Phan and Christian "ETR" Cain, both well-known figures in the fighting game community—made light of the *Cross Assault* sexual harassment affair during their live commentary, peppering their talk about the match with jokes about suing each other for sexual harassment and similar statements (including Marn, at one point, saying "That's so gay!" and then swiftly following with "Sorry, sorry, that's verbal harassment"). The commentators' actions on the stream, a Level|Up "Wednesday Night Fights" or "WNF," prompted a response article on Kotaku excoriating them for their "defensiveness" and blitheness about the issue, and perhaps more interestingly, a follow-up blog post from Tom Cannon on Shoryuken.com.

Cannon's blog post ("Hurtful speech: time to take a good look in the mirror," 2012) is notable mostly in the context of the message described above, one that was barely even a full day old by the time he responded to Marn and ETR's actions from the WNF stream. By comparison, Cannon's second post takes an entirely different tone. His first post focuses on getting "past" drama and arguing that not every fighting gamer is like that; the second post is much more aggressive on the subject of community self-policing. The writing for his earlier post feels hopeful, wishing to put the community back on track; by contrast, in the second post his frustration and annoyance are much more apparent—phrases like "there are way too many ignorant children among us" and referring to this behavior as "our dark side" drive that point home.

A key point in this second post is also Cannon's argument that it's the responsibility of the entire community to police this behavior, which is a sharp contrast to the earlier rhetoric about people like Aris Bakhtanians being isolated, atypical, idiosyncratic social actors. He is quick to emphasize that the online presence and character of the fighting game community is important for a number of reasons: "Our online presence is the face of the community. It is our recruiting tool. Increasingly it will be a source of revenue. A strong, positive online presence is critical to the growth of the scene." Consider that statement in the context of Bakhtanians' fear that the fighting game community was headed in a sanitized, "e-sports"-like direction that was trying to change the culture into something it is not. This brings us back to competing rhetorics about how the community should act in the public eye: a devil-may-care, "this is just how we are" attitude versus a push toward a more constructed, more reserved public image designed to attract new blood to the scene.

In fact, Cannon even addresses the idea of spokespersonship and public perception directly:

> Another excuse is that we're being unfairly singled out, and that "these few bad apples don't speak for the community." These guys don't speak for all of us? We just let them speak for us on-stream, and many of us want to let them off the hook when someone calls them out! For those of you accusing Kotaku of over-reacting and nit-picking, Kotaku didn't invent a story here. We gave them the story with this shockingly insensitive reaction to a very serious topic. So it's time to stand up. If we continue to let the worst elements in the scene speak for us or excuse their bad behavior, we deserve whatever criticism we get.

This description of group culpability is a stark contrast to the message of positivity and in some sense even partly dismissive message from a mere one day before, where the encouragement that "we're still a good community" and the use of the term "drama" to imply a needless furor were the big sell.

The end of the post speaks to a break between Shoryuken.com and Level|Up over the incident, and a postscript that links to Level|Up's official condemnation of what went down on the WNF livestream and a statement that neither Phan nor Cain would be invited back as commentators. So in some sense, there was an official rejection/calling to the carpet, as well as Cannon's statement as a community leader. Beyond that, however, this second article from Cannon points to and discusses, if not reflects, a very common response to the *Cross Assault* events and subsequent media coverage: the idea that the fighting game community has been unfairly attacked, chosen for persecution that it doesn't deserve solely for the purpose of harming that community. However, one example in particular stands out as an example of how writers and journalists—even those with no interest in attacking the fighting game community—can see the worst sides of the community arise from everyday moments of the culture.

THE CASE OF MADDY MYERS AND
THE MISOGYNIST FEEDBACK

Later in 2012, games journalist and fighting game fan Maddy Myers, a writer for the *Boston Phoenix* who has been covering games and gaming culture for over five years, pitched a story on "fight nights," the local meet ups for fighters discussed in earlier chapters. As a player of fighting games, Myers was interested in writing about them, and particularly about fight nights as a social phenomenon. So, she pitched the idea to her editor: "I told my editor that fight nights existed, that I had been to some, that it could be nice to talk about how these events developed locally. So I said I'd attend and see if there was a story there, basically" (personal communication, June 4, 2013). Myers got the go-ahead and began to attend local fight nights in the Boston area, both as an observer and a participant, someone who was attending to sit down and play games. As her eventual story for the *Phoenix* notes in the very opening lines, "[y]ou can't get real *Street Fighter* skills if you play by yourself. . . . You have to leave your house. You have to lose, hundreds of times, to better players. . . . You have to go to Fight Night" (Myers, 2012). She wasn't coming at the story with the intent to badmouth, criticize, or chastise the fighting game community.

Yet when she actually began attending events, the treatment she received in these fight night spaces was overwhelmingly negative. Rather than being welcomed with open arms, her very presence was viewed with suspicion or outright disbelief. Male players worked off a set of assumptions that presumed Myers had no experience, interest, or skill at fighting games in particular (or fighting games in general) and when the universally male crowds at these events chose to speak with her, they were frequently patronizing, abusive, or outright harassing. The piece she would eventually write for the *Phoenix*—"One woman's battle against the anxious masculinity of the fighting-games scene"—focused on the treatment she received, citing example after example of how her being a woman in a male-dominated social fighting game space was a thoroughly unsettling experience.

I want to focus on Myers and her experiences here in particular because many of the problems she faced, both at the fight nights *and* after her story was published, echo the behaviors of the fighting game community during the *Cross Assault* scandal. In discussing her experiences, Myers described to me scenarios that often reproduced *to the letter* statements made to or about Miranda Pakozdi, or the gaming media reporting on that particular situation. Examining these commonalities and behaviors points very strongly to a fighting game culture that has serious, unresolved issues with its handling of gender.

Reading Myers' write up of her experiences, one finds echoes of many of the issues already mentioned in this chapter. She describes the male players at fight nights as being more confused than anything when seeing her walk in the door or sit down at a game, as if they don't understand why she should be there at all. When Myers does get a game in on her first night—after a long wait, as she didn't feel comfortable "forcing" herself into the line of arcade-like "I got next"s going on—it's against an opponent who is not taking her seriously:

> It's my turn to play another round of [*Ultimate Marvel vs. Capcom 3*]. I'm up against the one guy using a controller instead of an arcade stick. I start out by asking him about his settings, which I've heard are unusual. He interrupts me.
>
> "So, are we all supposed to go easy on you?" He gives me a crooked smile.
>
> I pause. Because I'm a girl? Because I'm a girl. I stare at him with serious eyes, giving him more than enough time to backpedal. But he keeps grinning. So I give him a "no" in my best Daria deadpan.
>
> He laughs. He sounds nervous and a little too high-pitched. "Come on, I thought we were having fun here."
>
> I pause for a while, watching him. "I'm sorry, I'm just confused," I say. "What did you mean by that?"
>
> He laughs. He won't answer.
>
> "What did you mean?" I ask again.
>
> "See, if I don't go easy on you, you won't have any fun," he says.
>
> "I'm not here to have fun," I say. "I'm here to learn. Go ahead and beat me."

It's this final exchange that really drives home the point of this experience: Myers is attempting to engage the fighting game culture in the context of its own rhetorics, as discussed earlier in the book: the notion that one learns through competition, that "fair" competition is the core of being a fighting game fan, and that everyone is equal on the battlefield. Yet because of her gender, Myers' opponent makes a number of problematic assumptions: that she's not there to compete, that she won't have any fun if she loses, and that broadly speaking she probably isn't a "serious" fighting game fan.

Later in the story she describes a game against a male challenger in very tense terms; it's a close game that comes down to the wire and which Myers wins. She describes her victory in terms very much like those of the fighting gamers interviewed in the previous chapters: "this must be the reason to keep coming back. To get better, to watch your own progress, to feel this good about yourself." Yet she follows this description by noting that when she went to shake her opponent's hand and say "good game"—a common act of sportsmanship and politeness in the community—she found her opponent standing up, back to her, before throwing his controller down and leaving the venue without a word. It's impossible to say why this particular opponent reacted this way, though it's a moment situated within and framed by Myers' description of the players in the space as already hostile and wary about a (lone) woman player in their midst. It could have been any of a number of factors, either personal or situational, that would make that player act in such a way. But it is worth noting if only for the way in which that behavior goes against the rhetoric of the fighting game culture as it was expressed to me by players within it, and observed by me at events like EVO. The ideal is that, regardless of who beat him, that player should be gracious in defeat and seek to learn from his loss.

DIFFERENCE SHOULDN'T MATTER (EXCEPT WHEN IT DOES)

In looking at the fighting game community's handling of issues of ethnicity and gender, this chapter returns again and again to a particular paradox. On the one hand, the rhetoric of the community espouses equality, a meritocracy where only skill and the love of the game matter. Fighting gamers see themselves as inclusive and, generally speaking, color/gender-blind. If you have the skills, you can succeed. However, on the other hand, these supposedly invisible—and, by inference, *inoperable*—differences crop up in the community's behavior all the time. Only skill matters, but Asian players are just naturally better at the game, and women are simply not cut out to be part of the competitive world. Everyone's equal on the battlefield, but if the player is a woman then we have every right to make jokes that either border on or simply *are* sexual harassment, because if you don't have the thick skin to take some trash talk, then you're not really serious about being part of the community.

This false meritocracy is not new to video games or to competitive communities; as previously mentioned, T. L. Taylor has spoken at some length about how this is a behavior pattern resonant with physical sports, where the persistent narrative of the level playing field makes any sort of long-term solution a complex matter. However, the case of Aris Bakhtanians and Miranda Pakozdi on *Cross Assault* highlights just how deeply this unwillingness (or even inability!) to acknowledge barriers to equality in the scene goes. Bakhtanians' claim that fighting games without sexual harassment is "just Starcraft," for all its hyperbolic quality, is fundamentally about his perception of the community's resistance to changing its behavior, especially to suit what are perceived as outside moral and ethical standards. Because playstyle and the mores of social play are so deeply entwined in the identity of "fighting gamer," asking people like Bakhtanians—and he is not alone in the community, by far—to shift their behavior and reduce some of the abusive acts that serve as barriers to a diverse community is, in their eyes, tantamount to asking them to give up being fighting game fans.

Of course, this puts the part of the community on the opposite side of that spectrum in a problematic space, especially since many of the players talked about in this chapter who've engaged in this sort of behavior—Bakhtanians, Phan, Cain—are popular, well-known, and iconic. For the community to change its mores and practices on this front, it's likely—as Tom Cannon observed, blogging about *Cross Assault*—that this change needs to be internally motivated and involve a large degree of internal "watchdogging" and ally support behaviors. In short, the community needs to police itself. Yet things like the bystander effect work against this, for one, and for two, in some contexts standing up against the community's bad behaviors means loss of face and/or favor on the part of the ally

OTHER INTERSECTIONS?

Race and gender are certainly areas where the fighting game fan identity seems to intersect most frequently and visibly, but they're hardly the only ones, and these examples, while important, are only part of the broader picture themselves. One consideration mentioned in passing earlier is the way in which social class impacts the community. Depending on one's investment in the competitive scene, being a fighting gamer is not cheap; at minimum it requires a regular monetary investment in arcade play or a larger single amount of money on a home console and games to play on it. Above and beyond that, recall that the arcade stick is *de rigueur* in the fighting game community, and the most popular, basic, pre-assembled sticks—such as MadCatz's *Street Fighter IV* Fight Stick—still run upwards of US$200 at minimum. And this is merely the cost involved in *playing*, let alone the cost of attending and entering tournaments across the country, or even the globe. Much like the professionalization of e-sports that Taylor discusses, "professional fighting gamer" is difficult to do on the career level as well. In short, money is a major factor in how much participation one can engage with in terms of actual play in the pro community; it would be worth the time of researchers to identify just what the extent of that influence is.

Interestingly, when I spoke to Sola Adesiji, she expressed the idea that it should be *easier* for the fighting game community to come to grips with players of different genders and backgrounds because "it is one of the most diverse" communities she's encountered. From her point of view, that ethnic diversity should encourage players to have a more accepting and open attitude. I asked her directly what she thought the fighting game community's next steps needed to be, to improve their image and their relationships with players of various backgrounds. In particular, I asked her about the tension between maintaining their "rowdy," free-wheeling identity and perhaps "cleaning things up" more for public acceptability. Adesiji believes that these aren't irreconcilable, and some trash talk or rowdiness is just part of the scene's arcade roots, but some change is necessary, and she equates that change with maturity:

> Sola: People need to look at that and determine what's more important. Twenty years from now, are we still gonna be doing this? Are you still gonna be . . . is the fighting game community still gonna be in the dark while other tournament and leagues are just out there, with more money? No, you're gonna want more. So you have to sacrifice. And a lot of people don't like that.
>
> Todd: So it seems like, it's kind of like, you can keep your informal, kind of . . . rough and tumble community if you want, but what you're giving up there might be this public acceptance that you've been saying you want.
>
> Sola: Exactly. You can't have your cake and eat it too. <laughs>

She goes on to say that she still loves and appreciates the "hype" of the rowdy fighting game culture, but argues that it needs to happen in "a smarter way." To her, it's not about removing the things about the fighting game community that define it; it's about finding a way to express those ideas and energy in a way that isn't harmful within and without the community. That said, she had one simple injunction to the fighting game community, in the end: "You have to grow up."

Also, while we've discussed various aspects of the relationship between gender and the fighting game community here, there is comparatively little to say about LGBTQ representation and participation. It's difficult to say how many players are queer-identifying and out in their lives, but the number of players who choose to blend their sexuality and their identity as a fighting game fan (or public figure within that community) is relatively low. It may be that, as has been observed in physical sports, the mere perception of possible backlash or other negative consequences from a culture seen as hostile to queer identities (see Cavalier, 2011) may be enough to ensure any out, queer-identified players keep things low key. Alternately, it may be that such players don't feel a need to mix their private sexuality and their fighting game community participation, especially if there's no perceivable *benefit* to doing so. Sadly, without more out queer fighting game players willing to discuss their experiences and more research on their participation with the community, the best we can do is speculate.

What the examples in this chapter make clear, however, is that players do not always live up to the positive, skill-determinant, outreach-oriented rhetoric of a fighting game community determined to add every player it can to its ranks. Sometimes the ways it handles issues of ethnicity and gender are, if not benign, then at least not intentionally hurtful; the push-pull tension of the US fighting game community's views on Japan, for example, straddle the strange line between racist othering and "compliment" that makes it difficult for in-group members to fully internalize the potential problems with such views.

On the other hand, the treatment of women observed in the examples above is almost universally on the level of abuse, and vocal members of the community have gone out of their way to imply that the attitudes which lead to that sort of abusive behavior are essential to their identity as fighting game players and, indeed, to the fighting game culture as a whole. While there are certainly examples presented here of members of the community who attempt to use their privilege and social capital to counteract that message, the schism itself points to a community that has serious unresolved issues with its treatment of women, issues that in the eyes of some are actively preventing the community from acquiring the respect and prestige that they believe it deserves. Only time will tell if the community can generate the momentum needed for a paradigm shift away from being a "boy's club" or not.

NOTES

1. This refers specifically to the character Zangief, a massive Russian wrestler. The earliest *Street Fighter 2* games predate the fall of the Soviet Union. Indeed, in Zangief's story "ending" after defeating the final enemy in single player mode, Mikhail Gorbachev—unnamed, but featuring the mark on his head that "identified" him—appears and congratulates Zangief, even doing the "Cossack dance" with him!
2. See Chapter 3's description of the importance of the crowd for some description of Yipes's commentary in context.
3. I want to be clear: Mendoza also made this sort of commentary, and is a skilled *Marvel* player in his own right. However, his additional "color" commentary was something that was distinctly absent from the other games' final tournaments, and thus is worthy of note.
4. Viewable online at http://youtu.be/sZZUMjoxfZA.
5. Presumably, as opposed to doing it entirely by accident; the common stereotype of the unskilled in the fighting game community is someone who just slams the buttons/moves the stick at random rather than attempting to perform moves skillfully.
6. Viewable online at http://youtu.be/0SLDgPbjp0M.
7. Viewable at the 4:50 mark of http://youtu.be/X6Ii-5KknyY.

7 Defining the Game and Defining the Self

We've examined a number of facets of the fighting game culture by now: the arcades that represent a shared history and an ideal place to play; the gameplay practices that define their interaction with the games themselves, their social interactions and online communities; and how issues of ethnicity and gender intersect with and complicate many of these things. Building on all of that, this chapter posits the question: What is the fighting game performance like? How do all of these factors come together to create a way of understanding and enacting the self as a fighting game fan? How does it compare to the public conception of fighting games, or indeed, likely of many types of digital games in general? In that imaginary, games are for children, primarily boys; they are reflex tests where the winner is determined not by who has the strongest strategy or the sharpest wit, but by whoever has the fastest fingers and the best reaction time. Undoubtedly violent, they are played solely for slaking a prurient and pointless need to simulate violence. Certainly, fighting games seem to fit that preconceived notion reasonably well at a cursory view. Their most visible fans are male. They're fundamentally about combat, and at high levels of play the action is so fast and furious that those without superior reflexes will be left behind. Even I, as a longtime gamer and even as a fan of fighting games, envisioned competitive fighting gaming as being all about who has the fastest fingers in the West.

However, the picture of fighting game play that I observed at EVO, and which players and fans described to me in great detail, couldn't be less like the description I gave above. To those fans—fans who take the enterprise "seriously"—having good reflexes is only the most basic part of the equation, and certainly no guarantee of victory. To them, fighting games have more in common with chess than with *Pac-Man*; winning comes not from having the fastest fingers but rather the sharpest mind: internalizing the necessary expertise, doing research into what works best, and continually striving to find the right level of challenge in order to create constant, dedicated improvement in the art. Although they perform their punches and kicks with the press of a button rather than moving their actual bodies, these "serious" fighters are very much like many of the martial artist characters that serve as their representatives in digital bouts. In many ways, this echoes the construction Reeves, Brown, and Laurier (2009) have of expertise in the FPS game *Counterstrike*, where expertise in play is gained through "gradually developed competencies" (p. 223). As Garrett put it, "the top players of these games, they never drop [controller] inputs, they don't mess up, and they never miss anything . . ." For expert players, the reflex issue of muscle memory and speed is the entry barrier to online play, rather than—as the common view would have it—the totality of the experience. This dissonance between the public conception and the lived reality for these players serves as a useful entry for discussing the implications and interpretations of the data I collected on this subject.

In this concluding chapter I will shed some light on exactly how these factors position the "game" in "gameplay," much as Butler aimed to clarify the relationship between the body and gender. In both these scenarios, what we consider materiality—be it the physical body of human beings or the metaphorical "body" of a game in its code—serves only as an influence. Ultimately, what defines a game is as dependent, if not more, on the social practices of play as it is on what the designers code into the game in the first place. Rather than viewing the game text and its affordances and limitations as central in analyzing games, I argue that considering them as one influence in a cloud of interconnected elements—social play, technology, and personal identity being only a few—that come together to create the experience. I argue that in addition to being experiential in nature, the play of these games is heavily discursive, to the point that two people engaged in different discourses of play are no longer playing "the same game" anymore in many ways. I'll also examine some of the limitations of this research, and what both these findings and those limitations imply for future study of both this community and game studies at large.

BEING A GOOD PLAYER: CORE ELEMENTS OF THE IDEAL FIGHTING GAME PERFORMANCE

As detailed in previous chapters, it is possible to construct a vision of the ideal performance when it comes to serious fighting game fans. Speaking generally, the ideal fighting game player takes the game seriously, is a gracious winner, seeks self-improvement, has an investment in both gamer culture broadly and fighting game culture specifically, considers fighting games to primarily be a social activity and a test of skill, and both appreciates and seeks to emulate the (American) arcade ideal of two fighters challenging each other one on one. The various elements of this ideal performance come from both social and gameplay angles; how these players interact with each other is equally critical to understanding them as looking at what they do with a controller—or more accurately/specifically, an arcade stick—in hand.

The arcade ideal as an environment of play is a major contributor to this. Remember that the arcade ideal encompasses a number of sub-factors. For example, it's the origin of the idea that games are played side by side or face to face, in full view of a crowd, as many arcades in the United States would allow for. EVO itself is, according to one of its organizers, an attempt to recapture the spirit of the arcade in a larger event; the earliest EVO tournaments were held in actual arcades around the country before they grew to be larger events and thus needed to switch to a consistent location and consoles. However, as I observed at EVO itself, playing on console equipment—PS3s on tables, an endless array of TVs and monitors—does not necessarily diminish the arcade experience. The behaviors of players, such as the tendency to gather in crowds, the "I got next" method of inserting oneself into play, even crowd reactions to major matches—these are all arcade behaviors that translated over into the new setting. Even part of the technology of play, in the form of the mostly ubiquitous arcade stick, has some of its roots in the arcade, though as I've noted, there are other concerns that make the arcade stick desirable over the alternatives.

More to the point, the use of technology is itself a way of expressing adherence to the performance. While the description of arcade sticks and their technological benefits above does indeed provide a number of practical reasons for using a stick, doing so also identifies the user as a serious fighting game player in the first place. Arcade sticks and even the homemade arcade cabinets I observed at EVO are both interfaces for the game and ways of showing that the person who uses or creates them plays a certain way. In terms of Goffman's *The Presentation of Everyday Life* (1959), these are necessary "props" for the performance; like an actor's costume or held items serve to cue our interpretation of what kind of character s/he is portraying, even the *use* of an arcade stick or the creation of a homemade arcade cabinet cues us to understand what sort of player someone is.

Remember too that these fans construct fighting games as a primarily social activity. When describing play, interviewees consistently framed it in terms of competition, and when they did speak of playing single-player scenarios against the CPU, it was only "for fun" or as a method of training oneself for the eventual goal of fighting against other people. At EVO, nobody who played was alone for long; not only did people regularly insert themselves into available stations for play in the bring-your-own-console (BYOC) area, but even standing near one and observing was good enough to garner repeated invitations to join in from people playing alone there. It is a central, defining assumption that verged on the exominative. It was just assumed, unless I asked otherwise, that of course I was talking about fighting games as played with others. To do otherwise was unthinkable and of no real use.

Being a good sport and a gracious winner, rather than a sore loser, is also part of the package, and it has both social and gameplay ties. Winning, as I saw at EVO, was not particularly important. When the crowd cheered, it was not always for the winner, and an easy or fait accompli win wasn't particularly interesting. Speaking with players, they indicated almost to a person that the critical aspect of the fight is not winning or losing, but the challenge; losing to someone more skilled is a chance to improve one's own game and, in the process, improve the play of future opponents as well. It is almost as if winning or losing is incidental, a consequence of the game code: A winner must be determined, but the gaming process itself is more important. In short, winning is nice, but being a strong, gracious competitor and giving your opponent a good match is better by far.

This is naturally a consequence of the idea of fighting games as agon, a skill challenge between competitors. Discussions of banning, tournament rules, and exactly where the line is crossed between "social restriction necessary" (for example, Hilde's crowd boo phenomenon at EVO) and "official ban necessary" (Akuma in *Street Fighter 2 Turbo: HD Remix*) have a lot to do with the idea of creating a level playing field and allowing a situation where skill shines through to illuminate the stronger competitor. Though the camps at Shoryuken.com and Smashboards have differing views on the nature of a fighting game, both of them create tournament rules with the same goal in mind: a fair fight. To them, casual players care about nebulously-defined fun (which often means winning) and not necessarily about skill; this is why they "nerdrage" after losing on XBox Live, why they play *Smash* with items turned on, and why "home rules" such as "throws are cheap, we won't use them" emerge. To the casual player, when everyone has a chance to win, the game is more fun; to the serious player, the source of fun is determining the better player by matching skills. As T. L. Taylor (2006) points out, "fun" is a highly abused notion in video game study. What is fun for one player group quite clearly might not be for another.

Butler argues that a performance is a series of iterated events and experiences, moving through time. Part of the way in which this performance maintains itself is through normative play. The ways in which these players choose to pursue playing the game—their normative opinions on the hobby itself—both reflect and reinforce a particular ideological character. In turn, as more players adopt that style of play, the social strength of that playstyle as a norm increases, and the social force of that ideology of play also increases. Much like a gender performance, repetition and indoctrination over time help to turn praxis into a norm, with all the pressures that go along with it.

Chapter 3 on the practice of play is the strongest example of this in action. The clash over house rules and tournament restrictions between the community at SRK and the *Smash* community (and even within the *Smash* community) is fundamentally about the "skill challenge" aspect of the performance. Mapped out in a cause and effect fashion, the argument for turning off items in *Smash* reads like so:

1. What are fighting games for? Competition with another player.
2. Competition with another player needs to be fair and even, with skill as the only determinant.

3. Thus, fighting games need to be fair and even.
4. Items present uncontrollable situations where player skill doesn't determine the outcome of the match.
5. Items are not fair and even.
6. Items must be banned.

While this is somewhat simplified, it shows how one might start with a social norm—fighting games as perfect, Caillois-defined agon—and how that social norm then becomes a gameplay norm. The process isn't limited to *Smash*, either; you can replace the last three lines with the following:

4. Akuma's double air fireball and other moves present situations where even skilled players will be entirely without options or recourse.
5. Akuma is not fair and even.
6. Akuma must be banned.

That process would more or less describe why Akuma isn't legal in tournament play for *Street Fighter 2 Turbo: HD Remix* despite David Sirlin's attempts to balance him. Though within the greater community arguments rage about that first step—"What are fighting games for?"—the process that comes after resolving said step is consistent.

In both of these scenarios, however, the affordances of the game code are the relative constant. *Smash* can be played with items or without; *SF2T* can be played with Akuma, or without him. There is nothing elemental in the code, nothing written onto the CD/DVD media, which says "this is a fighting game" in an incontrovertible way. Recall the discussion in Chapter 1 on the many influences—genre, historical, market—that go into defining what a fighting game is. Despite differing opinions on all of that, norms about play affect player expectations about the experience, which then affect how they perform play itself. What's on the medium for the digital artifact is just a starting point.

BEING A SOCIAL PLAYER: PERFORMING THE FIGHTING GAME IDENTITY SOCIALLY

In research examining the potential of massively multiplayer online games as third spaces, Steinkuehler and Williams (2006) suggest that some MMOs start as third spaces for players, but over time, that status starts to fade away. They link bridging relationships[1]—less deep, more inclusive ones—with third spaces, arguing that the complex relationships of bonding are less likely to flourish in the light and playful atmosphere of a third space. From the outside, my initial assessment of SRK was that it was a place for fans of fighting games to hang out, to share their love of fighting games, and perhaps to share tips about better play. For the most part, the image fits Oldenburg's (1999) eight criteria[2] for a third place as Steinkuehler and Williams describe them.

Now, after speaking to players who participate in those communities, observing their forums myself, and attending events which those forums help to organize and structure, I don't believe forums like SRK are primarily that sort of space. It was clear that Shoryuken.com is somewhere that serious fighting gamers go to engage in serious fighting game play. Even when they weren't actually interfacing with the game, they were engaged not only in the production of gaming capital (Consalvo, 2007) but also in the reproduction of the playstyle favored by that community. Though the literal content varied, communities based on other games such as Dustloop, Smashboards, or 8 Way Run.com functioned in much the same way. This isn't to say that no casual, informal socialization goes on in these spaces; it clearly does. But the image these sites present, and which of the behaviors of their users support the best, is a place where the work of social play happens.

A second focus area for this study sought to examine the impact of ways of playing on social participation, as well as community formation: how do ways of playing affect social interaction, particularly in the context and formation of gamer culture and gaming communities? The ways in which forums such as those mentioned above are *not* third places help to make salient the answer to that question. Certainly, there is a social element to those forums—most have at least one "general discussion" forum for topics unrelated to fighting games, if not more—but first and foremost, these are communities of expertise, much as Elitist Jerks.com is for *World of Warcraft* (Paul, 2011). As an earlier quote from an SRK user noted, users there consider it first and foremost a space for discussing high-level play. Rather than building a community as a socializing space, the sun around which these forums orbit is ways of playing. The three aspects of that—play practice, normative play, and social play—all encompass different expressions of the community of expertise concept. Further, social participation in that space, and in related spaces such as the EVO tournament, is heavily shaped by this concept of the expertise-based collective. Though genuine friendships and social connections can and do emerge from such participation, the primary *motivation* for doing so is adherence to and development of a particular way of playing.

The many stories of players I interviewed about their introduction to fighting games are another useful entry point on the topic. As mentioned earlier, the arcade setting features prominently into the history of many of these players. Even for those who started on home consoles rather than arcades, such as Nicholas, the *idea* of the arcade still has an influence on their eventual participation. Beyond that, there are also stories of how players new to fighting games learned "the right way to play" early on, abandoning their old style and adopting the serious fighting gamer performance. Gene's story is perhaps the most dramatic, in the sense that he outright says that he was taught the proper way to play, but there are more subtle examples. Ibrahim, Garrett, Jeff, Jordan, Nicholas, and others all became exposed to the fighting game community via an online forum, often because they were in need of expertise that was available on those forums/expertise-based communities. Before that point, they describe scenarios where they were primarily casual players in scope: They played "for fun," sometimes by themselves, and typically not in a competitive setting. Exposure to places such as Shoryuken.com and 8WayRun.com opened their eyes in some ways to this new way of doing things, and they've been part of that ever since. As mentioned earlier, viewing fighting games as a competitive thing between two players rather than a solo activity is practically exnominative among these players; this speaks quite strongly to the influence participating in these communities can have.

However, the result wasn't just a change in playstyle. It was also participation socially, be it via online forum postings or attending local get-togethers to play in person (which is also part of the performance!) rather than alone or online. Attending EVO or other such tournaments is also part of the process. Isaac and Aaron both framed their desire to attend EVO not just as wanting to participate as a player, but simply for the experience of it all. Entry into the fighting game community wasn't just about playing fighting games a certain way; it was about making new social contacts with like-minded people, and building a social network as well. Of course, in the process, they also reinforce the power of the norms that build the community. Some players on XBox Live respond to trash-talking, unskilled "scrubs" by offering advice, attempting to sway them to the right way to play. In areas with a smaller population, respondents spoke about always wanting to bring new blood into the fold, and even in more "saturated" cities such as in southern California, the idea is that if someone shows promise, s/he should be welcomed into the community to strengthen it.

Social participation is much the same. The norms of play and behaviors of social play of the arcade ideal extended outward even to total strangers at events like EVO. In that regard, they doesn't so much reflect the norms of fighting game play as *embody* them. By coming to tournaments to compete, players reaffirm the idea that players *worth playing against* will be in attendance. The fact that Isaac and Aaron both wished so strongly to attend EVO despite their relatively low estimation of their chances for winning certainly suggests that the expense of travel was worth it on the experience alone. What was important to them was that they could experience play in a particular way at EVO: "real" play, against skilled and like-minded competitors. The role of the matchmaking forum is the same way. While socialization assuredly can result from meeting another player to battle via matchmaking, the *point* of it—the reason for the social contact in the first place—is the norm of play. Fighting games are *supposed* to be played against other people, so social contact with other players first and foremost is a way of satisfying that.

In the context of Steinkuehler and Williams, this process of acculturation is much like the "bridging period" they describe for MMO players, a period where light social contact in a third space increases interest in the activity, but once "their activities became more hardcore . . . the function of MMOs as third places began to wane" (2006, p. 903). When Gene and Evan encountered players from a different arcade who introduced them to SRK, when Garrett or Ibrahim discovered online communities of players who were also fans of *Soul Calibur*, and when Jeff was introduced to the world of serious fighting gaming by a stranger at a tournament, these players were creating bridging relationships. They were light, low-impact, focused on interest. As time went by, however, participation in the community—and gaining the proper capital to do so—went hand-in-hand with a certain style of play, and these lighter associations gave way to a focus on serious play.

As the '09er phenomenon on SRK shows—and as Christopher Paul observes with Elitist Jerks—the membership of such communities rarely have patience for those unwilling to engage the norms seriously. The complaints leveled against '09ers and forum participants of all stripes suggest a more casual and light use of the online space that isn't consistent with the instrumental ways regulars use them. Jordan, for example, noted that one major complaint was that new users would post new threads speculating about the game's fiction, or simply expressing what parts of the games they thought were interesting; in other words, approaching the forum as a third space. To the regulars of SRK, this was not how they experienced the site. Shoryuken. com is a place for the "work" of play: sharing expertise, setting up games, and furthering the norms of serious play. Much like the difference between casual players and hardcore players noted above, these two frames for social participation were so different as to be incompatible.

In short, ways of playing—particularly gameplay norms—serve as a framework and motivation for both community formation and social participation. Serious players create communities to share expertise and further their style of serious play, and attend social events in order to play the game with others who share the same normative views on the matter. When these ways of playing are not shared between communities, conflict, even schisms, result. Whether it's Ibrahim and Garrett mentioning how community opinions on *Soul Calibur 3* threatened to split the community, or Matthew's dire prediction that the *Smash* community is about to split in half on the issue of Metaknight, the key issue in structuring social participation—be it online or at events—always comes back to the norms of play.

LIMITATIONS AND DIRECTIONS FOR FUTURE INQUIRY

It is relatively clear that, as Bloor (2002) argues while discussing Wittgenstein on rules, that ways of playing—a set of socially-constructed rules and behaviors—are his "collective pattern of self-referring activity" (p. 33). Just as the literal rules of the game built into the computer code shape the possibilities of the experience, the social rules of play become an institution with demonstrable effects on the players. However, this "collective pattern of self-referring activity" is also a "stylized repetition of acts" (Butler, p. 179); in other words, this collective way of playing that fighting gamers exhibit—a combination of actual play practice, opinions on how play should ideally be, and their social play with each other—is a performance, a discursive structure that, through repetition, becomes an institution: a creator and arbiter of rules.

However, it is not only players that are affected by this fact. As a thought experiment, consider three people on a tennis court. Two are playing a standard singles game, volleying the ball back and forth with their rackets and adhering to known conventions of scoring. A third is standing off to the side, bouncing a ball up and down on his/her racket, trying to keep it from falling on the ground. In both cases, people are playing a game with rules of a sort, using the same basic equipment: a tennis court, a racket, a tennis ball. However, to say they are playing the same game is a mistake. Certainly, there are similarities; they are both focusing on keeping the ball in play, for example, but in the end it is adherence to conventions—rules—that defines the activity itself. In the case of fighting games, the code (i.e. the actual literal game) is the ball, and the technology used to play it, the racket. After that, the game experience is defined much more heavily by play convention than by anything elemental about the game itself. If one were to walk by this taking place on a tennis court, which of the two groups of players would have the "authenticity" of "real tennis" behind them? It is easy to imagine a scenario where asking the two people playing traditional tennis what they're doing would earn the person asking an incredulous "What does it look like?" response, whereas the one bouncing the ball on his/her racket might sheepishly respond, "Just passing the time."

This is Consalvo's (2007) gaming paratext at work. Her description of the paratext in *Cheating* focused primarily on peripheral consumption and how extratextual consumption relates to the actual experience of playing the game in the first place: "[p]aratexts surround, shape, support, and provide context for texts. They may alter the meanings of texts, further enhance meanings, or provide challenges to sedimented meanings" (p. 182). One of her examples is strategy guides, which not only provide a literal guide to in-game knowledge, but also guide the reader to play in a specific way. The key issue here is that the paratext has the capability to fundamentally alter the experience of the text, which is why she quotes Lunenfeld's (1999) claim that in the modern era, text and paratext are inseparable. In a similar fashion, the practice of playing competitive fighting games is not just about the game code. A network of social play practices surrounds and informs it; through its paratextual elements, the performance of fighting game play takes shape.

I believe that this research not only contributes to recent studies that argue for interpreting games as more situated between the game text itself and social play (Soltis, 2008; Kolos, 2010), but also suggests a new way to conceptualize how different player communities define themselves. Rather than thinking of different types of gamer playing the same game in different ways, it seems more fruitful—based on the experiences of players observed in this study—to conceptualize them as in essence playing two separate games entirely. Much as with performative gender, the "body" of a game—the computer code—is only one point among many; a consistent material influence, but one that is ultimately wrapped in how it is used.

However, this research is primarily about a single type of gamer community and playstyle: serious fighting game players. More research is required to examine if the ways of playing observed here are consistent across different genres of game, both digital and non-digital. Are these behaviors observable in, for example, players of board games or collectible card games such as *Magic: the Gathering*? Exploring the potential impact on other gaming communities will help cement if this is a behavior that's endemic to fighting gamers or if it has broader applications across game studies.

It is also critical to note that while the analysis of the data made every effort to identify intersectional notions, the fighting gamers that were interviewed were all male, and within a relatively narrow age range. I also did not investigate the ethnicity of the players to whom I spoke. The gendered and ethnic dimensions of the performance discussed in Chapter 6 suggest that these norms in the community would have a large impact on the experiences of women players and players of color, for example. Research that focuses specifically on their experience would be invaluable, particularly as a comparison to the experiences discussed here.

Similarly, a second direction for future research would be to analyze how players construct ways of play across genres. Juul (2010) suggests that hardcore players, for example, are flexible in terms of the time and investment they will devote to games while casual players are more inflexible, with more strict constructions of what they are looking for. The fighting game players in this study clearly set aside much of their available time and energy for fighting games. However, they were capable of playing those games in a casual way, whereas it seems as if casual players can't approach it the other way (hence, "Stop Having Fun Guys" memes emerge). Examining how hardcore players of one game type perform play of another type would help to increase our understanding of how players move between performances in differing scenarios, as well as how durable certain gameplay norms are across different social situations.

Methodologically, I made a specific decision not to engage in participant observation, choosing to distance myself from actual play. However, in conducting this research—particularly in noticing how players observed locally responded to my participating socially in the activity rather than remaining distant—I believe that a more thoroughly participatory approach might provide insights into this phenomenon that a more detached approach would not. For example, how might have these findings been different if I had been an entrant in the EVO tournament rather than an observer? A more participant-oriented approach would be poised to answer that question and, ideally, uncover additional facets of that experience.

On one hand, it is somewhat disheartening that many of the casual/hardcore player rifts I observed in this research seem, at first glance, unresolvable. With their differing expectations of the experience and their conflicting styles of satisfying those expectations, never the twain shall meet. However, I believe that this research is among the first steps to closing that gap. The more we understand about how these ways of play get formed, and how people identify with those ways of play, the better our ability to design games that take this into account and create situations where those unresolvable conflicts are less divisive. If this research can help me to overcome my frustration, to see the different perspective of the hardcore players that who were once the bane of my *Smash Bros.* experience, then anything is possible.

FIGHT FOR THE FUTURE

Considering that this book opens with a few anecdotes about how I personally viewed the fighting game community and culture, it's only fitting that it closes with some commentary on those views as well. My experiences over the course of gathering this data were quite varied. In some cases, I learned many new things I had no idea about: the origin of Michael Mendoza's "Pringles" commentary in the *Marvel* world, how critical the arcade was to these players despite their decline in the United States, and how to read a sheet of frame data, among other things. In other cases things I already knew were confirmed: fighting gamers see the characters they play primarily in mechanical rather than aesthetic terms, for example, and are a community that has mixed feelings about letting strangers and newbies inside. In either case, though, delving into the culture was really eye-opening.

From an observational standpoint, I recommend to anyone that has an interest in studying this kind of community that they find an event like the EVO tournament and attend it for a day or two, either just to watch or even as a participant. I say this because these events are proof of perhaps the most positive and striking thing about this culture: its energy, verve, and passion. Fighting gamers bring to their chosen play a level of energy—"hype," in their terms—that is incredibly striking. During the final days of EVO, watching famous players battle it out on the big screen while the rest of us watched, just being in the room was an amazing experience. Even when I didn't know what was *technically* going on, I could still feel the tension. This was as true for the wild and rambunctious *Marvel vs. Capcom 2* finals as it was for the more quietly intense *Street Fighter 4* fights; whether the crowd was on its feet and shouting or simply watching with bated breath, the electricity still came across.

Of course, it's worth noting that I'm white, and identify as a cisgendered male, and that gives me an in to vanish into that crowd semi-invisibly that other researchers might not have, and perhaps this gets to the crux of my interpretation of the fighting game community's major stumbling blocks. A key rhetoric that the fighting game community espouses is that they wish to grow the base of potential players. As I quoted one interviewee as saying earlier, the idea is that by bringing new blood into the community, the range of potential opponents gets wider and as a result, everybody benefits. After all, playing against skilled opponents is how you improve, and underlying so much of fighting games culture is the idea that everyone wants to be the best. Yet there are multiple examples in this book of ways in which the fighting game community is absolutely unwilling to change for anyone, least of all new blood, and this is a major issue they will have to resolve if the culture wants to put this inclusive rhetoric into actual practice.

Consider, for example, Shoryuken.com and the '09ers. I don't want to imply that the way the old guard treated new forum members was universally problematic; that said, it was hardly welcoming, either. Many SRK users felt that the new fans hadn't paid their dues yet, and so being unwelcoming and harsh was an effective method of weeding out people who "couldn't take the heat," as it were. In its own way, this is the same rhetoric that got deployed in discussions about the EVO 2010 women's invitational; many players—including women players, importantly—argued that any sort of "special treatment" would be more harmful than helpful. If women want to play and participate, then they have to pay their dues and work their way up without any "help." And of course there are Bakhtanians' comments about how his misogynist acts on *Cross Assault* are born from a desire not to whitewash the core fighting game culture for the sake of something like e-sports, a tension between what the fighting gamers view as a professional and whitewashed corporate sellout and their own self-concept as an aggressively "indie" scene that's been boiling for quite some time (Groen, 2013).

The result is an interesting set of contradictions. Fighting gamers want their games and events to be popular; they want new players, and they want recognition for what they see as a great and amazing scene and culture in which to play games. Yet at the same time, the public face of that culture is openly hostile to what sometimes feels like practically anything: new members have to "pay their dues" first but have trouble getting started doing that thanks to a hostile community. Women players have to "prove that women can play" but systemic mistreatment of women makes it impossible to engage in the types of social play they need to be involved in to accomplish that goal. Fighting gamers want their tournaments to be of interest to the e-sports world at large, but they don't want to "clean up" or compromise in order to do that. When events like the *Cross Assault* debacle make it into the gaming press the fighting game culture argues that they are being unfairly treated, and that they do a lot of good, but the pair of stories by Tom Cannon mentioned in Chapter 6 emphasize the duality of that as well. Day one involves calls for sanity and a slick video arguing the scene is mostly about hype and energy; day two involves excoriating commentators—symbols of the community—who were dismissive about the problems that made the day one post necessary in the first place, and so on.

The image I am left with of the fighting game culture is one of a passionate community that nevertheless has serious challenges ahead of it when it comes to relating to the world around it. Understanding how these players relate to each other and to the games is an important step in looking at competitive communities of game practice. However, the ways in which the fighting game community's practice falls short of the mark of its rhetoric are also important to consider. They highlight how that sense of community identity that binds its members together can also reinforce harmful norms, and even serve to segregate the community into its own niche space, counter to its ideals of inclusion and growth. It is my hope that, with time, that community will begin to address those issues and help to share its members' tremendous, exciting energy and drive with a broader world.

NOTES

1. See Putnam, 2000.
2. Specifically: that they are neutral ground where individuals can come/go as they please, they are a leveler that reduces or eliminates the importance of rank and status, conversation is the primary activity, they are easily accessible/accommodating, that there is a cadre of regulars, that a low profile is sufficient, that the mood is playful, and that the space feels like a "home away from home."

References

"2010 SSF4 Women's Invitational: More Info and FAQ." (2010). Retrieved July 21, 2010 from http://shoryuken.com/f8/2010-ssf4-womens-invitational-more-info-faq-223895

"About Evolution." (2009). Retrieved March 14, 2009 from http://evo2k.com/?page_id=50

"About Us." (2009). Retrieved March 14, 2009 from http://www.gamefaqs.com/features/aboutus.html

"Back to basics, getting beyond the drama." (2012, February). Retrieved June 10, 2013 from http://shoryuken.com/2012/02/29/back-to-basics-getting-beyond-the-drama/.

"Beat 'em up." (2010). Retrieved July 27, 2010 from http://en.wikipedia.org/wiki/Beat_'em_up

"BBR Recommended Rule List v2.0." (2009). Retrieved June 27, 2010 from http://www.smashboards.com/showthread.php?t=230481

"BurnYourBra discusses the difficulties of being a female gamer." (2011). Retrieved June 10, 2013 from http://www.eventhubs.com/news/2011/apr/15/dmgburnyourbra-discusses-difficulties-being-female-gamer/

"Character Ranking Notes (Tier lists + more)." (2009). Retrieved November 9, 2009 from http://shoryuken.com/f241/character-ranking-notes-tier-lists-more-174600

"Chill out. Metaknight won't ever be banned." (2010). Retrieved June 27, 2010 from http://www.smashboards.com/showthread.php?t=263145

"Counterpicking Made Easy." (2008). Retrieved June 27, 2010 from http://www.smashboards.com/showthread.php?t=187501

"Counter Picking.. Your thoughts?" (2009). Retrieved June 27, 2010 from http://shoryuken.com/f266/counter-picking-your-thoughts-184741

"Cross Assault: Introducing Team Street Fighter." (2012). Retrieved June 10, 2013 from http://shoryuken.com/2012/02/15/cross-assault-introducing-team-street-fighter/

"Cross Assault: Introducing Team Tekken." (2012). Retrieved June 10, 2013 from http://shoryuken.com/2012/02/16/cross-assault-introducing-team-tekken/

"Evo Championship Series >> Tournament Rules." (2010). Retrieved June 27, 2010 from http://evo2k.com/?page_id=47

"Evo Reminder: Wireless Dualshock3 Controllers Are Banned!" (2013). Retrieved June 25, 2013 from http://shoryuken.com/2013/05/30/evo-reminder-wireless-dualshock-3-controllers-are-banned/

"Game Shark Store—Arcade Sticks." (n.d.) Retrieved November 9, 2009 from http://store.gameshark.com/listCategoriesAndProducts.asp?idCategory=274

"Guilty Gear XX Accent Core I System." (n.d.). Retrieved July 27, 2010 from http://www.aksysgames.com/ggxxac/system_15.html

"Hilde's Tier w/o Combo?" (2009). Retrieved November 9, 2009 from http://www.8wayrun.com/f28/hildes-tier-w-o-combo-t6755

"Hurtful speech: time to take a good look in the mirror." (2012, March). Retrieved June 10, 2013 from http://shoryuken.com/2012/03/01/hurtful-speech-time-to-take-a-good-look-in-the-mirror/

"Infinite Dimensional Cape." (n.d.) Retrieved June 27, 2010 from http://super-smash-bros.wikia.com/wiki/Infinite_Dimensional_Cape

"Information and Updates from the Brawl Back Room." (2010). Retrieved June 27, 2010 from http://www.smashboards.com/showthread.php?t=264241

"Message to Newcomers who feel Unwelcome." (2009). Retrieved July 21, 2010 from http://shoryuken.com/f241/message-newcomers-who-feel-unwelcome-177860

"No items. Fox only. FD." (2008). Retrieved July 27, 2010 from http://www.smashboards.com/showthread.php?t=146849

"Official Metaknight Discussion." (2010). Retrieved June 27, 2010 from http://www.smashboards.com/showthread.php?t=263165

"Official SC4 Tier List And Character Guides." (2009). Retrieved November 9, 2009 from http://www.8wayrun.com/f21/official-sc4-tier-list-and-character-guides-t5967

"READ ME FIRST: MVC3 FORUM RULES." (2012). Retrieved June 10, 2013 from http://forums.shoryuken.com/discussion/101124/read-me-first-mvc3-forum-rules-updated-8-26-12

"Real Arcade Pro. EXSE." (2009). Retrieved November 9, 2009 from http://www.hori.jp/us/products/xbox360/xbox360_rap_ex_se/index.html

"So You Wanna Go For a Ride?: Syke and Windy's MvC3 Basics Thread." Retrieved June 30, 2013 from http://forums.shoryuken.com/discussion/comment/4771605/#Comment_4771605

"Stop Having Fun Guys." (2009). Retrieved March 5, 2009 from http://tvtropes.org/pmwiki/pmwiki.php/Main/StopHavingFunGuys

"Television Interview about Harassment in Gaming." (2012). Retrieved June 10, 2013 from http://www.feministfrequency.com/2012/11/television-interview-about-harassment-in-gaming/

"The Importance of Counter Picking." (2010). Retrieved June 27, 2010 from http://allisbrawl.com/blogpost.aspx?id=71218

"The Role of Girls and Women in the FGC." (2010). Retrieved June 10, 2010 from http://shoryuken.com/f2/role-girls-women-fgc-223786

"The Sanwa and Seimitsu FAQ." (2006). Retrieved November 9, 2009 from http://shoryuken.com/f177/sanwa-seimitsu-faq-118289

"The future of Algol, Hilde and Star Wars." (2009). Retrieved June 27, 2010 from http://www.8wayrun.com/f21/the-future-of-algol-hilde-and-star-wars-t4502/page9.html

"Tournament legal (SSBM)." (2010). Retrieved June 27, 2010 from http://super-smash-bros.wikia.com/wiki/Tournament_legal_(SSBM)#Controversy

"USB Gecko is the new Action Replay!" (2008). Retrieved March 5, 2009 from http://www.smashboards.com/showthread.php?t=165363

"Video Games and Violence." (2010). Retrieved March 5, 2009 from http://www.theeca.com/video_games_violence

"Why we can't wait to ban Metaknight." (2010). Retrieved June 27, 2010 from http://www.smashboards.com/showthread.php?t=263082

"Wreaking Havoc in Wolfkrone: The anti-Hilde Thread." (2009). Retrieved June 27, 2010 from http://www.8wayrun.com/f28/wreaking-havoc-in-wolfkrone-the-anti-hilde-thread-t2165

"Xbox 360 Real Arcade Pro. VX SA." (2013). Retrieved June 25, 2013 from http://stores.horiusa.com/-strse-103/Xbox-360-Real-Arcade/Detail.bok

"XBox Live Marketplace | Games." (2010). Retrieved July 27, 2010 from http://marketplace.xbox.com/en-US/games/catalog.aspx?d=0&r=-1&g=3006&mt=0&ot=0&sb=2&rl=0&p=1

Aarseth, E. (1997). *Cybertext: Perspectives on Ergodic Literature*. Baltimore: Johns Hopkins University Press.

Aho, J. A. (1998). *Things of the World: A Social Phenomenology*. Westport, CT: Praeger Publishers.

Althusser, L. (1971). *Lenin and Philosophy and Other Essays* (Brewster, B., Trans.). New York: Monthly Review Press.

Altman, R. (1984). A semantic/syntactic approach to film genre. *Cinema Journal*, 23 (3), 6–18.

Apperley, T. H. (2006). Genre and game studies: towards a critical approach to video game genres. *Simulation and Gaming*, 37 (1), 6–23.

Ashcraft, B. (2008). *Arcade Mania! The Turbo-Charged World of Japan's Game Centers*. New York: Kodansha International.

Bartle, R. (1996). Hearts, clubs, diamonds, spades: players who suit MUDS. Retrieved March 11, 2009 from http://www.mud.co.uk/richard/hcds.htm

Berger, P. L. & Luckmann, T. (1966). *The Social Construction of Reality: A Treatise in the Sociology of Knowledge*. New York: Anchor Books.

Bertrand, I. & Hughes, P. (2005). *Media Research Methods*. New York: Palgrave-Macmillan.

Blaut, J. M. (1992). The theory of cultural racism. *Antipode*, 24 (4), 289–299.

Bloor, D. (2002). *Wittgenstein, Rules and Institutions*. New York: Routledge.

Bogost, I. (2007). *Persuasive Games: the Expressive Power of Videogames*. Cambridge, MA: MIT Press.

Brooker, W. (2002). *Using the Force: Creativity, Community, and Star Wars Fans*. New York: Continuum Publishing.

Bryant, J., Rockwell, S. C., & Owens, J. W. (1994). "Buzzer beaters" and "barn burners": the effects on enjoyment of watching the game go "down to the wire." *Journal of Sport and Social Issues*, 18 (4), 326–339.

Burrill, D. A. (2008). *Die Tryin': Videogames, Masculinity, Culture*. New York: Peter Lang.

Butler, J. (1988). Performative acts and gender constitution: an essay in phenomenology and feminist theory. *Theatre Journal*, 40 (4), 519–531.

Butler, J. P. (1990). *Gender Trouble: Feminism and the Subversion of Identity*. New York: Routledge.

Butler, J. P. (1993). *Bodies that Matter: On the Discursive Limits of "Sex"*. New York: Routledge.

Caillois, R. (1958). *Man, Play and Games*. Urbana, IL: University of Illinois Press.

Cavalier, E. S. (2011). Men at sport: gay men's experiences in the sport workplace. *Journal of Homosexuality*, 58 (5), 626–646.

Chen, M. (2008). Communication, coordination, and camaraderie in *World of Warcraft*. *Games and Culture*, 4 (1), 47–73.

Chen, M. (2012). *Leet Noobs: the Life and Death of an Expert Player Group in World of Warcraft*. New York: Peter Lang.

Cofino, I. (2010). *I Got Next: A Documentary on the Fighting Game Scene*. Available online at http://www.igotnextmovie.com

Consalvo, M. (2003). The monsters next door: media constructions of boys and masculinity. *Feminist Media Studies*, 3 (1), 27–45.

Consalvo, M. (2007). *Cheating: Gaining Advantage in Videogames*. Cambridge, MA: MIT Press.

Consalvo, M. (2009a). Persistence meets performance: *Phoenix Wright, Ace Attorney*. In Davidson (Ed.), *Well Played 1.0: Video Games, Value, and Meaning* (pp. 145–158). Pittsburgh, PA: ETC Press.

Consalvo, M. (2009b). Lag, language, and lingo: theorizing noise in online game spaces. In Wolf & Perron (Eds.), *The Video Game Theory Reader 2* (pp. 295–312). New York: Routledge.

Consalvo, M. & Harper, T. (2009). The sexi(e)st of all: avatars, gender, and online games. In Panteli (Ed.), *Virtual Social Networks: Mediated, Massive and Multiplayer Sites* (pp. 98–113). New York: Palgrave Macmillan.

Crawford, G. & Rutter, J. (2007). Playing the game: performance in digital game audiences. In Gray, Sandvoss, & Harrington (Eds.), *Fandom: Identities and Communities in a Mediated World* (pp. 271–281). New York: New York University Press.

Crecente, B. (2008). Fighting to play: the history of the longest lived fighting game tournament in the world. *Kotaku*. Available online at http://kotaku.com/5054856/fighting-to-play-the-history-of-the-longest-lived-fighting-game-tournament-in-the-world.

Crenshaw, K. (1991). Mapping the margins: intersectionality, identity politics, and violence against women of color. *Stanford Law Review*, 43 (6), 1241–1299.

Creswell, J.W. (1998). *Qualitative Inquiry and Research Design: Choosing Among Five Traditions*. Thousand Oaks, CA: Sage Publications.

Creswell, J.W. (2003). *Research Design: Qualitative, Quantitative, and Mixed Methods Approaches*. Thousand Oaks, CA: Sage Publications.

Dannenberg, R. (2005). Patent arcade: Case: Capcom v. Data East (N.D. Cal 1994) [C]. Retrieved July 27, 2010 from http://www.patentarcade.com/2005/08/case-capcom-v-data-east-nd-cal-1994-c.html

Davis, K. (2008). Intersectionality as buzzword: a sociology of science perspective on what makes a feminist theory successful. *Feminist Theory*, 9 (1), 67–85.

DiSalvo, B. & Bruckman, A. (2010, June). Race and gender in play practices: young African American males. Paper presented at the Foundations of Digital Games 2010 Conference, Monterey, California.

Dutton, N. (2007). Roundhouse kicks and melting faces: Chuck Norris and *World of Warcraft* fan culture. Paper presented at the Association of Internet Researchers 8.0 Conference, Vancouver, Canada.

Eastman, S.T. & Billings, A.C. (2001). Biased voices of sports: racial and gender stereotyping in college basketball announcing. *Howard Journal of Communication*, 12, 183–201.

Ebert, T.L. (1993). Ludic feminism, the body, performance, and labor: bringing *materialism* back into feminist cultural studies. *Cultural Critique*, 23, 5–50.

Fausto-Sterling, A. (2005). The bare bones of sex: part 1—sex and gender. *Signs: Journal of Women and Culture in Society*, 30 (2), 1493–1527.

Feuer, J. (1992). Genre study and television. In Allen (Ed.), *Channels of Discourse, Reassembled* (pp. 139–160). Chapel Hill, NC: University of North Carolina Press.

Fine, G.A. (1983). *Shared Fantasy: Role-playing Games as Social Worlds*. Chicago: University of Chicago Press.

Fishbein, R. (2012, May). Chinatown Fair returns with less fighting, more toys. *The Gothamist*. Retrieved from http://gothamist.com/2012/05/05/chinatown_fairs_backsort_of.php.

Foucault, M. (1978). *The History of Sexuality, Vol. 1: An Introduction* (R. Hurley, trans.). New York: Pantheon Books.

Frasca, G. (1999). "Ludology meets narratology: similitude and differences between (video)games and narrative." Retrieved March 5, 2009 from http://www.ludology.org/articles/ludology.htm

Frasca, G. (2003). Simulation versus narrative: introduction to ludology. In Wolf & Perron (Eds.), *The Video Game Theory Reader* (pp. 221–235). New York: Routledge.

Gan, S., et al. (1997). The thrill of a close game: who enjoys it and who doesn't? *Journal of Sport & Social Issues*, 21 (1), 53–64.

Genette, G. (1997). *Paratexts: Thresholds of Interpretation*. New York: Cambridge University Press.

Goldfarb, A. (2012, February). Capcom and IGN present Cross Assault. Retrieved June 10, 2013 from http://www.ign.com/articles/2012/02/22/capcom-and-ign-present-cross-assault.

Golub, A. (2010). Being in the world (of Warcraft): raiding, realism, and knowledge production in a massively multiplayer online game. *Anthropological Quarterly*, 83 (1), 17–46.

Goffman, E. (1959). *The Presentation of Self in Everyday Life*. New York: Anchor Books.

Goffman, E. (1974). *Frame Analysis: an Essay on the Organization of Experience*. Boston: Northeastern University Press.

Gray, K. (2013). Collective organizing, individual resistance, or asshole griefers? An ethnographic analysis of women of color in Xbox Live. *Ada: Journal of Gender, New Media, & Technology*, 1 (2), available online at http://adanewmedia. org/2013/06/issue2-gray/.

Gregory, K. (2012, June). Chinatown Fair is back, without chickens playing tick-tack-toe. *The New York Times*. Retrieved from http://www.nytimes.com/2012/06/11/ nyregion/chinatown-fair-returns-but-without-chicken-playing-tick-tack-toe. html.

Groen, A. (2013, May). Why the fighting game community hates the word "eSports". *Penny Arcade Report*. Available online at http://penny-arcade.com/ report/article/why-the-fighting-game-community-hates-the-word-esports.

Harper, T. (2007, October). The six-process gameplay model: a proposal for examining meaning and gameplay. Paper presented at the Association of Internet Researchers 8.0 Conference, Vancouver, British Columbia, Canada.

Harper, T. (2011). Rules, rhetoric, and genre: procedural rhetoric in *Persona 3*. *Games and Culture*, 6 (5), 395–413.

Heider, D. (2000). *White News: Why Local News Programs Don't Cover People of Color*. Mahwah, NJ: Lawrence Erlbaum Associates.

Heilman, M.E. (2001). Description and prescription: how gender stereotypes prevent women's ascent up the organizational ladder. *Journal of Science Issues*, 57 (4), 657–674.

Heilman, M.E., et al. (2004). Penalties for success: reactions to women who succeed at male gender-typed tasks. *Journal of Applied Psychology*, 89 (3), 416–427.

Horwitz, J., et al. (n.d.) The history of *Street Fighter*. Retrieved November 9, 2009 from http://www.gamespot.com/features/vgs/universal/sfhistory

Huizinga, J. (1950). *Homo Ludens*. Boston: Beacon Press.

Jakobsson, M. (2007). Playing with the rules: social and cultural aspects of game rules in a console game club. Proceedings of the Digital Games Research Association 2007 Conference.

Jansz, J. & Martens, L. (2005). Gaming at a LAN event: the social context of playing video games. *New Media & Society*, 7 (3), 333–355.

Jenkins, H. (2006). *Fans, Bloggers, and Gamers: Exploring Participatory Culture*. New York: New York University Press.

Jorgensen, D.L. (1989). *Participant Observation: A Methodology for Human Studies*. Newbury Park, CA: Sage Publications.

Juul, J. (2005). *Half-Real: Video Games Between Real Rules and Fictional Worlds*. Cambridge, MA: MIT Press.

Juul, J. (2009). Fear of failing? The many meanings of difficulty in video games. In Wolf & Perron (Eds.), *The Video Game Theory Reader 2* (pp. 237–252). New York: Routledge.

Juul, J. (2010). *A Casual Revolution: Reinventing Video Games and Their Players*. Cambridge, MA: MIT Press.

Kendall, L. (2000). "Oh no! I'm a nerd!": hegemonic masculinity on an online forum. *Gender and Society*, 14 (2), 256–274.

Kennedy, T. (2007, August). Women's online gaming communities: don't hate the game, hate the players. Presentation at the American Sociology Association Communication, Information & Technologies Mini-Conference, New York, New York.

Kennedy, T. (2009, October). "The voices in my head are idiots": rethinking barriers for female gamers and the importance of online communities. Paper presented at the Association of Internet Researchers 10.0 Conference, Milwaukee, Wisconsin.

Killian, S. & Sirlin, D. (2007). *Super Street Fighter II Turbo HD Remix* FAQ. Retrieved July 23, 2010 from http://blog.capcom.com/archives/577

Kirkland, E. (2005). Restless dreams in *Silent Hill*: approaches to video game analysis. *Journal of Media Practice*, 6 (3), 167–178.

Kirschner, A. & Schumacher, A. (2008). Treatise on the existence of tiers. Retrieved November 9, 2009 from http://super-smash-bros.wikia.com/wiki/User:Semicolon/Treatise_on_the_Existence_of_Tiers

Klepek, P. (2012, February). When passions flare, lines are crossed. Available online at http://www.giantbomb.com/articles/when-passions-flare-lines-are-crossed-updated/1100-4006/.

Kline, S., Dyer-Witheford, N., & de Peuter, G. (2003). *Digital Play: the Interaction of Technology, Culture, and Marketing*. Montreal: McGill University Press.

Kolos, H. (2010). *Not just in it to win it: inclusive game play in an MIT dorm* (Master's thesis). Retrieved from http://cms.mit.edu/research/theses.php

Koster, R. (2004). *A Theory of Fun for Game Design*. Scottsdale, AZ: Paraglyph Press.

Kvale, S. (1996). *InterViews: An Introduction to Qualitative Research Interviewing*. Thousand Oaks, CA: Sage Publications.

Leonard, D. (2003). "Live in your world, play in ours": race, video games, and consuming the other. *Studies in Media & Information Literacy Education*, 3 (4), 1–9.

Leonard, D. (2009). Young, black (& brown) and don't give a fuck: virtual gangstas in the era of state violence. *Cultural Studies Critical Methodologies*, 9 (2), 248–272.

Lin, H. & Sun, C. (2011). The role of onlookers in arcade gaming: frame analysis of public behaviors. *Convergence*, 17 (2), 125–137.

Lunenfeld, P. (1999). *The Digital Dialectic: New Essays on New Media*. Cambridge, MA: MIT Press.

MacCallum-Stewart, E. & Parsler, J. (2008). Role-play vs. gameplay: the difficulties of playing a role in *World of Warcraft*. In Corneliussen & Rettberg (Eds.), *Digital Culture, Play, and Identity: a World of Warcraft Reader* (pp. 225–246). Cambridge, MA: MIT Press.

Markman, K.M. (2005, May). *Star Trek*, fan film, and the internet: possibilities and constraints of fan-based vernacular cultures. Paper presented at the 2005 International Communication Association Conference, New York, New York.

Mason, J. (2002). *Qualitative Researching (2nd Edition)*. Thousand Oaks, CA: Sage Publications.

McCall, L. (2005). The complexity of intersectionality. *Signs*, 30 (3), 1771–1800.

McKee, A. (2003). *Textual Analysis: a Beginner's Guide*. Thousand Oaks, CA: Sage.

Mittell, J. (2001). A cultural approach to television genre theory. *Cinema Journal*, 40 (3), 3–24.

Murray, J. (1997). *Hamlet on the Holodeck: the Future of Narrative in Cyberspace*. Cambridge, MA: MIT Press.

Myers, M. (2012, October). One woman's battle against the anxious masculinity of the fighting games scene. *Boston Phoenix*. Available online at http://thephoenix.com/boston/recroom/145892-one-womans-battle-against-the-anxious-masculinity/.

Navarro, A. (2012, May). From fighting games to family fun: NYC's Chinatown Fair Arcade ain't what it used to be. *Giant Bomb*. Retrieved from http://www.giantbomb.com/articles/from-fighting-games-to-family-fun-nycs-chinatown-f/1100-4129/.

Neale, S. (1990). Questions of genre. *Screen*, 31 (1), 45–66.

Nelson, J.L. (1989). Phenomenology as feminist methodology: explicating interviews. In Carter & Spitzack (Eds.), *Doing Research on Women's Communication*:

Perspectives on Theory and Method (pp. 221–241). Norwood, NJ: Ablex Publishing.

Oldenburg, R. (1999). *The Great Good Place: Cafés, Coffee Shops, Community Centers, Beauty Parlors, General Stores, Bars, Hangouts, and How They Get You Through The Day*. New York: Marlowe & Company.

Paul, C. (2009, October). Theorycraft: structuring *World of Warcraft* from outside the game. Paper presented at the Association of Internet Researchers 10.0 Conference, Milwaukee, Wisconsin.

Paul, C. (2011). Optimizing play: how theorycraft changes gameplay and design. *Game Studies*, 11 (2), available online at http://gamestudies.org/1102/articles/paul.

Paul, C. (2012). *Wordplay and the Discourse of Video Games: Analyzing Words, Design, and Play*. New York: Routledge.

Pearce, C. (2009). *Communities of Play: Emergent Cultures in Multiplayer Games and Virtual Worlds*. Cambridge, MA: MIT Press.

Putnam, R. D. (2000). *Bowling Alone: the Collapse and Revival of American Community*. New York: Simon & Schuster.

Reeves, S., Brown, B., & Laurier, E. (2009). Experts at play: understanding skilled expertise. *Games and Culture*, 4 (3), 205–227.

Risman, B. J. (2004). Gender as a social structure: theory wrestling with activism. *Gender and Society*, 18 (4), 429–450.

Ryder, M. & Wilson, B. (1996). Affordances and constraints of the Internet for learning and instruction. Proceedings of Selected Research and Development Presentations at the 1996 National Convention of the Association for Educational Communications and Technology, Indianapolis, IN.

Said, E. W. (1978). *Orientalism*. New York: Random House.

Schiesel, S. (2008, February 1). In the list of top-selling games, clear evidence of a sea change. *The New York Times*. Retrieved from http://www.nytimes.com/2008/02/01/arts/01game.html?_r=1

Schrock, D., Reid, L., & Boyd, E. M. (2005). Transsexuals' embodiment of womanhood. *Gender & Society*, 19 (3), 317–335.

Shanahan, I. (2004). Bow nigger. Retrieved July 20, 2010 from http://www.alwaysblack.com/?p=10

Simon, B. (2007). Geek chic: machine aesthetics, digital gaming, and the cultural politics of the case mod. *Games and Culture*, 2 (3), 175–193.

Sirlin, D. (2006). *Playing to Win: Becoming the Champion*. Raleigh, NC: Lulu.com.

Sirlin, D. (2009). A few things about *Street Fighter 4*. Retrieved June 27, 2010, from http://www.sirlin.net/blog/2009/2/22/a-few-things-about-street-fighter-4.html

Smith, J. H. (2005, October). The aesthetics of antagonism. Paper presented at the Aesthetics of Play Conference, Bergen, Norway. Retrieved July 23, 2010 from http://www.aestheticsofplay.org/smith.php

Soltis, D. (2008, August). Moving parts: the interdependence of game play and social dynamics in digital games. Paper presented at the ACM Sandbox Symposium, Los Angeles, CA.

Stein, A. (2013). Indie sports games: performance and performativity. *Loading . . . The Journal of the Canadian Game Studies Association*, 7 (11), 61–77.

Steinkuehler, C. A. & Williams, D. (2006). Where everybody knows your (screen) name: online games as "third places." *Journal of Computer-Mediated Communication*, 11, 885–909.

Sterling, J. (2012, February). Sexual harassment and fightin' drama, together at last!. Available online at http://www.destructoid.com/sexual-harassment-and-fightin-drama-together-at-last—222877.phtml.

Stoller, S. (2010). Expressivity and performativity: Merleau-Ponty and Butler. *Continental Philosophy Review*, 43, 97–110.

Sudnow, D. (1995). *Ways of the Hand: the Organization of Improvised Conduct*. Cambridge, MA: MIT Press.

Sze-fai Shiu, A. (2006). What yellowface hides: video games, whiteness, and the American racial order. *The Journal of Popular Culture*, 39 (1), 109–125.

Taylor, N., Jenson, J., & de Castells, S. (2009). Cheerleaders/booth babes/*Halo* hoes: pro-gaming, gender and jobs for the boys. *Digital Creativity*, 20 (4), 239–252.

Taylor, T. L. (2006). *Play Between Worlds: Exploring Online Game Culture*. Cambridge, MA: MIT Press.

Taylor, T. L. (2008). Does *World of Warcraft* change everything? How a PvP Server, Multinational Playerbase, and Surveillance Mod Scene Caused Me Pause. In Corneliussen and Rettberg (eds.), *Digital Culture, Play, and Identity: a World of Warcraft Reader* (pp. 187–202). Cambridge, MA: MIT Press.

Taylor, T. L. (2012). *Raising the Stakes: E-Sports and the Professionalization of Computer Gaming*. Cambridge, MA: MIT Press.

Taylor, T. L. & Witkowski, E. (2010, June). This is how we play it: what a mega-LAN can teach us about games. Paper presented at the Foundations of Digital Games 2010 Conference, Monterey, California.

Thornham, H. (2008). "It's a boy thing": gender, gaming, and geeks. *Feminist Media Studies*, 8 (2), 127–142.

van Manen, H. (1990). *Researching Lived Experience: Human Science for an Action Sensitive Pedagogy*. Albany, NY: State University of New York Press.

Walkerdine, V. (2006). Playing the game: young girls performing femininity in video game play. *Feminist Media Studies*, 6 (4), 519–537.

West, C. & Zimmerman, D. H. (1987). Doing gender. *Gender and Society*, 1 (2), 125–151.

Wenz, K. (2013). Theorycrafting: knowledge production and surveillance. *Information, Communication, & Society*, 16 (2), 178–193.

Williams, D. (2004). *Trouble in River City: the Social Life of Video Games*. (Doctoral dissertation). University of Michigan: Ann Arbor, MI.

Witkowski, E. (2012). *Inside the Huddle: the Phenomenology and Sociology of Team Play in Networked Computer Games*. (Doctoral dissertation). IT University of Copenhagen, Copenhagen, Denmark.

Wittgenstein, L. (1953). *Philosophical Investigations* (Anscombe, G. E. M., Trans.). Malden, MA: Blackwell Publishing.

Wolf, M. J. P. (2001). Genre and the video game. In Wolf (Ed.), *The Medium of the Video Game* (pp. 113–134). Austin, TX: University of Texas Press.

Woods, S. (2008). Last man standing: risk and elimination in social game play. *Leonards Electronic Almanac*, 16 (2–3).

Yee, N. (2007). Motivations of play in online games. *Journal of CyberPsychology and Behavior*, 9, 772–775.

Zelizer, B. (1993). Journalists as interpretive communities. *Critical Studies in Mass Communication*, 10, 219–237.

Index

For Product Safety Concerns and Information please contact our
EU representative GPSR@taylorandfrancis.com Taylor & Francis
Verlag GmbH, Kaufingerstraße 24, 80331 München, Germany